RIVERSIDE COMMUNITY COLLEGE
1916

P9-DVH-955

OTHER BOOKS BY BERNARD BAILYN

Voyagers to the West
The Peopling of British North America
The Great Republic (co-author)
The Ordeal of Thomas Hutchinson
The Origins of American Politics
The Ideological Origins of the American Revolution
Education in the Forming of American Society
Massachusetts Shipping, 1697–1714 (with Lotte Bailyn)
The New England Merchants in the Seventeenth Century

Edited and Co-edited Works
The Apologia of Robert Keayne
Pamphlets of the American Revolution
The Intellectual Migration: Europe and America, 1930–1960
Law in American History
The Press and the American Revolution
Strangers Within the Realm: Cultural Margins
of the First British Empire

FACES OF
REVOLUTION

FACES OF REVOLUTION

*Personalities and Themes in the
Struggle for American Independence*

BERNARD BAILYN

ALFRED A. KNOPF

New York · 1990

Riverside Community College
Library
4800 Magnolia Avenue
Riverside, California 92506

JUN 19 '92

THIS IS A BORZOI BOOK
PUBLISHED BY ALFRED A. KNOPF, INC.

Copyright © 1990 by Bernard Bailyn
All rights reserved under International and Pan-American
Copyright Conventions. Published in the United States by
Alfred A. Knopf, Inc., New York, and simultaneously in Canada
by Random House of Canada Limited, Toronto. Distributed
by Random House, Inc., New York.

"Mind" from *Things of This World* by Richard Wilbur,
copyright © 1956 by Harcourt Brace Jovanovich, Inc. and renewed
1984 by Richard Wilbur, reprinted by permission of the publisher.

Library of Congress Cataloging-in-Publication Data
Bailyn, Bernard.
Faces of revolution: personalities and themes in the struggle for
American independence / by Bernard Bailyn.—1st ed.
p. cm.
Includes bibliographical references.
ISBN 0-394-49895-X
1. United States—History—Revolution, 1775–1783.
2. United States—History—Revolution, 1775–1783—Biography.
3. United States—Biography. I. Title.
E208.B2 1990
973.3'0922—dc20
[B]   89-43368   CIP

Manufactured in the United States of America
First Edition

Riverside Community College
Library
4800 Magnolia Avenue
Riverside, California 92506

for
My Graduate Students
Past and Present

Contents

Contents

II
THEMES

Preface

When I began writing on the American Revolution many years ago I planned a series of personality sketches and interpretative essays to be published separately, as time permitted, and then, eventually, brought together as a unit. The pieces, according to the plan, would be carefully matched in subject matter, and so closely related to one another that certain episodes and ideas, even certain phrases, that appeared in one would reappear in others, but in different contexts, with the result that what would have seemed at first to be a casual collection of biographical and thematic sketches would in the end form in the reader's mind an integrated and rounded picture. At certain angles of perception the various faces—facets—of the Revolution would reflect each other and deepen the perspective of the composition as a whole.

It was an ambitious plan, but many other projects intervened, and the occasions for writing the pieces required formats difficult to fit into the general pattern. Only two of the planned pieces (the first two in this volume, which originally had matching titles) were written precisely according to the original scheme. Yet the intent must have lodged itself in some vital lobe or other, for over the years I have come back again and again to the purpose that lay behind that scheme and have written—no longer according to an intricate plan but to satisfy immediate commitments—pieces which in cruder ways come within at least the general boundaries of the book I had in mind. Personalities and ideas, even phrases, reappear in different contexts; themes are touched on, anticipated, in one essay and developed more fully in another; key issues are approached in one way in one essay, in another way in the next.

I wish these pieces, brought together in this volume, were closer to the original plan; I wish they could do all the things I originally hoped they would do. As it is, I shall be satisfied if they give some pleasure and information to readers interested in our origins as a nation, and if they convey clearly certain basic ideas.

I believe, in the first place, that there was nothing inevitable about the American Revolution. It did not need to happen, and as late as 1772 or 1773 the best-informed people of the time (Franklin, for example) thought it could be deflected. As I put it at one point (Chapter 9 in the present volume):

> Deep flows of potentially revolutionary beliefs and apprehensions had moved through the delicate structure of mid-eighteenth-century American politics, but in the constitutional crisis of the 1770s there had been no necessity for these passionate concerns to break through the channels of civility. . . . What was inevitable—what no one could have restrained—was America's emergence into the modern world as a liberal, more or less democratic, and capitalist society. That would have happened in any case. But that this emergence took place as it did—that it was impelled forward by a peculiar ideological explosion generated within a society less traditional than any then known in the Western world—this crucial fact has colored the whole of our subsequent history, and not only our own, but the world's.

The implications, I think, are important. While there were deep forces at work which in time would have led inescapably to a greater and greater attenuation of Anglo-American political relations until the connection became mere friendly cooperation, the fact that the break was violent and revolutionary meant that in important ways it was the product of human decision and of the impact of personalities and ideas upon the events of the time. During the years of disruption it therefore mattered who was in charge, who led the struggle, and who led the opposition to it; it mattered what kinds of people they were, what patterns of personal responses they brought to the public life of their time. Above all, it mattered what they believed, what motivated them, how they perceived the world and the events in which they participated. No one can understand why there was a revolution, what kind of a revolution it was, and what consequences it had, without some sense of the personalities involved and some sense, too, of the complex relationship among personalities, ideas, and events. In seven of the chapters I have attempted to explore this problem with respect to four major figures (Thomas Jefferson, John Adams, Thomas Hutchinson, and Thomas Paine) and three minor personalities (Jonathan Mayhew, Andrew Eliot, and Stephen Johnson, whose careers illustrate particularly well the role of religion in the Revolutionary movement).

A second implication of the idea that the Revolution was not inevitable goes more directly to the currently controversial issues of interpretation. In its origins, the Revolution, I believe, was no product of social or economic forces developing inexorably toward an explosion; it was not a product of social conflict. Shaping circumstances, of course there were, as well as important social struggles that accompanied the revolt and that played into it in complicated ways. And the Revolution had profound social consequences. But social conflict did not determine the outbreak of the Revolution, which in its essence was

> a response to acts of imperial power deemed arbitrary, degrading, and uncontrollable—a response that was inflamed to the point of explosion by ideological currents generating fears everywhere in America that irresponsible and self-seeking adventurers—what the twentieth century would call political gangsters—had gained the power of the British government and were turning first to the colonies. [Chapter 9]

Some great events have indeed arisen from social discontent: explosions of the long-smoldering anger of the dispossessed. But the American Revolution was not one of them, however much it expressed the failure of public institutions to adjust to social and economic change, however much it evoked the aspirations of ordinary people, drew into public roles new men unaccustomed to power, freed certain American businessmen from the constraints of overseas control, and produced a wave of social and political reform. These were consequences, not causes. What accounts for the outbreak of the Revolution, which proved in the end to be a radically transforming event, was the inter-action of events with a set of beliefs and ideals that were deeply and widely disseminated through the population and were comprehended with various degrees of detail and precision and with various empha-ses at different levels of society, beliefs bearing mainly on the uses of power and the meaning of political liberty.

Not a very startling proposition; but it has occasionally been de-nounced with, to me, astonishing asperity as some kind of home-brewed Hegelianism, a species of "neo-Whig" idealism, presumably (oddly enough) conservative, which attributes the moving forces of history to abstract ideas. Such a notion never occurred to me. I am well aware of the social conditioning of human behavior and the cir-cumstantial molding of belief and intellection; one essay (Chapter 8) is devoted precisely to exploring the social and economic conditions that shaped the reception of radical ideas in America and the trans-forming force those ideas acquired because of the peculiar circum-stances that existed here. I do not believe that ideas move history; people do, and people are products of their time and place. What I have asserted, and assert here once again, is that what people do bears some relation to what they think and feel and believe. The world is never perceived raw, pure, and immaculate; it is filtered through human minds, and it behooves someone who seeks to un-derstand the public upheavals of the past to determine what lay in people's minds, the maps of the political and social world they carried in their heads, the common fears and frustrations they sought to relieve, the aspirations they shared—and then examine how that sub-jective, inner world was related to the external world of social and economic circumstances and political events.

And there is a further idea, touched on in several of the essays but drawn out at length only in the final piece (published here for the first time). The powerful set of ideas, ideals, and political sensibilities that shaped the origin and development of the Revolution did not drop dead with the Constitution. That document, in my view, does not mark a Thermidorean reaction to the idealism of the early period engineered by either a capitalist junta or the proponents of rule by a leisured patriciate, nor did the tenth *Federalist* paper mark the death knell of earlier political beliefs or introduce at a crack a new political science. Madison was the most penetrating and original political thinker of his generation, but the ideas of the tenth *Federalist* were commonly discussed at the time, by writers far less original than he, and discussed without any sense that the ideals of the Revolution were being rejected. Modifications in the basic doctrines had to be made to accommodate the urgencies of the time; fundamental beliefs had to be tested, refined, modernized, and ingeniously reapplied— but they were not repudiated. The Constitution created, of course, a potentially powerful central government, with powers that served certain economic groups particularly well, and this new government could be seen—as the antifederalists saw it—as just the kind of arbitrary, absolute, and concentrated power that the Revolution had set out to destroy. But in fact, as almost all the antifederalists sooner or later came to see, it was not. For the earlier principles remained, though in new, more complicated forms, embodied in new institutions devised to perpetuate the received tradition into the modern world. The essential spirit of eighteenth-century reform—its idealism, its determination to protect the individual from the power of the state—lived on, and lives on still.

My aim, in these few pieces, is to convey something of the vividness of the personalities involved in the Revolution; to comment on some of the ways in which personalities and ideas intersected with circumstances and events; to sketch briefly my understanding of the background, origins, character, and legacy of the Revolutionary movement; and to probe, I hope not too solemnly or argumentatively, some of the issues that agitate historians two centuries after the event.

The essays in Part I are reprinted as they originally appeared except for some clarification and elaboration here and there, and some updating of publishing information. The last three essays have been extensively revised to take into account my own second thoughts, recent publications, and criticism, direct and indirect. I have retained some of the original introductions to the essays in Part I, but have set them off in italics so that readers who wish to go directly to the substance of the biographical sketches may do so without difficulty. Except for the last essay, the annotation has been omitted since it is available in the initial publications (listed on page 279).

B.B.

NOTE: In quotations from eighteenth-century writings, capitalization and punctuation have been modernized where modern usage would assist in conveying the writer's thought, and ampersands have been spelled out; but the original emphases and orthography have otherwise been retained.

I

PERSONALITIES

1

John Adams

"It Is My Destiny to Dig Treasures
with My Own Fingers"

In 1954 the Adams Trust, the legal custodian of the hitherto inaccessible archives of the Presidential family, announced the opening of its fantastically rich repository to qualified scholars and a large-scale program of microfilming and publishing the documents. Life *magazine, which through* Time Inc. *underwrote the editorial costs of the initial publications, began an elaborate coverage of the event, printing first a picture story of the meeting of dignitaries at which the program was launched, and subsequently treating its five million readers to large photographic displays of Adamses through the ages, together with generous selections from the first four-volume set of the* Papers *scheduled for publication, the* Diary and Autobiography of John Adams. *Twelve-page prospectuses of these first volumes, published, as all the rest will be, by the Harvard University Press, were widely distributed. The publication day—September 22, 1961—was celebrated not only by reviews, notices, and advertisements of the books in every newspaper in the country that pretended to interest in cultural affairs, but also at the Massachusetts Historical Society by the greatest reception in the 170-year history of that organization, at the American Academy of Arts and Sciences by a splendid testimonial dinner, and at a commemorative luncheon in Washington by the presence of and an address by the President of the United States. Congratulations, President Kennedy said in toasting the editors: "four volumes out and only eighty or a hundred more to go." He was*

3

optimistic. The present editors estimate that there will be at least 150 volumes in three series, of which, by 1990, 32 have appeared.

The sheer scope of this project is extraordinary. No family in American history has produced such a succession of important public figures: two Presidents, a diplomat and ambassador to England, a Secretary of the Navy, two authors of worldwide reputation and influence, and two leading industrialists—to name only the most prominent. And they wrote more, surely, and left more writing behind, than any other family in history: diaries that fill ten, twenty, thirty volumes; trunkfuls of letters—a family correspondence that runs unbroken for more than a century; whole depositories of state papers; reams of poetry (President John Quincy Adams wrote, and left behind intact, more than twenty volumes of poetry, besides a diary that covers, in detail, seventy years of his life and that will occupy an estimated thirty-five volumes in the present edition; his son Charles Francis's diary will fill a mere twenty-four)—writings in all forms, contributed by every generation of the family for over two centuries. The publication project will only include the papers of three generations of the family (the generations of John, John Quincy, and Charles Francis, covering the years 1755–1889), but the 35 mm microfilms of this portion of the archive alone, if unrolled from their 608 reels, would extend for over five miles.

What comes of it all? What good is it? No one, not even the most dedicated scholar, will ever attempt to read all these volumes through. The original manuscripts are available on microfilm; historians who wish to consult them may do so. Why edit them? Why publish them? Who benefits?

A close reading of the first four volumes of The Adams Papers *and an examination of the contribution to the* Papers *themselves made by the editor, the late Lyman Butterfield, and his assistants, Leonard Faber and Wendell Garrett, suggest at least a partial answer.*

We knew, or thought we knew, a great deal about John Adams before the present edition of his diary and autobiography appeared. For so much of his long life was spent in public service that a great deal of it can be reconstructed from public documents. In addition, his grandson Charles Francis Adams, the Civil War diplomat, published between 1850 and 1856 a ten-volume edition of the President's Works *based not only on the state papers but on the documents in the then closely guarded family archive as well. Charles Francis was in many ways an excellent editor, but he was, nevertheless, a man of his age, and he shared some of its prim tastes. Moreover, unlike his grandfather, he had been born into a family of the highest cultivation and refinement. He naturally, instinctively, altered in his editing certain words and passages of the diary and autobiography. "He omitted all sheer indecencies," the present editors explain, and "passages containing suggestive words or actions"; bowdlerized some of John Adams's shocked descriptions of Parisian society; suppressed some of his "frequent references to the coarser side of farm and barnyard life"; "balked at too revealing glimpses of the diarist and his family"; "laid a very heavy hand on John Adams' moonings and mopings, his 'gallanting' and 'hustling' with the girls of the neighborhood"; and purged "unsavory descriptions of, and harsh observations on, the diarist's acquaintances."*

All of this, of course, the new edition faithfully restores, and in reproducing fully and exactly what Adams wrote and in supplying the reader with the information necessary for understanding the circumstances in which the documents were written, the editors have made possible a deeper penetration into the personality of this complicated man and a firmer grasp on the meaning of certain of the ideals and ideas of the American Revolution than we have yet had. For it is now possible to see more clearly than ever before the fundamental pattern of Adams's character and motivation, to observe both the basic continuity and the critical transitions in his development, and, above all, to perceive, to some degree at least, the intensely personal roots of the ideas and beliefs which this leading Revolutionary statesman introduced into one of the most creative debates in modern history.

I

HE WAS, FROM HIS EARLIEST recorded years, a driven and uneasy man. Born forty years before the Revolution into a family of very modest means (his father was a farmer and shoemaker), he was impelled by a frantic desire for affluence and fame. But he had little besides a decent education to start with: "no books," he wrote despondently, "no time, no friends"; "it is my destiny to dig treasures with my own fingers. No body will lend me or sell me a pick axe." Launched, after a stretch of schoolteaching, upon a career in law, he turned to his only resources, those within him, and these, in years of desperate work, he cultivated with grim and almost morbid concentration. He drove himself relentlessly. He assigned himself books to master, shelves of books, difficult, technical books, on metaphysics, on chemistry, on history, on religion, and above all on law—not merely common law and canon law but also civil law "in its native languages, those of Greece and Rome," which "few of my contemporary beginners in the study of the law have the resolution to aim at. . . . I shall gain the consideration and perhaps favour of Mr. Gridley and Mr. Pratt [Boston's leading lawyers] by this means." Repeatedly he set himself tasks to accomplish and schedules to meet. There are resolutions everywhere in the early years of the diary.

> I am resolved [he wrote at the commencement of a new year] to rise with the sun and to study the scriptures on Thursday, Friday, Saturday, and Sunday mornings, and to study some Latin author the other 3 mornings. Noons and nights I intend to read English authors. This is my fixt determination, and I will set down every neglect and every compliance with this resolution. May I blush whenever I suffer one hour to pass unimproved. I will rouse up my mind, and fix my attention. I will stand collected within my self and think upon what I read and what I see.

He will seize upon every opportunity life offers him, and create some that it does not. He pledges himself to "attempt some uncommon, unexpected enterprize in law. . . . I swear I will push myself into business. I will watch my opportunity to speak in court, and will strike with surprize—surprize bench, bar, jury, auditors, and all. Activity, boldness, forwardness, will draw attention. . . . I'll have some boon in return, exchange: fame, fortune, or something." Reputation, he tells himself, "ought to be the perpetual subject of my thoughts," and he considers ways and means to "spread an opinion of myself as a lawyer of distinguished genius, learning, and virtue." Perhaps he should mingle with ordinary people "and converse familiarly . . . on the common tittletattle of the town and the ordinary concerns of a family, and so take every fair opportunity of showing my knowledge in the law." Or perhaps he should "endeavour to renew my acquaintance with those young gentlemen in Boston who were at colledge with me." In any event, he must "look out for a cause to speak to, and exert all the soul and all the body I own to cut a flash, strike amazement, to catch the vulgar." It was this that he longed for above all: to do something, to produce something "that will surprize the world." A single thought would serve, he calculated, to raise him "at once to fame" if it were sufficiently "new, grand, wild, yet regular."

Such fist-clenched entries, repeated with endless variations through the first ten years of the diary, record the passion of the young Adams's assault upon an adverse and seemingly impenetrable world. But they merely set the stage for the most intense struggles of his youth and early manhood, which were directed not outward to a hostile environment, but inward, into the ambiguities and tensions of his own nature. For he was anything but a single-minded careerist. Powerful elements within him beat against his determination to make a name for himself, impeded the easy satisfaction of his ambition, set limits to the possibilities of his success.

He was, in the first place, a man of fierce integrity and strict Christian morality—a Puritan, at least to the extent of having unconsciously and unquestioningly accepted as his own the exacting behavioral standards of the Bible Commonwealth. If he sought fame, reputation, and success, he despised them, too, and excoriated himself in one breath for the very efforts he urged upon himself in another. The happiness he really sought, he wrote at a time when his quest for recognition and security was almost obsessive, would come not from "fortune, fame, beauty, praise and all such things," but from "an habitual contempt" of them. In the end "we shall find that we have applied our whole vigour, all our faculties, in the pursuit of honour, or wealth, or learning or some other such delusive trifle, instead of the real and everlasting excellences of piety and virtue." Only "habits of contemplating the deity and his transcendent excellences . . . and habits of love and compassion to our fellow men . . . will afford us a real and substantial pleasure." He was young, in his early twenties, when he wrote these words, but he meant them, and continued to mean them, and he loathed himself for violating their spirit. They rose from as deep a source, as keen and permanent a need, as did his worldly ambitions.

Though he suffered from this conflict all his life, his eventual success in the world, with its consequent easing of the need to push and strike and plan and promote, blunted its edge. A feeling of gracelessness and social clumsiness, an admitted naïveté of manner, hurt him more; and this he never overcame. As a young man he was driven into fits of despair over his shyness, his social stiffness and maladroit conversation, all grimly recorded in diary entries that are painful to read. At times it was only a matter of having "behaved with too much reserve to some and with too stiff a face and air, and with a face and air and tone of voice of pale timidity." At other times it was a failure easily to "chatter with a girl." Often he was tongue-tied: "objects before me don't suggest proper questions to ask, and proper observations to make"; and then he overcompensated, babbled, overextended himself to make a figure, and was easily tripped up by calmer men with sharper wits. The problem seemed self-intensifying. The more he tried, the more affected he became, the more vulnerable he was, and so the more cautious and paralyzingly self-conscious. "I talk to Paine about Greek, that makes him laugh. I talk to Sam Quincy about resolution and being a great man and study and improving time, which makes him laugh. . . . I talk to Hannah and Easther about the folly of love, about despising it . . . which makes them laugh. . . . Besides this I have insensibly fallen into a habit of affecting wit and humour, of shrugging my shoulders and moving [and] distorting the muscles of my face. My motions are stiff and uneasy, ungraceful, and my attention is unsteady and irregular." He cringed at slights, dreaded ridicule, and bled at contempt, painfully probing wounds playfully inflicted. At night, alone, he brooded on, rehearsed, the devastating responses he should have made.

He was born naïve. The world was always bigger, more impressive, than expected, and it continuously caught him by surprise. He could not help but gawk. In Boston after a day at court where he "felt shy, under awe and concern," he attended a "consort" where he came upon "the most spacious and elegant room, the gayest company of gentlemen and the finest row of ladies that I ever saw." The scene from the meeting-house steeple in Wethersfield, Connecticut, was "the most grand and beautifull prospect in the world, at least that I ever saw." At John Morin Scott's house in New York, "a more elegant breakfast I never saw"; at the Exchange, "the most splendid dinner I ever saw." Wealth, sophistication, and elegance always impressed him, despise them as he might. In a sense it was always true, as he later said of himself in Paris, that he "did not know the world," and what was worse, he knew he did not know.

But if in this way he was naïve, untutored and unskilled in the ways of the world, in another way he was not, and this other knowledge and skill, which could at times be exhilarating, at other times proved to be the most wearisome burden of all. He had—to an extraordinary degree; to an extent that can only now, in the fully restored text of the diary and autobiography, be properly appreciated—a sensuous apprehension of experience. For all his mental efforts and intellectual accomplishments, his knowledge and ideas, he responded first and fundamentally to the physical—the tangible, audible, visual—qualities of life. He felt the world, directly and sensitively, before he thought about it; and he expressed his feelings with a vividness and an accuracy of phrasing that make his prose the most alive and readable of any written in eighteenth-century America.

His writing sparkles with unstylized, personally idiomatic images of the tangible world: "a cabbin filled with straw where . . . the master of the house, his wife and four children all pigged in together"; a cow's teats that "strutt with milk"; a Moravian prayer meeting where "the women's heads resembled a garden of white cabbage heads"; kissed girls "glowing like furnaces"; the Spanish landscape, "like a bird deprived of its feathers"; England's navy weakened "like a girdled tree"; "the tyrannical bell that dongled me out of my house every morning"; a "small, spungy, muscular substance growing fast to the rock, in figure and feeling resembling a young girl's breast."

Such sensuous vividness, such idiomatic concreteness, was not restricted to the single metaphor or phrase. There are long sections in the *Diary and Autobiography*—a twenty-page description of Adams's first, terrifying transatlantic voyage; a detailed account of a month-long midwinter trip across Spain by mule and wagon; a 1,500-word picture of the procession of the knights of the *cordon bleu* at Versailles and a view of the royal family at supper—that are of sustained literary brilliance. Let a few sentences from an almost routine description of a tour in France (a visit to Chantilly) illustrate the interest his prose can generate.

> Walked around the gardens, fish ponds, grottoes, and water-
> spouts. And looked at the carps and swan that came up to us
> for bread. Nothing is more curious than this. Whistle or throw
> a bit of bread into the water and hundreds of carps, large and

fat as butter, will be seen swimming near the top of the water towards you, and will assemble all in a huddle before you. Some of them will thrust up their mouths to the surface, and gape at you like young birds in a nest to their parents for food.

While we were viewing the statue of Montmorency, Mademoiselle de Bourbon came out into the round house at the corner of the castle dressed in beautifull white, her hair uncombed, hanging and flowing about her shoulders, with a book in her hand, and leaned over the bar of iron; but soon perceiving that she had caught my eye and that I viewed her more attentively than she fancied, she rose up with that majesty and grace which persons of her birth affect if they are not taught, turned her hair off of both her showlders with her hands in a manner that I could not comprehend, and decently stepped back into the chamber and was seen no more.

This profoundly sensuous experience of life expressed itself in many ways. Events were never abstractions to him: they were human encounters, exchanges between sentient, visible and audible, people. Repeatedly, in entry after entry in these four volumes, he slips into dramatic dialogue, quoting in direct discourse the words of the actors, placing them, often, in separate paragraphs introduced by the speakers' names: *"Coll. Q.," "B. Fessenden"; "Lincoln," "I."* It was not a self-conscious effort to dramatize. Anecdotes—of which there are literally dozens in these volumes—were renderings of human exchanges, and they drifted naturally and insensibly into at least low-key theatrics; it took very little conscious art on Adams's part to blow these naturally glowing embers into crackling little tragedies and comedies. Thus his wonderful account of the night in 1776 when "but one bed could be procured for Dr. Franklin and me in a chamber little larger than the bed . . . with only one small window." The episode had emerged from the surrounding narrative naturally, without design, but once the scene was before him again he instantly shifted from description to dialogue. The curtain goes up. There on the stage is Franklin, that "old conjurer," that "Egyptian mummy," snug in bed; and there is JA, "an invalid and afraid of the air in the night," drawing the one small window shut.

Oh! says Franklin, don't shut the window. We shall be suffocated. I answered I was afraid of the evening air. Dr. Franklin replied . . . come! open the window and come to bed, and I will convince you: I believe you are not acquainted with my theory of colds. Opening the window and leaping into bed, I said I had read his letters to Dr. Cooper . . . but the theory was so little consistent with my experience that I thought it a paradox. However, I had so much curiosity to hear his reasons that I would run the risque of a cold. The Doctor then began an harrangue upon air and cold and respiration and perspiration, with which I was so much amused that I soon fell asleep, and left him and his philosophy together.

Humor flowed naturally from Adams's dramatic objectification of himself and the world he saw. At times, when the diarist places himself too prominently downstage and gives himself too grandiloquent a script, the humor is unintentional, and the reader ends up smiling indulgently at the overacting self-dramatist. At one point he pictures himself, alone, heroically declaiming the Catilinarian orations at the top of his lungs, and then explains that doing so gives him not only aesthetic and intellectual rewards but physical ones as well: it "opens my porr[s], quickens the circulations, and so contributes much to health." He snaps up an Englishman's compliment to his wife, but then stops short: "Down, vanity," he writes, "for you don't know who this Englishman is." But most often the humor is intentional, based squarely on Adams's dramatic imagination which exaggerated the ridiculousness of people and things: of poor Aunt Nell, who broke two teeth "at table in company, and to avoid exposing her self, swallowed them"; of B. Bicknal's wife, who was anxious and trembled on her wedding night, until "she recollected she had put her hand to the plow and could not look back, so she mustered up her spirits, committed her soul to G[od] and her body to B. Bicknal, and into bed she leaped"; and above all, of JA, who found himself, to his own great relief, in comic as well as tragic roles. Twenty years after it happened he recalled, and wrote into the autobiography, the exact words uttered by the enraptured secretary of the Tripolitan minister to London with whom Adams had been smoking a pipe "more than two yards in length . . . in awful pomp, reciprocating whiff for whiff":

"Monsieur," Adams remembered the secretary saying, "vous etes un Turk."

But it was not all good humor and enjoyable scenes. The same source in his personality from which his vivid prose and his dramatic instinct flowed generated also his most difficult problems. The difficulties arose not from the fact that he was, as he wrote in the autobiography, "of an amorous disposition, and very early, from ten or eleven years of age, was very fond of the society of females"; for he came of parents who "held every species of libertinage in such contempt and horror . . . that my natural temperament was always overawed by my principles and sense of decorum." The problem was more general and more permanent than that. He loved to daydream, to lie late in bed, to laze away the afternoon, to succumb in whatever way to languor and indolence. But neither his culture nor his situation in life would allow him such satisfactions. From both, from his stern Calvinist heritage and even more from the desperate necessity he felt to forge a career for himself, came violently abusive but only unevenly successful assaults upon this weaker self.

"Dreams and slumbers, sloth and negligence, will be the ruin of my schemes. . . . Why can't I keep awake?" "Laziness, languor, inattention are my bane; am too lazy to rise early and make a fire, and when my fire is made, at 10 o'clock, my passion for knowledge, fame, fortune, or any good is too languid to make me apply with some spirit to my books." He hates himself, torments himself—for his "slothful memory" and his wandering mind; for wasting time meandering in the woods, musing, "indolent and thoughtless"; for "gaping and gazing"; for spending a day "in absolute idleness, or what is worse, gallanting the girls"; for allowing his "rambling imagination" to soar. "Law and not poetry," he instructed himself, "is to be the business of my life." But how nice it was to recall the "shady thicketts and gloomy grottos" of Worcester where he had "sat by the hour together to ruminate and listen to the falls of water."

II

Such problems and tensions—between ambition and integrity, between the desire to appear knowing and sophisticated and the inability to be so, between the longing to retreat into a sensitive inner world of feeling and the need for self-mastery and control over external reality—these are the classic problems of adolescence. What is so striking about Adams is not only the acuteness of his experience of them and his vividness in expressing them but the extent of his life that they dominated. The tormented tossings and turnings and the corrosive self-examinations that resulted from these conflicts dominate completely the first 250 pages of this edition of the diary, which bring Adams to the age of thirty. But then, suddenly, there is a change—a rapid growth; a sudden emergence into maturity.

Three circumstances converged to create the change. The first was his marriage in 1764, on the eve of his thirtieth birthday, to a remarkable woman. Mr. Butterfield's first volume contains two eloquent testimonies to the powers and the probable effect on John of his marriage to Abigail Smith. The diary breaks off fifteen months before the marriage, and when it was resumed three months after the event, what was then, and thereafter, written in it is strikingly different in character from what had earlier been entered: less confessional, more objective, factual, and closed to inner feelings.

But an even more revealing witness of the significance of the marriage—more revealing in some ways even than the famous correspondence between John and Abigail—is the portraits of the two, drawn in pastel by an obscure but evidently discerning colonial artist, Benjamin Blyth, two years after the marriage. John's is a likable but unimpressive face: round, rather soft-looking, bland, and withdrawn. It is an unfinished, uncertain face, with no decisive lines or distinguishing feature. The composure seems artificial and posed, and one turns the page easily—but then is caught up, startled, by what appears on the opposite side. Abigail's face is extraordinary, not so much for its beauty, which, in a somewhat masculine way, is clearly enough there, as for the maturity and the power of personality it expresses. The face is oval in shape, ending in a sharp, almost fleshless, chin; a firm, thin, but graceful mouth; a rather long arched nose; brilliant, piercing, wide-spaced eyes. It is about as confident, controlled, and commanding a face as a woman can have and still remain feminine. The mystery is not so much why Adams no longer poured his soul out into his notebooks after 1764 as why he did not burn the ones in which he had.

But there is more to the change than this. By 1765 the years of labor, planning, and striving were beginning to pay off. Adams's fears of failure and need for reinforcement were dissipating as more and more cases came his way and his reputation for unusual competence in law spread. The first diary entry after his marriage records his membership and activity in the Sodality, a private club of lawyers, in which he found himself, to his great satisfaction, an equal with the most learned and distinguished practitioners in Boston—famous and successful men, among them the venerable Jeremiah Gridley, who had once, not so long before, sponsored and counseled him in his entry into the profession.

But 1765 was also the year of the Stamp Act, and it marks Adams's emergence into the world of public controversy. In the last half of that year he published his Dissertation on the Canon and Feudal Law, one of the early statements of American Revolutionary theory; composed the equally distinguished if less famous Braintree Instructions denouncing the Stamp Act; and was appointed counsel for Boston to plead for the reopening of the courts in defiance of Parliament's law. At the time, he hated the growing Anglo-American controversy, not merely for the public upheaval it threatened but also for the disturbance he believed it would create in the progress of his own career. But he could not have been more wrong. It gave him a platform he was eminently capable of using; it vaulted him suddenly into the fame he had so long sought; ultimately it placed him in the halls of kings. Later, he recognized the fact (though he overstated it): "I am but an ordinary man. The times alone have destined me to fame."

If the *Diary and Autobiography* revealed only this sudden halt in the extended adolescence of John Adams it would still be a unique and valuable set of documents. But it becomes evidence of important elements in our early national history by documenting the continuities as well as the critical transition in the life of the second President. For though Adams changed, around his thirtieth year, he was not transformed. The earlier characteristics were transmuted, not eliminated; and they continued to shape his, and in part the nation's, history.

He remained a man of fierce and stubborn, at times almost flamboyant, integrity. His unbending rectitude, his moral courage, and his selflessness in public office became famous. He knew there was a right, believed himself capable of finding it, and once he perceived it clung to it steadfastly. How could he—why should he—compromise? If he felt an office in Governor Hutchinson's administration was offered to him with implied strings—strings that might involve "a sacrifice of my honour, my conscience, my friends, my country, my God"—why should he think twice about it? If he saw, what Franklin probably knew as well but was not likely to do anything about, that three commissioners from the United States were not needed in France, that one, in all likelihood, would do better than three, why should he not report the fact to Congress even if it meant his own retirement from the greatest scene he had ever beheld? He never knew the value of, nor was he able to use, the saving gesture, the stabilizing concession. He may have been a statesman, but, "unpractised in intrigues for power," as he once accurately described himself, he was never a politician—which is what that pliant old fox Franklin, whose slack hedonism in Paris drove Adams into fits of righteousness and suspicion, meant when he described his colleague as one who "means well for his country, is always an honest man, often a wise one but sometimes, and in some things, absolutely out of his senses."

And if he lost the naïveté of his early years, he remained, to his everlasting chagrin, clumsy in society, awkward, and self-conscious. He was impressed by what he saw of high society and grand affairs in Paris, as well he might have been; but sometimes he was overcome. "It is vain to attempt a description of the magnificence of [the Duchesse d'Anville's] house, gardens, library, furniture, or the entertainment of the table." "The Queen was . . . an object too sublime and beautiful for my dull pen to describe." Mercy Warren, who knew him well, wrote—correctly, though Adams never forgave her for it—that in Paris he was "ridiculed by the fashionable and polite as deficient in the *je ne scai quoi* so necessary in highly polished society." He had nothing of Franklin's casual wit or of Jefferson's natural elegance of address. One can sympathize with his embarrassment and with the woodenness of his reply (what *would* have been the graceful but pointed response?) to the twitting Frenchwoman who in the midst of a sumptuous feast asked him, since his name indicated a peculiar descent "from the first man and woman," to explain to the assembled company "how the first couple found out the art of lying together." And one cannot help respecting his resolute decision, when suddenly the eyes of a vast and brilliant throng turned on him, to imitate the composure, the "power of face," of Indian chiefs exposed to the stares of the white men. But it is hard to see how else but wearisome he must have seemed to that succession of French dinner partners from whom he doggedly insisted on extracting bibliographies—of "the purest writers of French," of the best historians of France, of the best dictionary and grammar of Italian and of German.

He never overcame his sensitivity to slights and ridicule. His self-esteem was always vulnerable and frequently injured, and he was continually on his guard to defend it by stubborn self-assertion. In the end this vulnerability, growing wildly in the intense heat of domestic politics and international intrigue, became paranoiac. He became morbidly suspicious—of Hancock, who had launched a "persecution against me across the Atlantic"; of Charles Thomson, the secretary of the Continental Congress, who, Adams insisted, had doctored the official records of that body to favor his enemies; of Hamilton, and not only for the obvious political reasons. The true source of the trouble between Hamilton and himself, Adams believed, was personal: it lay in the speeches he had once made opposing a military appointment for Hamilton's brother-in-law, Philip Schuyler; they "had been rankling in Hamilton's heart from 1776 till he wrote his libel against me in 1799." Above all, he suspected Franklin. He suspected him of all sorts of things: of hiring a secretary as "a spy on me"; of withholding official information from him; of having held "mysterious intercourse or correspondence" with George III; of "backstairs intrigues" in behalf of his illegitimate son, the "base born brat" William, and other favorites. Retired from the Presidency, at ease with Abigail in the security of Quincy, Adams was consumed with thoughts of the abuse, secret and open, to which he had been subjected. "A perpetual vulcano of slander," he wrote in 1804, has been "pouring on my flesh all my life time."

And he never lost his sensuous, physical response to the things and the people around him. The recollections and descriptions of his old age are as sharp and vivid as those of his youth. He recalls the color of unusual soils and the amount of pepper the double agent Bancroft had used on his food. He likens sleeping with others to being "buried in hot embers." He remembers Lafayette "panting for glory." He comments on, and in so doing demonstrates, the "dissagreable sibillations" of the English language, and attempts to imitate the precise sound of English names pronounced with a French accent (Washington: "VAUGSTAINGSTOUNG"). Anecdotes, dialogues—graphic representations of people vividly alive, talking, twisting their faces, shrugging their shoulders—fill the autobiography, written by a bitter and weary man of seventy, as they had the diary of a passionate adolescent.

III

It is with these central personality characteristics in mind—characteristics formed in a troubled youth, modified and consolidated in maturity—that one can best understand Adams's response to the Revolutionary crisis and the sources of his political theory. For unlike Jefferson, whose political and social ideas seem somehow to have been kept immaculate, unaffected by the grinding abrasions of everyday life, Adams drew his ideas as much from his feelings, from his sensitive reactions to the human realities about him, as he did from the great array of writings, ancient and modern, that he had mastered.

He never doubted that England's policy toward the colonies after the Stamp Act was evil, and not simply because abstract rights were being violated. The evil that first moved him into strong opposition could not have been more specific or personal. Royal authority in Massachusetts in the 1760s was coming to rest increasingly, as Adams saw it, in the hands of a single family, the Hutchinsons, who, with their Oliver kin and a number of dependents and hangers-on, were becoming absolute monopolists of public office. His fear and hatred of this group flowed from his general resentment of the unassailable social superiority that existed in the world he was seeking to conquer. He envied and despised "all the great notions of high family that you find in Winslows, Hutchinsons, Quincys, Saltonstals, Chandlers, Leonards, Otis's," for " 'tis vain and mean to esteem oneself for his ancestors' merit." When it became evident that Thomas Hutchinson, admittedly a man of "great merit," was using his influence to advance not only his own career but that of his personal following "to the exclusion of much better men," and when it appeared that his avid place-seeking was closely tied in to England's new colonial policies,

Adams's social animosities took fire and became the source of a flaming hatred of state authority which placed him, ordinarily a cautious
man, in the vanguard of the Revolutionary radicals.

Again and again he struck out at "this amazing ascendancy of one
family." Dazzled by Thomas Hutchinson's glare, he wrote, bewildered by "the mazy windings of [his] heart and the serpentine wiles
of his head, . . . the bigotted, the superstitious, the enthusiastical, the
tools, the interested, the timid" had become his "creatures" just as
Hutchinson himself, in turn, by his insatiable lust for office, had become the puppet of a power-mad ministry bent on destroying the
constitution. It all fitted together—the objective world of strange
Parliamentary laws, of troops stationed in peaceful towns, of plural
officeholding and prejudiced courts; and the subjective world of
long-remembered slights, of frustrated ambition, and envy. By 1774
he was convinced that he was witnessing the culmination of a deliberate conspiracy "against the public liberty . . . first regularly formed
and begun to be executed in 1763 or 4." The result, unless the plot
were exposed and destroyed, would be tyranny—not some vague,
unfamiliar historical tyranny but one imposed by people he knew,
executed by hands he had shaken.

Each phase of the Revolutionary crisis and the subsequent reconstruction of public authority appeared to Adams with the same
vividness and the same high degree of personification. There are, of
course, abstractions—glittering generalities—in his political writings
as there are in those of all the leading figures of the Revolution. But
there is a concreteness, too, built up by his sensuous imagination and
tactile grasp of reality that is entirely distinctive. It is not enough for
him first to qualify "taxation" with "hideous" and then to specify it
further by adding "more cruel and ruinous than Danegeld of old"; the
drama in his mind's eye must be fully played out, and he refers the
reader to Shakespeare, *Henry VIII*, Act I, Scene ii. There is nothing
abstract about the need for free elections and for trial by jury: they
are the only security we have "against being ridden like horses, and
fleeced like sheep, and worked like cattle, and fed and cloathed like
hoggs and hounds. Nay no other security against fines, imprison-
ments, loss of limbs, whipping posts, gibbetts, bastinadoes, and
racks." Lexington was not simply an infuriating provocation and proof
of evil intentions; it made perfectly clear that "if we did not defend

ourselves they would kill us." So, too, later, in France, when a Dutchman argued that for his people to support the United States openly would be to split the Protestant interest in Europe and throw the balance of power to France, and that America might do well to consider such issues in deciding its policies, Adams replied that no one should be so deluded as to expect that America would

> tamely suffer Great Britain to tear up from the foundations all the governments in America . . . and submit to the unlimited domination of Parliament who knew little more of us than they did of Kamshatska and who cared not half so much for us as they did for their flocks and herds. The inhumanity too with which they conducted the war . . . not only hiring European mercenaries, but instigating Indians and corrupting domesticks as if we were fit for nothing but to be cutt to pieces by savages and negroes. Americans would not submit to these things merely from prophecies and precarious speculations about the Protestant interest and the ballance of power in Europe.

In passing he refers to England's Hessian allies who sell "their subjects like cattle to [be] slaughtered in America for the humane purpose of butchering us."

It was the same when he came to consider the principles of politics to be used in the reconstruction of public authority after independence. His ideas on government were anchored as deeply in his understanding of himself and of human nature as they were in his knowledge of history and of political theory. Long years of raking self-examination and an extraordinary sensitivity to other people's feelings and motivations had left him with attitudes to human possibilities more akin to those of his Calvinist forebears and of the twentieth century than of the eighteenth-century Enlightenment. He saw more darkness than light. He had felt in himself and had acknowledged to himself the powerful irrationalities of his own nature, and while he admitted that "human nature, depraved as it is, has interwoven in its very frame a love of truth, sincerity, and integrity," it was the passion of man, his boundless ambition, his love of fame and honor—forces he had fought within himself—that he knew to be controlling. What is it, he asked, that decides men's opinions of others? "It is avidity, envy, revenge, interest." Who knew better than he that ambition was "one of the more ungovernable passions"? Control and discipline were as necessary to restrain the passions of society as they were to create order in the life of the individual.

He accepted none of the current clichés that placed the burden of corruption on institutions and saw the promise of felicity in the release of natural instincts. All men, in high station or low, primitive or sophisticated, contained within them the same destructive elements, and must be equally constrained for the common good. His political theory was an effort to express in the constitutional language of his day the implications of this dark, introspective psychology.

It was a difficult task, and he was never optimistic about the chances of success. But certain pitfalls could at least be avoided. Provision could be made against what seemed the most obvious danger, the tyranny of an unchecked aristocracy. He had little hope that "men in high life" would ever completely forgo the attraction of "titles, ribbons, stars, garters, crosses, keys," or that "princes and nobles and great ministers" would cease to "commit high crimes and misdemeanors which no other authority would be powerful enough to prevent or punish." Such behavior by the favored few would continue to exist; it could not be eliminated; but it might be controlled, to some extent at least, by confining its expression. Make provision for the inevitable. Allow the aristocracy, however it might be defined, a legal, constitutional role in government, but limit it to a special institution, the traditional middle chamber of the legislature, and place it in isolation, one among several elements of government in constant tension and competition with others.

But this was not the only, or even necessarily the chief, danger to the general good. The mass of humanity was no better than the aristocracy. From his earliest recorded years Adams feared "the errors to which the public opinions of the people were liable in times of great heat and danger as well as . . . the extravagances of which the populace of cities were capable when artfully excited to passion." The principles and judgments of "at least one third of mankind" easily "give way to their fears." "The poor people," once stirred to action, "are seldom aware of the purposes for which they are set in motion . . . and when once heated and in full career they can neither manage themselves nor be regulated by others." He never believed that "a perfect equality of suffrage was essential to liberty." Limits and controls must always be present, and means must be found to build into the structure of government counterweights to the force of the many as well as of the few.

Fearful of human passions, he was a passionate advocate of the separation of powers—governmental and social—and of maintaining a competitive balance among them. If the power of the "democratical" element were allowed full sway "our lives, liberties, reputations, and estates will lie at the mercy of a majority and of a tryumphant party." So the popular element of the constitution must also be constrained, sealed off, confined. It too must be subject to law interpreted by a fully independent judiciary and enforced by a powerful, impartial, in effect disciplinarian, executive.

He despised, too easily perhaps, the optimism of a Paine or a Jefferson who looked for major solutions in the elimination of monarchy or of aristocracy. He shared their fears of both; but he feared himself—those elements of ambition, of irrationality, and of sensuous satisfaction which he had fought so fiercely and so knowingly—even more. He knew no peace, and saw no peace for mankind, until they too were brought under control.

2

Thomas Jefferson

"No American Should Come to Europe
under 30 Years of Age"

*S*o far twenty-five of the projected seventy-five volumes of The Papers
of Thomas Jefferson *have been published, and it is now clear that
this enterprise, set on foot in 1943 by the Thomas Jefferson Bicentennial
Commission and originally edited by the late Julian P. Boyd and his associates at Princeton, introduced a new era in the history of American
documentary publications.*

The full effect of The Jefferson Papers *can be properly assessed, of
course, only when the entire set has been published—a date somewhat far
off, since the volumes published between 1950 and 1989 carry the story only
to 1792, just under a decade before Jefferson became President, three and
a half decades before he died. Few of us writing now are likely to see the
completion of the series, and some kind of interim assessment would seem to
be in order. For this edition is one of a number of such major publication
series underway: the* Franklin Papers, *so far twenty-seven volumes, published with remarkable speed and thoroughness at Yale; the* Adams Papers,
at the Massachusetts Historical Society and Harvard; the Madison Papers,
at Chicago and the University of Virginia; the Hamilton Papers, *recently
completed at Columbia; Wilson's at Princeton; and others: Clay's, Cal-
houn's—an extraordinary series of projects whose appearance is in itself a
phenomenon worth some consideration. An examination of the first of these
ventures, which has set standards and suggested styles for the others, may*

lead to some appreciation of the meaning of this remarkable development in publishing and scholarship.

The volumes of the Jefferson Papers *so far published in chronological sequence cover the period 1760–92, usually designated the era of the American Revolution, and are thus in the structure of American history complete in themselves. They are also complete in the chronology of Jefferson's career, for they cover his early years and his sojourn in France, where he lived for five years (1784–89), first as commissioner to negotiate commercial treaties and then as minister to France. These years abroad have long been recognized as forming a crucial transition in Jefferson's life. If he had died in Europe he would be known to history as a successful revolutionary leader, a lawyer who had eloquently stated the principles of the American cause and who had turned thereafter to the arduous task of incorporating these ideas into constitutional and statutory forms. But he survived, to become almost immediately upon his return the central and most controversial political figure of the early national period, and subsequently a dominant force in the intellectual history of American politics. Even in Jefferson's lifetime the years abroad were seen as critical in his development, for, it was said, it was then that he acquired a lifelong fascination with Enlightenment radicalism and a devotion to France that lured him into a variety of unsound policies which, as Secretary of State and as President, he pursued to the hazard of the national interest. Modern historians lacking such animus have carried on the discussion, finding in the French sojourn a source if not of political delusion then of formative ideas and experience.*

The years in France (Volumes VII-XV) are important also in another way. A host of recent publications, especially Dumas Malone's heroic six-volume biography, Merrill Peterson's deft one-volume life, and most recently Jack McLaughlin's fascinating account of Jefferson's lifelong involvement in the building and rebuilding of Monticello, make clear how much there is to know about this Olympian figure and how difficult it is to understand him as a person, an actual human being. Even before his death Jefferson's personality had become lost in polemics and political symbolism; he died a cause, an idea, a national institution. Since then, each major political battle, each era of American literature, historiography, and politics, has added another layer to the image of this extraordinary man until, in the late twentieth century, all human substance seems to have been lost. "Jefferson" is all things to all men. He emerges now a culture hero, a luminous presence known only and in some misty way to be liberal, good, learned, and complicated. The man himself, the personality, has vanished; and in seeking to recover it one comes back repeatedly to the half decade in France. Those years are peculiarly revealing. The public personality was fully formed, but it had not yet completely absorbed the private; the materials and design of the mature figure were all there, but they had not yet acquired that hard-glazed surface which has proved so difficult to penetrate; the characteristic ideas and use of ideas were all there, but they were almost inert, suspended by force of circumstance above full commitment. The essential elements of personality stand out more clearly then than at any other time, and may be grasped with greater assurance.

The natural importance of this period of Jefferson's life for an understanding of his personality is enlarged by the peculiar character of Boyd's edition of the Papers *as "writings" or "works." The project as a whole will eventually consist of two series: one, the longer, chronological in character; the other, comprised of the large integral items such as the* Autobiography *and the* Notes on the State of Virginia. *The former series is not a mere collection of Jefferson's letters and smaller writings. It includes, in addition to these, all the letters, memoranda, and other communications sent to him, and also everything else "legitimately Jeffersonian by reason of authorship or of relationship." Thus the* Papers *contain documents written but not signed by Jefferson, those "about which he expressed his views or took some course of action," and those neither written by him nor addressed to him but which "because of their importance or because of their allusion to him or because they passed through his hands, deserve to be printed or at least recorded among his papers." The result is a presentation, as complete as possible, of the writings* "and recorded actions" *of Thomas Jefferson.*

I have stressed the phrase "recorded actions," which appears in the first sentence of the general introduction to the project, because it is the key to the uniqueness of the Papers. *Bringing to print as consecutive documents not only everything Jefferson wrote and that was written to him but everything that bears on his "recorded actions," the editors have compiled, and in their annotation have written, a running commentary on, an exhaustive documentary biography of one of the most important figures of the late eighteenth and early nineteenth centuries.*

The effect they have achieved by the mere quantity of material included is heightened by the manner of presentation. This is no hodgepodge collection. The great array of material is strictly controlled to keep the central chronology clear. Documents not in the major to-from *category are, with* rare exceptions, reduced to footnotes, and in this subordinate position discreetly fill in this "record of a man's career" when the primary papers are thin or missing. Furthermore, the editors have devised an unusual scheme which emphasizes the special character of the Papers as documentary biography and history. At a number of points (on an average twice or three times a volume) they have broken into the chronological order to introduce separate sections containing several documentary items and a detailed editorial comment, all bearing on a single unusually important episode or document. The separate section entitled "The Declaration of Independence" in Volume I, for example, includes five documents—four draft versions of the Declaration and the final "fair copy"—dated from June 11 to July 4, preceded by a 2,000-word essay by the editors on the textual changes from Jefferson's first draft to the one finally adopted. Similarly, a 360-page section in Volume II on the revisal of the laws of Virginia—in itself a major achievement of textual reconstruction and historical analysis—brings together under three main headings and a five-part appendix documents from the entire decade 1776–86.

It is not only by these documentary clusters that the editing contributes to the overall effect. Throughout the volumes, the presentation and annotation of individual items are such as to transcend the ordinary requirements of textual clarification and to indicate the editors' concern with the meaning of the documents, their bearing on the interpretation of Jefferson and his time. Thus, puzzled by Jefferson's uncharacteristic "cold dismissal," while minister to France, of his erstwhile intimate, the mysterious Charles Williamos, the editors append to a one-page letter a 2,500-word examination of the relationship between the two men and of the circumstances of the break, arriving at the "almost inescapable" conclusion that Jefferson had been informed that "he had admitted a British spy to his confidence." But perhaps the editors' most imaginative analysis is in the section in Volume XV entitled "The Earth Belongs in Usufruct to the Living," which consists principally of a letter to Madison of September 6, 1789, prefaced by an extensive editorial comment. This letter contains Jefferson's first full statement of his deceptively simple belief that the world belongs to the living and not to the dead, a notion that, as he came to apply it, had enormous political and social implications which he did not hesitate to draw. But the letter purports to be not merely an epistolary "speculation" but a concrete proposal to Madison to include a declaration of this principle in the "preamble to our first law for appropriating the public revenue"—a proposal that can *only be described as fantastic. In their introduction to the section the editors scour the circumstances of the immediate situation in which the letter was written for some reasonable explanation. They find one. Their argument, based to a large extent on their discovery of "a common (homoeoteleutic) copyist's error," is that the document was not meant to be a letter to Madison at all; it was, rather, a "thesis" written for Lafayette's use in the French National Assembly in early September 1789, providing theoretical grounds for the wholesale revision of* France's *fundamental law. The strange form of its appearance was a hastily constructed "protective device" by which Jefferson hoped to disguise what, if the editors' argument is correct, was improper interference in the internal affairs of the sovereign state to which he was accredited. The letter in any case is important; the editors' analysis of it adds both a deeper dimension to its meaning as social and political theory and an episode in the history of the eighteenth-century revolutionary international.*

All of these editorial characteristics—the scope of the materials included as the "papers" proper; their arrangement and presentation, particularly the grouping of certain documents into clusters; and the extensive editorial analysis and interpretation in which are included generous extracts from non-Jeffersonian sources—all of this creates a density in the portrayal of Jefferson that no biography, no matter how extensive, could possibly convey. In fact, it is the very weaknesses of the volumes as biography in the ordinary sense—the repetitiousness, the inclusion of false starts—that contribute most significantly to an enrichment of the portrait.

I

WHAT DO THE PAPERS OF THOMAS JEFFERSON reveal of the Virginian's personality? What can be said of his character, the pattern of his responses, the way in which he engaged with the world?

Beneath the familiar, manifest features there appear to be two dominant elements, two controlling groups of traits or instincts or habits of mind.

The first was a surprisingly uncritical willingness to accept, a generous receptivity to preformed patterns, a reluctance to scrutinize critically what was given: conventionality of the liberal mind, conventionality of behavior.

Jefferson's central experience in the five years after 1784 was his encounter with the realities of European life. His reaction to French, and more generally to European, culture and society, which he expressed in letter after letter, was as highly stylized, as formally patterned and shaped to expectation, as those carefully trimmed gardens he examined in England. His response was an eighteenth-century stereotype—a boldly liberal, high-minded, enlightened stereotype, but a stereotype nonetheless—a configuration of liberal attitudes and ideas which he accepted uncritically, embellishing them with his beautifully wrought prose but questioning little and adding little.

Europe was the obverse of America, which appeared to him more arcadian, more idyllically pastoral, more ideal and natural, the longer he stayed in France. Europe was effete, sunk in corruption, dragged down into near-hopelessness by the weight of despotism and aristocratic privilege. Emphasis became exaggeration and hyperbole. "I was much an enemy to monarchy," he wrote to Washington, "before I came to Europe. I am ten thousand times more so since I have seen what they are. There is scarcely an evil known in these countries which may not be traced to their king as its source, nor a good which is not derived from the small fibres of republicanism existing among them. I can further say with safety there is not a crowned head in Europe whose talents or merit would entitle him to be elected a vestryman by the people of any parish in America." After a year in France he was confident that "of twenty millions of people supposed to be in France . . . nineteen millions are more wretched, more accursed in every circumstance of human existence, than the most conspicuously wretched individual of the whole United States."

There was much, of course, he could not deny admiring: "polite manners," for example, and the arts; but they were easily outbalanced by the malignant, festering corruption.

> The truth of Voltaire's observation offers itself perpetually, that every man here must be either the hammer or the anvil. . . . Intrigues of love occupy the younger, and those of ambition the more elderly part of the great. Conjugal love having no existence among them, domestic happiness, of

which that is the basis, is utterly unknown. In lieu of this are substituted pursuits which nourish and invigorate all our bad passions, and which offer only moments of extasy amidst days and months of restlessness and torment. Much, very much inferior this to the tranquil permanent felicity with which domestic society in America blesses most of its inhabitants, leaving them to follow steadily those pursuits which health and reason approve, and rendering truly delicious the intervals of these pursuits.

This theme, of sexual promiscuity as the ultimate corruption, had a special meaning to this typically Puritan revolutionary and recent widower. He returned to it again and again; it formed the substance of some of his most lyric and passionate letters: letters to his regular correspondents at home; to the glamorous Philadelphian Anne Bingham, swept up in the whirl of Paris high society; and above all, since its threat was greatest to the young whose habits were still unformed, to the youthful Americans traveling in Europe and to those who sought his opinion of European education. "Why send an American youth to Europe for education?" he wrote to John Bannister, Jr.

He acquires a fondness for European luxury and dissipation and a contempt for the simplicity of his own country; he is fascinated with the privileges of the European aristocrats, and sees with abhorrence the lovely equality which the poor enjoy with the rich in his own country: . . . he is led by the strongest of all human passions into a spirit for female intrigue destructive of his own and others' happiness, or a passion for whores destructive of his health, and in both cases learns to consider fidelity to the marriage bed as an ungentlemanly practice and inconsistent with happiness: he recollects the voluptuary dress and arts of the European women and pities and despises the chaste affections and simplicity of those of his own country. . . .

"No American," he concluded, "should come to Europe under 30 years of age."

This stereotyped response to European culture did nothing to interfere with Jefferson's enjoyment of Parisian society; but it was not without important effects. It limited his understanding of Europe and, particularly, of the great upheaval whose premonitory motions took place while he was in Paris and of whose initial violence he was a close witness. For a corollary of this Enlightenment creed was an exaggerated belief in the influence of formal institutions and particularly in the determinative effect upon society of the formal structure of government. A simplistic constitutionalism lay at the bottom of Jefferson's thoughts on politics. "It is difficult to conceive," he wrote of the French, "how so good a people, with so good a king, so well disposed rulers in general, so genial a climate, so fertile a soil, should be rendered so ineffectual for producing human happiness by one single curse, that of a bad form of government. But it is a fact." Observe, he wrote in his notes on his tour through Holland and the Rhine Valley, "the effect of the difference of government" as you "pass the line between the republic [of Frankfurt] and the Landgraviate of Hesse. . . . In Francfort all is life, bustle, and motion. In Hanau the silence and quiet of the mansions of the dead. Nobody is seen moving in the streets; every door is shut; no sound of the saw, the hammer, or other utensil of industry."

Jefferson may have been convinced by his own argument that "vices in the form of government" lay at the heart of Europe's miseries, but others—more consistent empiricists, more original, dissatisfied, quizzical minds—were not. Madison, whose letters in these years, if less graceful, were consistently more original and penetrating in analysis than Jefferson's, was no less a republican than he, but he thought Jefferson's interpretation was superficial. "I have no doubt," he wrote in reply, "that the misery of the lower classes will be found to abate wherever the government assumes a freer aspect, and the laws favor a subdivision of property. Yet I suspect that the difference will not fully account for the comparative comfort of the mass of people in the United States." Just what the main cause of the difference was, Madison confessed he was not sure; but he suspected that "our limited population has probably as large a share in producing this effect as the political advantages which distinguish us." The thought intrigued him; and he followed it out into an original, probing, far-ranging if inconclusive speculation on "the most proper distribution of the inhabitants of a country fully peopled."

It was this liberal conventionality and not an innate conservatism or preference for aristocratic government that accounts for Jefferson's uncritical approval of the early phases of the French Revolution and for his optimism in predicting its outcome. For what engrossed his attention as he witnessed the disturbances of 1788 and 1789 was the manifest purpose of the Revolutionary leaders to remodel the institutions of government to conform to Enlightenment principles. All else—the latent, irrational elements involved in a social upheaval: the powerful, desperate resistance of entrenched privilege, the capricious violence of inflamed mobs, the murderous irresponsibility of demagogues—took him by surprise; they were distractions, dangerous irrelevancies, whose importance to the central drama he only reluctantly acknowledged and which he never fully incorporated into his understanding of what was happening.

The same ingenuousness, the same inability to exceed the limits of conventional enlightened theory, stands out even more clearly in Jefferson's letters on the Constitution. His correspondence with Madison on this issue—part of "the most extended, the most elevated, and the most significant exchange of letters," the editors write, "between any two men in the whole sweep of American history"—is especially revealing. Where before the Philadelphia convention Jefferson saw the problem in traditional liberal terms, as a dilemma created by the necessity to increase the powers of the national government and the threat that such powers would constitute to the liberties of the people, Madison, long since convinced that central authority must be enhanced if the Union was to survive, took nothing for granted and reexamined with searching skepticism and imagination the nature of liberty and of the dangers to it as a preliminary to devising solutions. When the Constitution finally appeared, Jefferson's response was a perfect cliché of enlightened political theory: it had no bill of rights and it did not require rotation in office, particularly in the case of the President. Madison, of course, was no enemy to bills of rights as such; ultimately he drafted the first ten amendments. But he had not argued for them, he told Jefferson, not merely because he, like others, believed the rights in question were reserved to the states by the manner in which federal powers had been granted, but because "there is great reason to fear that a positive declaration of some of the most essential rights could not be obtained in the requisite latitude." The act of defining them, in other words, would necessarily limit their scope: "the rights of conscience in particular, if submitted to public definition, would be narrowed more than they are likely ever to be by an assumed power." And in any case, how effective, he asked, are such "parchment barriers"? The real threats to liberty in a republican government come not from the power of the state but from "overbearing majorities." In every state, he observed, bills of rights had already been violated by the legislative action of majority opinion. "Wherever the real power in a government lies," he concluded in a brilliantly prophetic passage,

> there is the danger of oppression. In our governments the real power lies in the majority of the community, and the invasion of private rights is *chiefly* to be apprehended, not from acts of government contrary to the sense of its constituents, but from acts in which the government is the mere instrument of the major number of the constituents. This is a truth of great importance, but not yet sufficiently attended to: and is probably more strongly impressed on my mind by facts and reflections suggested by them, than on yours, which has contemplated abuses of power issuing from a very different quarter. Wherever there is an interest and power to do wrong, wrong will generally be done, and not less readily by a powerful and interested party than by a powerful and interested prince.

It was upon these assumptions that he launched his own, original interpretation of the function of bills of rights.

Throughout this exchange of letters on the Constitution, Jefferson's views are the simpler and more obvious. Nothing Jefferson wrote in these years comes close in perception and originality to Madison's letter of October 24, 1787, which includes in its fifteen printed pages not only a history of the Philadelphia convention and a razor-edged analysis of the Constitution, but a theory of politics, which, cleverly adapted from an earlier formulation and presented in a more polished form, would become famous as the tenth *Federalist* paper.

Jefferson's style in private, personal affairs as reflected in the *Papers* was consistent with the pattern of his political thought and of his analysis of the great public events of his time. His personal relations also appear to have been formal and stylized; not stiff, always, nor mannered, precisely—though at times they were both—but controlled and correct beyond the demands of eighteenth-century respectability. There was about him a kind of dignity, an implacable *gravitas,* that kept his personal behavior within the most predictable patterns. His letters to his daughter Patsy, then attending a convent boarding school in Paris, are formal, unbending, and unimaginatively parental to an extraordinary degree. Repeatedly he points out to her "that you do not employ yourself so closely as I could wish," and lectures her on the virtues of "industry and activity." "Idleness," he explains to the fourteen-year-old girl, "begets ennui, ennui the hypochondria, and that a diseased body. No laborious person was ever yet hysterical." Inevitably, even in this case, his bland high seriousness, lacking the slightest wrinkle of humor, became political and ideological. Thus his prim reply to Patsy's perky resistance to grubbing through a fifteenth-century Italian translation of Livy that Jefferson had given her (it "puts me out of my wits," she complained):

> I do not like your saying that you are unable to read the antient print of your Livy but with the aid of your master. We are always equal to what we undertake with resolution. . . . It is a part of the American character to consider nothing as desperate; to surmount every difficulty by resolution and con- trivance. . . . Consider therefore the conquering your Livy as an exercise in the habit of surmounting difficulties, a habit which will be necessary to you in the country where you are to live.

And he ends his admonition with a discourse on the unique impor- tance of "the needle, and domestic oeconomy" in a republican society.

There was a relaxation of sorts in a series of letters to Abigail Adams, with whom he seems to have been on what for him were quite familiar terms, until distance and a difference of opinion on Shays' Rebellion cooled things off. But even in these letters, where Jefferson clearly sought to strike a light, informal, even flippant note, he achieved at best a kind of elegant, courtly badinage, which inevi- tably ended in political satire. There is no real, spontaneous humor, based, as it must be, on a sense of the ridiculousness of people and things, in all the hundreds of letters Jefferson wrote in this period;

nothing, for example, like John Adams's detailed account to Jefferson of his interview with the Tripolitan minister to London: "I took the pipe with great complacency, placed the bowl upon the carpet, for the stem was fit for a walking cane, and I believe more than two yards in length, and smoked in aweful pomp, reciprocating whiff for whiff with His Excellency . . . the two secretaries appeared in raptures and the superiour of them who speaks a few words of French cryed out in extacy, Monsieur vous etes un Turk."

There was, of course, one interval during which, as far as can be told from the paucity of evidence, Jefferson did break through his instinctive reserve and conventionality of behavior. His famous romance in 1786 with the English artist Maria Cosway was not merely a surge of affection for that attractive, rather light-headed woman, but a flirtation with the whole careless, semi-bohemian, café-society world of the Anglo-French artistic set. That his attachment to Mrs. Cosway was sincere and for several months consuming there can be no doubt, but if he was for a while passionately in love it was not with her so much as with the abandon, the heedlessness, and the devotion to sensibility that he took to be her way of life. In the letters with which he overwhelmed her after her departure and by which he revealed to her with such inadvertent cruelty the poverty of her literary resources and her inadequacy to cope with his Olympian talents ("Your letters they are so well wrote," she complained, "so full of a thousand preaty things that it is not possible for me to answer such charming letters. . . . my letters must appear sad scrawls to you")—in these letters it is less an individual than an atmosphere that Jefferson affectionately recalled.

The episode was for Jefferson a fling at unconventionality, at irresponsibility; but it was only a fling: brief, confined almost entirely to the late summer of 1786, and never completely cut loose from control. There was awareness throughout, and it was ultimately the internal tension created by this awareness that came to symbolize the whole experience. By the time he sat down to write the famous "dialogue . . . between my Head and my Heart" which so bewildered Mrs. Cosway, he had recovered whatever composure he may have lost, and, in the form of an eighteenth-century set piece full of carefully constructed casualness, he proceeded to straighten himself out.

> This is not a world to live at random in as you do [the Head
> informed the Heart]. To avoid these eternal distresses to
> which you are for ever exposing us, you must learn to look
> forward before you take a step which may interest our peace.
> Everything in this world is a matter of calculation. Advance
> then with caution, the balance in your hand.

If, as the editors say, the letter owes much of its literary distinction
to the fact that Mrs. Cosway "could not be quite certain whether the
Head or the Heart had won the argument," it owes its historical importance to the fact that the reader of the *Papers* is never in doubt.
For the words of caution and control here spoken by the Head were
only variations of familiar Jeffersonian injunctions, written on other
occasions without disguise or apology.

Even Jefferson's prose, that elegant and efficient instrument, worked
within the same restrictions of conventional forms. The syntactical
balance, the rhythmic cadences, the consistency of tone which flowed
so freely from his pen are eighteenth-century mannerisms raised to
some remarkably high power. The miracle of what John Adams called
his "peculiar felicity of expression" was that in spite of the formal
patterning of phrase and sentence it could still be so supple, so ac-
commodating at once to rhetoric, to abstract reasoning, and to detailed description. It would seem as difficult to sharpen the precision
of Jefferson's description of "hanging the upper stone of a grist mill"
as to improve on the dignity and eloquence of the Declaration. But
the limitations are also prominent. Adams's statement in his *Autobiography* that Jefferson "can write ten times better than I can" is true
only if the force of naturalness, of the personally idiomatic twist, of
the unexpected, the blunt, raw, rough-edged, explosive phrase, is
discounted as a literary virtue. For in Jefferson's writings the direct
impact of experience is expressed in the same elegant patterning of
phrase as his most euphuistic courtesy. Spades are called many
things—"a spirit for female intrigue," "infidelity to the marriage bed,"
"dissipation," "ruin"—anything but spades; and while he achieves a
considerable dramatic effect by repeating the hissing sibilant "disease," it is a very different kind of effect from that of Adams's fistlike
phrases: "A Covent Garden rake will never be wise enough to take
warning from the claps caught by his companions"; "the putrefaction

of a great city in the summer heat"; "downright ignorance of the nature of coin, credit and circulation."

In part, of course, this is only to say that a reading of the *Papers*
supports Carl Becker's analysis in *The Declaration of Independence* of
the literary qualities of Jefferson's writings. But only in part, for if
Becker's description of the prose of that document applies to the rest
of Jefferson's writings, his explanation of its relation to Jefferson's
personality does not. Nothing in the *Papers* supports Becker's view
that Jefferson's "convictions, his sympathies, his ideas are essentially
of the intellect, somehow curiously abstracted from reality, a consciously woven drapery laid over the surface of a nature essentially
aristocratic, essentially fastidious, instinctively shrinking from close
contact with men and things as they are." This conclusion of Becker's
appears considerably overdrawn even as it relates to the Declaration;
as a general description of Jefferson's personality it is utterly mistaken.

II

For if a deep conventionality, an uncritical acceptance of enlightened
styles in matters of high culture, of social and political theory, of
personal behavior and literary form, stands out in the *Papers*, so too
does another, quite different cluster of traits which leaves one with
the impression of a personality the very opposite of excessively fastidious, shrinking from close contact with men and things as they are.
However stylized Jefferson's reaction to Europe may have been, however conventionally enlightened his political theory, however mannered his personal relations and literary style, in matters of "business,"
in his direct, tactical involvement with public affairs, he was as unconventional, as imaginative, resourceful, and tough as the best, or
worst, of Old World politicians, and more adroit than most.

Again, it is the completeness and the density of the record that
allow one to see a pattern otherwise easily obscured. Following Jefferson through all his activities week by week, even day by day and
at times hour by hour, for a number of years, one comes to realize
that Jefferson was a superb "man of business." The amount of correspondence he carried on personally, the number of intricate problems
he was able to deal with simultaneously, the sheer magnitude of his
participation in the public affairs of the day, would seem to have been

overwhelming. There was nothing superficial or merely formal in this participation. He could not have been more deeply committed, more industrious, or more efficient. The impression of Jefferson is always the same. He is managing things: parrying thrusts, satisfying demands, gathering information, consulting, planning, drafting propositions—and doing so not merely to fend off chaos, to keep things stable, but to create situations favorable to aggressive plans of his own, plans calculated to advance the cause of America, enlightenment, and liberty.

In the six months from October 1788 through March 1789, for example, Jefferson brought to a successful conclusion the intricate, protracted negotiations over the Consular Convention with France. Immediately afterward, working with great intensity, he drew up his *Observations on the Whale-Fishery,* a technical treatise for which he had been gathering information for years but which had been precipitated by an unexpected *arrêt* excluding American oil from French markets; the document illustrates not merely Jefferson's intellectual breadth but his originality as a diplomat and his skill as a politician. Simultaneously (October 1788) he wrote a proposal for funding the foreign debt of the United States, the culmination of efforts he had been making since 1784 to redeem the credit of the nation. A few days later he compiled a comprehensive memorandum on the case of Schweighauser and Dobrée, a complex business going back to 1779 and involving the cost of outfitting an American vessel temporarily placed in a French squadron. These major and official activities were carried out alongside an array of lesser ones. During the same months Jefferson consulted surreptitiously but continuously with Lafayette and others on the developing revolution in France, single-handedly kept the family affairs of the Virginia-born Lucy Ludwell Paradise from falling to pieces, continued the delicate maneuvering with the Dutch bankers which alone kept the United States solvent, handled the efforts being made to blackmail the American government with the threat of revealing the official papers of the corrupt Silas Deane, dealt with innumerable problems presented to him by Americans traveling in Europe, conducted lengthy discussions on political theory and practice with half a dozen correspondents, and kept his chief, John Jay, Secretary of Foreign Affairs, informed of everything.

He was an excellent ambassador. He had that same capacity to combine symbolic and practical representation that made Franklin's stay in France such an important episode in Franco-American relations. In a court almost paralyzed by ceremony and bored with excesses in dress and ornamentation, Jefferson's republican asceticism, his directness and apparent candor, lent him a distinction and significance which no amount of modishness could have gained for him. But the work he did was more important. He had begun his ambassadorial labors even before he left America, making a detailed survey of the needs of northern commerce as he traveled to Boston for embarkation, following up this personal investigation with a questionnaire "concerning government, labor, commerce etc." Once in France he began an endless series of negotiations in behalf of American commerce which he pursued tirelessly through the last twists of intrigue. His indefatigable but unsuccessful efforts to break the farmers-general's monopolistic control of French imports of American tobacco led him into the intricacies of French cabinet politics and the secret recesses of commercial privilege. His more successful campaign to reopen the markets for American whale oil forced him into a sharp encounter with a ruthless, apolitical clan of Nantucket whalers who, in defense of the special advantages they enjoyed at Dunkirk, in all probability had conspired with French officials to impose the anti-American restrictions. He did not triumph in all such situations—in some, no one could have succeeded—but his successes were notable, and throughout he was shrewd and aggressive.

At the level of daily, immediate decisions no conventionality, no stereotype of people or situations, weakened his judgment, limited his insight or originality. He was a natural tactician, with a nice touch in dealing with tangled situations and difficult people. At this level his judgment was authoritative, and it was universally sought. Washington, who apologized to him for having "accustomed myself to communicate matters of difficulty to you," consulted him on the most delicate questions of judgment and decision: on how far he should participate in developing western lands and new transportation routes, on what his attitude to the Cincinnati should be, on whether and how he should accept gifts from the Virginia legislature. Adams, who disagreed with Jefferson on many matters of politics and political theory, solicited his advice on procedures in diplomacy and even in finance, a subject in which the Bostonian was generally considered to be the superior in experience and knowledge. Madison, next to whose comments on constitutional principle and theory Jefferson's remarks were rigid and obvious, found his opinions of men and measures penetrating and reliable. And typical of Jefferson's relations with Lafayette was the letter he wrote him in May 1789 arguing for careful timing in breaking with his instructions as delegate of the *noblesse* to the States General, and the conference he held with him in June of that year in which he suggested a plan for royal initiative in reconciling the divisions in the States General, for which "excellent ideas" Lafayette thanked him, and promised to try "to bring matters to the issue you point out."

Throughout Jefferson's discussion of the revolutionary movement in France, the difference in the quality of his thought as an ideologist and high-level theorist and as a pragmatic tactician stands out sharply. However superficial his understanding of the total complex of forces at work and of the overall tendency of events, and however unjustifiably serene his optimism in the outcome, his sense of the moment to strike, his instinct for the saving gesture, the stabilizing concession, never deserted him. His conclusion in the crisis of June 1789 that a decisive move by the Crown "to side openly with the Commons" would complete the Revolution "without a convulsion" is, Professor Robert Palmer has written, "the judgment of most historians today." His reasoning, in sending Lafayette and Rabaut de St. Etienne a draft of a charter of rights to be presented by the king to the nation, was the quintessence of extemporized calculation:

> You will carry back to your constituents [Jefferson wrote] more good than ever was effected before without violence, and you will stop exactly at the point where violence would otherwise begin. Time will be gained, the public mind will continue to ripen and to be informed, a basis of support may be prepared with the people themselves, and expedients occur for gaining still something further at your next meeting, and for stopping again at the point of force.

At times, under pressure, in annoyance and embarrassment, this note of expediency became sharp and shrill, drowning out the softer, idealistic harmonies of his thought altogether. No one, of course, was

inclined to treat the Barbary states, just then commencing their depredations against the commerce of the new nation, with charity or
idealistic uplift. But even in the terms of hard calculation in which
the first American discussions of this problem were conducted, Jefferson's solution was notably belligerent. Offer them, he wrote, "an
equal treaty"; if they refuse it, "go to war with them." If we mean to
be a naval power, he explained, "can we begin it on a more honourable occasion or with a weaker foe?" "These pyrates," he continued
later, "are contemptibly weak. . . . The motives pleading for war
rather than tribute are numerous and honourable, those opposing
them are mean and shortsighted." There was a similar hard pragma-
tism in his expeditious handling of the recall of the newly appointed
French minister to America, his friend the Count de Moustier, whom
he had recommended to Jay as "open, communicative, candid, simple
in his manners, and a declared enemy to ostentation and luxury."
When Jefferson discovered through Madison and others that in America the count proved to be "unsocial, proud and niggardly and betrays
a sort of fastidiousness toward this country," when, in addition, his
sister-in-law, Madame de Brehan, than whom, Jefferson had written,
it is impossible to find "a better woman, more amiable, more modest,
more simple in her manners, dress, and way of thinking," impressed
Americans as finicky, snobbish, and "perfectly soured toward this
country," and when, on top of this, he heard that it was generally
believed in America that there was an "illicit connection" between the
two, which "on their journeys . . . they often neglect the most obvious
precautions for veiling," Jefferson promptly got rid of Moustier by
having Lafayette pressure the French Foreign Minister into constru-
ing "a loose expression in one of [Moustier's] letters . . . into a petition
for leave of absence."

There was nothing patterned, stylized, or imitative in Jefferson's
handling of the hundreds of practical problems and concrete situations
he faced; in none of this was he "abstracted from reality, . . . instinctively shrinking from close contact with men and things as they are."
His management of such matters was spontaneous and direct; he
responded sensitively and imaginatively to the very grain of reality.

III

These two groups of characteristics stand out clearly: in the broad outlines of Jefferson's world view, in his political theory, and in the style of his personal behavior, a conventionality, an uncritical acceptance of established formulations and patterns; in matters of "business," in the actual conduct of affairs, in politics and administration, a taut and critical aggressiveness, a sense of expediency, of flexibility and resourceful improvisation.

What counts in the last analysis, however, is not simply the existence of certain characteristics but the way in which they act upon each other, the way in which they combine within the total personality: the balance, the integration they achieve. In Jefferson's case the pattern is peculiarly complicated. These strands or elements of personality were never tightly integrated; their configuration was mobile and unstable, shifting from time to time and from situation to situation; there was no permanent, inflexible arrangement of priority, no settled rule of subordination and dominance. The consequences are of considerable historical importance.

At times it resulted in a syncopated response to problems and issues: an initial, instantaneous reaction, a reflex almost, in terms of one set of responses, subsequently qualified, even reversed, by another. Thus Jefferson's reception of the Constitution. At first, reacting in terms of a set theory of enlightened constitutionalism, he was sharply critical of that pragmatic document. So far was it from the model he had in mind that he thought "all the good of [it] might have been couched in three or four new articles to be added to the good, old, and venerable fabrick, which should have been preserved even as a religious relique." A month later he declared himself "nearly a neutral" on it. A month and a half after that he wrote that he hoped the first nine states to vote would ratify it, and the last four reject it, thus putting it into effect but forcing, by the threat of disunion, a new convention for amendments. Finally, in 1789, after much correspondence on the subject and debates with his friends in Paris, he declared quite simply that the new American constitution was "unquestionably the wisest ever yet presented to men." It was not so much that he had altered his view, but that a different set of considerations and attitudes had come into play as gradually he came to grips with the concrete problems, learned more of the political battles that had taken place in the convention, and became caught up, even at such a distance, in the campaign for ratification.

At other times, as in his involvement in the early stages of the French Revolution, this weak integration of contrasting characteristics led to simultaneous but quite different responses at different levels of activity. At still other times, as in the negotiation of commercial arrangements, it led to an appearance of applying different principles to similar circumstances. It could easily result in apparent inconsistencies which animosity could construe as hypocrisy.

Whether it would or not would depend to a large extent on external circumstances. Before the end of 1789 circumstances had been such as to minimize the possibility of trouble resulting from Jefferson's curiously uneven blend of characteristics. Before he left for Europe in 1784 he had experienced public affairs only during an extraordinary period of revolution and war, a crisis lasting almost two decades when means were necessarily subordinated to the end of survival, and the most effective ideas were the most ideological, the most universally evocative of idealism and self-sacrifice. In this situation of flux the conflict between self-sufficient abstractions and material and social reality was at a minimum. Similarly in Europe Jefferson's uncritical assertion—his mere existence as a symbol—of an obvious liberalism was a powerful public role and one that created for him no conflicts in politics or incongruities with the actual management of affairs. It was only after Jefferson's return to America in 1789 and his resumption of high public office in a society recovered from its revolutionary zeal and desirous not of change but of stability and development that circumstances forced the full realization of the problems of his personality. The way in which these problems appeared and the way in which they worked themselves out are not merely passages in an important biography; they are elements in our national history, which one can look forward to examining as they have not been examined before in the future volumes of *The Papers of Thomas Jefferson*.

3

Thomas Hutchinson

"My Temper Does Not Incline
to Enthusiasm"

I

O N THE FOURTH OF JULY 1776, Thomas Hutchinson, the exiled loyalist governor of Massachusetts, was awarded an honorary doctorate of civil laws by Oxford University. "Probably no distinction which Hutchinson ever attained was more valued by him," his nineteenth-century biographer wrote; certainly none so fittingly symbolizes the tragedy of his life. For he was honored as an American— the most distinguished as well as the most loyal colonial-born official of his time. Provincial assemblyman, speaker of the Massachusetts House of Representatives, councillor, lieutenant governor, chief justice, governor, he had gone through the entire course of public offices and of official honors, and he was in addition America's most accomplished historian. But to the people who on the day of Hutchinson's award proclaimed their nation's independence, he was one of the most hated men on earth—more hated than Lord North, more hated than George III (both of whom, it was believed, he had secretly influenced), and more feared than the sinister Earl of Bute.

The distrust and the animosity Thomas Hutchinson inspired surpass any ordinary bounds. The reactions he stirred are morbid, pathological, paranoiac in their intensity.

John Adams was transfixed by him: for fifteen years, suspicion, fear, and hatred of Hutchinson were ruling passions. He first recorded his suspicions of Hutchinson in 1760, when he was twenty-five. Five years later he poured out the first of a series of rhetorical cascades against Hutchinson's "very ambitious and avaricious disposition," condemned his taking "four of the most important offices in the province into his own hands," and spoke with bitterness of his secret network of officeholding kin who together created the "amazing ascendancy of one family, foundation sufficient on which to erect a tyranny." Hutchinson, he said, had not only "monopolized almost all the power of the government to himself and his family" but "has been endeavoring to procure more, both on this side and the other side of the Atlantic." He was a "courtier," Adams said, slyly manipulating "the passions and prejudices, the follies and vices of great men in order to obtain their smiles, esteem, and patronage and consequently their favors and preferments"; he was a dissembler, a man of a thousand disguises, hungry for power, for office, and for gain: from him "the liberties of this country [have] more to fear . . . than from any other man, nay from all other men in the world." A decade later Adams's hatred of Hutchinson had become obsessive: "the mazy windings of Hutchinson's heart and the serpentine wiles of his head," he wrote, were primary sources of the Anglo-American conflict, and in his "Novanglus" letters of 1774–75 he wrote an impassioned history of Hutchinson's "tyranny in the province" and his advancement of the ambitions of "Bute, Mansfield, and North," to which could be traced the entire source of the Anglo-American conflict.

Adams's opinions, in this case as in so many others, were extreme, but in differing degrees they were widely shared. Josiah Quincy, Jr., convinced "that all the measures against America were planned and pushed on by [Governor] Bernard and Hutchinson," went to England in the winter of 1774, with the support of the provincial leadership, in large part to counteract the malevolent influence of Hutchinson and other Tories on administration policy. In the same year John Dickinson lumped together "the Butes, Mansfields, Norths, Bernards, and Hutchinsons" as the "villains and idiots" whose "falsehoods and misrepresentations" were inflaming the people and creating hostilities. John Wilkes was informed from Boston that Hutchinson had inherited "a strange kind of attachment to what is called the King's prerogative, but being a man of the greatest duplicity, he had art enough to conceal it from the public"—art enough, apparently, to conceal it for no less than thirty years until finally, early in the reign of George III, he had felt safe to profess it. Samuel Adams, whose political life was formed in struggles with Hutchinson, denied that Hutchinson had true greatness even in evil, for while he was as mad with ambition and lust for power as Caesar, he lacked the courage and intrepidity needed to reduce a free people to slavery. And Mercy Otis Warren in her history of the Revolution devoted page after page to the pernicious influence of that "dark, intriguing, insinuating, haughty, and ambitious" man—so diligent a student of "the intricacies of *Machiavellian* policy," so subtle a solicitor of popular support, so hypocritical in his sanctity and ruthless in his lust for power—and to the fatal consequences of "his pernicious administration."

A "tool of tyrants," a "damn'd *arch traitor*," Hutchinson was hissed *in absentia* at the official dinner to welcome his successor, General Gage, and when later the Revolutionary mob found his portrait in his house in suburban Milton, they stabbed it with bayonets and tore out one of the eyes. The judicious Franklin spoke openly of Hutchinson's duplicity, and in 1772 decided that he would have to be destroyed politically if the British Empire were to be preserved. The London merchant and Member of Parliament William Baker prided himself on having denounced Hutchinson to the House of Commons as "a parricide who has attempted to ruin his country to save his own little narrow selfish purposes." And though Hutchinson was a hero to most of the loyalists, some of them too, like the former New York judge William Smith, believed him to be "a mere scribbling governor" and relished the nastiest scraps of gossip about him that came their way.

His official patrons distrusted him. Governor Thomas Pownall, who in 1757 recommended Hutchinson's appointment to the lieutenant governorship in a letter of elaborate praise, left Massachusetts three years later enraged at the conduct of his associate; for fourteen years thereafter the former governor sparred with Hutchinson from England, and he renewed their quarrel directly when Hutchinson arrived as an exile in England in 1774. Both Sir Francis Bernard, who succeeded Pownall as governor in 1760 and who served as Hutchinson's personal agent in London in 1769–71, and Lord Hillsborough, secretary of state for the colonies during the same years, who appointed Hutchinson to the governorship, disapproved of his conduct at several points, and at least on one occasion found his activities acutely

44

embarrassing. Even Hillsborough's benign successor, Lord Dartmouth, the soul of Christian charity, who was well disposed to Hutchinson and eventually became a friend of his, came to believe that Hutchinson had blundered badly as governor and in a bizarre episode attempted, at great cost to his official dignity as secretary of state, to correct what he considered to be Hutchinson's most costly error. And no less an authority than Lord North, according to the contemporary annalist George Chalmers, believed that Hutchinson, through his indiscretions, had personally precipitated the outbreak of the Revolution.

There were some, of course, who disagreed. Hutchinson's protégé, in-law, and colleague Peter Oliver, in his "Origin & Progress of the American Rebellion," wrote a lyric apostrophe to Hutchinson's virtues, which he summarized as "an acumen of genius united with a solidity of judgment and great regularity of manners"—qualities, he pointed out, that nature only sparingly confers. Some who knew Hutchinson only by reputation were amazed when they actually met him. The Bostonians, William Eden wrote in 1774, shortly after Hutchinson arrived in England, "thought Hutchinson a tyrant—I met him on Thursday last, at the Attorney General's—they might as well have taken a lamb for a tiger." Both Jonathan Mayhew and Andrew Eliot, Boston ministers of liberal views, spoke well of Hutchinson's "capacity and erudition" in their correspondence with the English libertarian Thomas Hollis and believed "he certainly wishes well to his country." But these were minority opinions. The feeling was widespread among well-informed Americans that Thomas Hutchinson had betrayed his country; that for sordid, selfish reasons he had accepted and abetted—even stimulated—oppressive measures against the colonies; that he had supported them even in the face of a threat of armed resistance; and that in this sense his personal actions lay at the heart of the Revolution.

So it was said, again and again and again. Was it true? Of what in fact was he guilty? He asked himself this question repeatedly, discussed it endlessly with himself, his friends, associates, with anyone of any importance who would listen, and left behind a voluminous record of his replies. Twice he drew up formal, official justifications of the whole course of his administration and of the character and effect of his opinions. One, written in 1775 in response to attacks made on him in the House of Commons, is his "Account and Defense of Conduct," which he called a "brief vindication of my character" and which he circulated privately to those he thought mattered most. The second he intended to be more public, the final volume of his *History of Massachusetts-Bay*, which he wrote in the leisure of his exile and left for posthumous publication, carefully pruned of all antagonistic phrases, all invidious portraits, anything that might detract from its central purpose of explaining what had happened and of clearing his reputation of slander.

But his fullest testament was written indeliberately. Hutchinson was a voluminous letter writer and, after 1774, a faithful diarist. His correspondence from 1765 until his departure for England in 1774, comprising hundreds of letters, drafts of letters, and notes related to his correspondence, survives intact—rescued accidentally from the oblivion to which Hutchinson assigned it at his departure from America. In addition, Hutchinson's personal correspondence and much of the correspondence of his immediate family survive in notebooks preserved in the British Museum. And finally, his diary, from his arrival in England until the year before his death, exists both in manuscript and in print, in an edition, only slightly expurgated, published by a loyal descendant.

The written record is therefore remarkably complete. The letters and diary form a documentary history not only of Hutchinson's administration but of his private life over the course of his last twenty years. In them one can find a detailed self-portrait, and whatever evidence there is of the claims laid against him.

II

It is hard to imagine anyone less disposed by background and heritage to betray his countrymen than Thomas Hutchinson. His family had helped to found New England, and they had prospered with its growth. Until Thomas, only one of the family had been famous: the notorious seventeenth-century Anne, who had refused to adjust her singular convictions to the will of the community (she was the last in the family—until Thomas—to do so), for which she had been banished, to die in exile. But the family's main interest had never been hers. The Hutchinsons had been tradesmen in London before the

Puritan migration; in New England they became merchants, and remained merchants, with remarkable consistency, generation after
generation. In the course of a century and a half they produced, in
the stem line of the family, not a single physician, not a single lawyer,
and not a single teacher or minister. The entire clan devoted itself to
developing its property and the network of trade, based on kinship
lines at every point, that Anne's brothers and nephews had created
in the mid-seventeenth century. They prospered solidly, but not
greatly. Their enterprises were careful, not grand. They were accu-
mulators, down-to-earth, unromantic middlemen, whose solid petit
bourgeois characteristics became steadily more concentrated in the
passage of years until in Thomas, in the fifth generation, they reached
an apparently absolute and perfect form.

He was born in Boston in 1711. His father, Colonel Thomas
Hutchinson, had risen somewhat, though not greatly, beyond the
level of his two prosperous merchant-shipowner relatives, Elisha and
Eliakim. The colonel served on the provincial council for over twenty
years, donated the building for a Latin grammar school (which his
son would attend), and improved into provincial magnificence the
imposing town house bequeathed to him by a widowed aunt. The
colonel's marriage fitted perfectly the pattern of his classically bourgeois existence. His wife, Sarah Foster, ten years his senior, was the
daughter of John Foster, the Boston merchant to whom he had been
apprenticed in trade, of status identical to the Hutchinson family's,
who engaged in the same kinds of trade as they did, and to whom,
by force of the remarkable endogamy that characterizes the family
history, Colonel Thomas became triply related by other marriages
between the two families.

Colonel Thomas set the pattern for young Thomas's life. He was
industrious (until prosperity and personal problems led him to relax
his attention to business), charitable, unaffected, unworldly, and clan-
nish. A straitlaced, pious provincial, he read the Scriptures to his
family mornings and evenings and devoted himself to trade and to
the welfare of his kin and community. For over thirty years, his son
later recorded, Colonel Thomas "kept a table on Saturdays with a
salt fish or bacalao [codfish] dinner." To this unpretentious feast he
regularly invited only four close friends, all of them merchants, two
of them relatives; only "now and then," his son recalled, was a clergy-

man added to the group. The colonel's life and young Thomas's boy-hood were deeply scarred by family tragedies, quite aside from the financial losses that severely reduced the family fortune. The colonel's eldest son, Foster, *"a most lovely son,"* an "amiable youth, the delight of [Harvard] College," died of a smallpox inoculation at seventeen. And then an infant son died, followed by a young daughter, of consumption; and finally in 1739 the twenty-three-year-old Elisha died of a fever, a loss which, coming as it did in the decline of the father's life, "broke his heart." Colonel Thomas himself had never been physically strong. For many years, his son candidly recorded, he had suffered secretly from a rupture, and all his life he had been subject to "indigestion and flatulencies at his stomach." More important for the legacy he may have passed on to his son, the colonel, young Thomas noted many years later, had had "two or three turns . . . of nervous disorders, which confined him several weeks at a time and deprived him of his sleep." He died soon after the loss of his son Elisha, of a "hectic fever" that followed "a languishing illness."

For young Thomas, the future governor, there was no break in the continuity of family and community life. He entered Harvard at the age of twelve, where he developed not so much the intellectual interests that later became important to him as his ability and resources in trade. At the time he entered college, he recalled half a century later, his father undertook his proper education by presenting him with "two or three quintals of fish." From this humble capital he managed to build, by "adventuring to sea" through his college years, a fund of £400–500 sterling, which, combined with an inheritance from his father, became a fortune, by provincial standards, by the time of the Revolution: in cash, fifteen times his original capital, and in real estate, eight houses, including the Boston mansion he had inherited, two wharves and a variety of lots and shop properties in Boston, and in suburban Milton a country house universally admired for its simple beauty and splendid setting, and a hundred acres of choice land.

Additional property in cash and real estate came to him through his marriage, which served for him as it had for his father to reinforce the family's dominant characteristics. The Sanfords of Rhode Island had been related to the Hutchinsons by marriage and in business for four generations; as early as the 1640s the two families had worked together to build the first important New England commercial network. Margaret Sanford, daughter, granddaughter, and great-granddaughter of New England merchants, was seventeen in 1734 when Hutchinson married her. At their marriage, the then governor of Massachusetts wrote in a businesslike letter of introduction for their honeymoon trip, the couple could claim a joint fortune of £5,000–6,000 sterling; Thomas, he said, was "a young gentleman of exact virtue [and] of good natural sense," a bit too modest, perhaps, but a successful merchant and universally esteemed.

Four years later, at the age of twenty-six, Hutchinson entered politics. He was never thereafter out of it, and he maintained an altogether consistent policy in defense of what, until the great issues of the 1760s intervened, were widely considered to be the basic interests of the colony. As representative of Boston to the Massachusetts House from 1737 to 1749 (with the exception of a single year) and a councillor for the succeeding seventeen years, he distinguished himself by his effective defense of a hard-money policy and by his equally determined defense of the territorial integrity of Massachusetts and of its chartered rights. As a leader of the hard-money forces, he inevitably made enemies, though no more than others on his side of that savagely divisive issue. His mastery of the economics involved was universally acknowledged, and while he was firm in his advocacy, he was never unreasonable, never fanatical. So convinced was the community of Hutchinson's "disinterestedness and integrity," Pownall reported in 1757, that even those who most sharply disagreed with him continued to respect him, even to revere him. In the end Hutchinson's views on the money question prevailed, in part because of the shrewd use that Massachusetts was able to make of the specie it received from the English government as repayment for its contribution to the war against France; and in part because when in 1741 the issue developed into a crisis that threatened violence, Governor Belcher had seized the initiative and stamped out the incipient rebellion by force.

But if Hutchinson's views on monetary matters were controversial, his defense of the colony's political and territorial rights was not. His service to Massachusetts as agent in all matters affecting its external relations was sustained through thirty years and was almost uniformly successful. He was turned to repeatedly, and year after year he extended himself in the public behalf. In 1740 he was sent by the colony to England to plead the case of certain Massachusetts landowners whose property had fallen to New Hampshire, and though, through no fault of his own, his official efforts came to little, he did not return empty-handed. The Holden bequest, which led to the construction of that handsome miniature of Georgian architecture, Holden Chapel, still standing in the Harvard Yard, was obtained by him for the College. He negotiated repeatedly, almost annually, with the border Indians in the interest of his native colony, managed the province's lottery, supervised the financing of the Louisbourg expedition of 1745, dealt with other colonies on joint military efforts, adjudicated boundary disputes with Connecticut and Rhode Island, and in 1754 represented the Bay Colony at the Albany Congress, where he played a major role. Before his appointment as lieutenant governor in 1758 he served as the Massachusetts agent of the commanding general of the British forces during the climax of the Seven Years' War, and when he quarreled with Governor Pownall it was in defense of the political interests that had maintained stability in Massachusetts for a decade and in opposition to what he felt were corrupt practices in handling the colony's war effort. Through all of this Hutchinson was a leading member of Harvard's Board of Overseers, with particular interests in the curriculum and investments, and served as judge both of the inferior court of common pleas and of the probate court of Suffolk County.

It is hard to see what more he could have done to serve his countrymen or how, as a leader of the establishment in trade and politics, he could have been more enlightened. It had been Hutchinson, more than anyone but Franklin, who saw at the Albany Congress the benefits of restructuring imperial and intercolonial relations, and he did what he could to implement these advanced ideas. Unlike many colonials in his position, he had never been a "courtier"; as a young man in London he had "found it very tiresome work to attend upon a British court," Isaac Watts reported, and he was never thereafter tempted to forsake local interests for advancement "at home."

Yet in the end his services were forgotten and he was cursed as a traitor in the land of his birth—cursed not merely by the wild men, the alarmists, the political paranoids, and the professional agitators, but by some of the most stable, sensible people of the time, many of whom knew him personally. There was, they said, some deep flaw in his character, some perversion of personality, some profound "malignancy of heart," that had turned his patriotism into treason, and led him to sacrifice the general good for the most sordid, selfish gain.

III

What do we know of the personality of Thomas Hutchinson, his character, his style and sensibility?

Surprisingly little. Of all the people who worked with him, struggled against him, cursed and denounced him, not one left a sketch of his character or even of his appearance more detailed or perceptive than James Otis's remark that he was "a tall, slender, fair-complexioned, fair-spoken, 'very good gentleman.'" John Adams, who wrote voluminously about him and was capable, beyond any other American of the eighteenth century, of casting a character, left polemics, but no account of his person. Edward Gibbon, who sought Hutchinson out in London in 1775 and knew him well, refers to him in his otherwise wonderfully expressive letters without a single adjective, without even the faintest shading of phrase that might reveal his perception of the man. Only one authentic portrait of Hutchinson exists, painted in London when Hutchinson was thirty. It is superficial but incidentally revealing. It shows a person dressed in utmost simplicity, slim in form, with a narrow face and undistinguished features. The lips are full but slightly compressed and pursed. There is a wisp of a smile, but no real attempt at expression. The overall effect is that of constraint, simplicity, and an almost total lack of emphasis, flair, or style.

It is not much to go on, but it is suggestive. For his prose conveys the same qualities. He wrote easily, abundantly, and logically. But the style is not only unaffected and unadorned in the extreme, devoid of images, figures of speech, thin even in adjectives, but so lacking in emphasis, so unpunctuated, so *still*, as to seem at times inarticulate. The reader finds himself again and again having to go back and reread passages because the thread is lost. The point, he invariably finds, is in fact there, but the stress is insufficient; the necessary emphases are missing. Hutchinson seems not to be attempting to reach the reader directly, not trying to convince him of what he is saying. One even-paced, unassertive paragraph follows another. This paragraph from the *History of Massachusetts-Bay* is typical:

> They distinguished civil subjection, into necessary and voluntary. From actual residence within any government, necessarily arose subjection, or an obligation to submit to the laws and authority thereof. But birth, was no necessary cause of subjection. The subjects of any prince or state had a natural right to remove to any other state, or to another quarter of the world, unless the state was weakned and exposed by such remove, and even in that case, if they were deprived of the right of all mankind, liberty of conscience, it would justify a separation, and upon their removal, their subjection determined and ceased.

Not only are there almost no figures of speech and few adjectives, but the nouns are frequently abstract and the word order inverted ("From actual residence within any government, necessarily arose subjection")—a combination perfectly calculated to trip the reader up and force him to retrace his steps. His narratives, his arguments, his explanations are bland in content and blandly told. Personalities rarely come into focus: "It is a delicate thing to hit off characters with justice," Ezra Stiles wrote Hutchinson upon reading Volume I of his *History*. "[Yet] the business of an historian is to paint, that we know the man and see him as he is. You have sometimes taken occasion to contrast the good and evil of character, without pointing out the result, the prevailing and ultimate complexion." The events themselves, Stiles concluded, were narrated with perspicuity and impartiality, but there was too much "cautiousness in character and motives."

The same could be said of almost every expression of Hutchinson's personality. He was by instinct political not philosophical, inductive not deductive; he sought to succeed in the world he knew, not transform it. At least as to his own career, he once wrote, he felt himself to be what he called "a quietist, being convinced that what is, is best." So he counseled a too stubborn political ally to "strive to be more of a willow and less of an oak. We don't live in Plato's Commonwealth, and when we can't have perfection we ought to comply with the measure that is least remote from it." He was circumspect in everything he did. Caution, control, and prudence were the guiding principles of his life. "My temper," he wrote in a characteristic understatement, "does not incline to enthusiasm." Everyone recognized it. You are, Governor Bernard wrote Hutchinson in 1769 after handing over to him the colony's government, "a much prudenter man than I ever pretended to be," and, he added, with more of a double meaning than he might have admitted, you "will take care of yourself." Hutchinson knew that his administration would be very burdensome and very precarious, but that, he said, would only "excite in me the more caution and circumspection." He tried never to overextend himself—"I don't love to promise too much"—and "never chose to give an opinion suddenly" on a matter of importance. Often he lectured others—his children, his colleagues, the constituted bodies of government—on the need for caution, at times lapsing into unappreciated moral discourses. To a correspondent seeking his approval of an unconventional marriage he pointed out that it was not enough to argue that in terms of "abstract morality" there was nothing wrong with it; "is not prudence a part of morality?" he asked with characteristic abstractness and underemphasis. Consider the consequences, he urged, consider your position, consider the use your enemies would make of such an obvious indiscretion.

Hutchinson himself never neglected such considerations—with results that his colleagues occasionally found disturbing. At one important point in his career he was officially consulted by the secretary of state on possible alterations in the constitution of Massachusetts which he was believed to have urged unofficially in the past. But his reply was said by the secretary, in words almost identical to Stiles's critique of the *History*, to be "like a lawyer's opinion, in which doubts and difficulties are stated but no conclusion is drawn." A great opportunity to strengthen government had been irretrievably lost by this too judicious, too cautious response, he was informed; an excess of caution, he was warned, could destroy the possibility of action.

It was not something Hutchinson could easily change in himself. Constraint was too deep a part of his nature. He rarely wrote an important letter only once. Drafts, notes, and revisions of letters abound in his papers; in them one can trace successive alterations and excisions that soften the edge of his original thought. Richard

53

Jackson was one of his most intimate correspondents; he was the only person, in England at least, to whom, for a brief period, Hutchinson expressed his more or less unqualified opinions. Yet in 1762, when affairs were in fact placid in Massachusetts, he carefully removed from a letter to Jackson the sentence: "We have violent parties in our little mock Parliament, and sometimes the public interest gives way to private piques and prejudices, as well as with you." Whole letters on important topics are drafted, redrafted, and then, if the sentiment is found still to be injudicious, or likely to be thought so, left in draft and filed away with the notation "not sent." Very little, however, was ever thrown away, and sometimes a passage eliminated from one piece of writing turns up in another, safer context. Hutchinson had originally drafted a lengthy paragraph for Volume II of his *History* critical of what he felt was the anarchic democracy of the Massachusetts town meetings, but then he "considered the times, and thought it would do more hurt than good." He therefore struck it out of the book and used the passage in a draft of a letter to Jackson explaining what must happen to society when every member of the town meetings "thinks it hard to be obliged to submit to laws which he does not like"—but then, thinking such a comment indiscreet even in a private communication, eliminated it from the letter too and suppressed the passage altogether. His *History* as a whole had originally been planned, he confessed to a friend (in a paragraph he deleted with a large X in his draft copy but which the Revolutionary leaders later published in full in the newspapers), as a history of his own times similar to Bishop Burnet's: "I shall paint characters as freely as he did, but it shall not be published while I live, and I expect the same satisfaction, which I doubt not the bishop had, of being revenged of some of the r[ogue]s after I am dead." But in fact he permitted himself no such indulgence. Partly, he explained to Stiles, it was simply that he knew he had "no talent at painting or describing characters." Partly too he had decided to take no chances: "My safest way was to avoid [personalities] and let facts speak for themselves. I was astonished after reading Robertson's *History of Scotland,* and having settled Mary Stuart's character in my own mind as one of the most infamous in history, to find him drawing her with scarce a blemish." But the great challenge came in Volume III, which Hutchinson wrote only for posthumous publication. Here if anywhere self-assertion would be justified and personal opinion might be spread upon the record. But it is one of the most impersonal, bland, and circumspect accounts of revolutionary events ever written by a participant—and not by accident. The chance survival of the heavily revised first draft shows how carefully and deliberately Hutchinson pruned his naturally unacerb style, how thoroughly he curbed his spontaneous thought, to achieve the final result.

He was cautious and temperate in everything he did. He permitted himself no ostentation in clothes. A laced coat, he said, was "too gay for me"; he preferred "a grave, genteel waistcoat," for, he wrote, he "would not be singular." As governor he had hoped to make do with his father's old carriage, but his friends told him his station required a more fashionable one. He agreed, then wrote his agents in England to get him one—secondhand, at a substantial saving: "it can't be too plain if neat and light," he wrote. None of this was senseless penny-pinching or dour prudery, and he was no misanthrope. He had no objection to stage plays, banned by the General Court of Massachusetts; he collected statuary (in cheap reproductions); and he hung in his hall a variety of paintings and fashionable prints, among them Hogarth's "Marriage à la Mode" series, in "rich frames and glass." He allowed himself at least one substantial extravagance, in furnishing, enlarging, and beautifying the Milton house, which was a joy to him from the time he built it in 1743 until he left for England thirty-one years later. Situated on a hilltop overlooking the Neponset River, with an unobstructed view north to Boston Bay, it was a "long, low structure with a central section rising a story and a half, flanked by dependent wings on either side each only one story high," and it has aptly been called "a Monticello in Massachusetts." Hutchinson spent as much time there as he could—every summer after 1754—and there he fully indulged what taste he had for physical, sensual refinement. It was a simple, modest taste. The habits of a lifetime were never overcome, even in Milton. Restraint and calculation had been part of his way of life since early childhood. "All the time he was at college," he wrote of himself with Franklinesque pride some fifty years later, he

kept a little paper journal and ledger, and entered in it every dinner, supper, breakfast, and every article of expense, even of a shilling; which practice soon became pleasant, and he found it of great use all his life, as so exact a knowledge of his cash kept him from involvement, of which he would have been in danger. And having been a very few instances negligent in this respect for a short time only, he saw the consequences of this neglect in a very strong light, and became more observant ever after.

In religion too he was rational, circumspect, and cool. He honored his family's traditional commitment to the Congregational Church, joining at the age of twenty-four the so-called New Brick Church of his college tutor and brother-in-law, the Reverend William Welsteed, to which he remained faithful, in formal terms at least, until he left America in 1774, and in which he baptized his children. He was closer in spirit, however, to his lifelong friend, the tolerant, rationalist, nondoctrinaire Reverend Andrew Eliot and to the Episcopal preacher Henry Caner, whose Anglican church he frequently attended, than he was to Welsteed or his Calvinist successor, Ebenezer Pemberton. For he despised the fanaticism of the Puritans, either in its ancestral form, laced as it was with those fine-spun doctrinal subtleties that led men to torture each other in passionate self-righteousness, or in its more modern, more pietistic form whose crankish adherents "scarce ever settled an account with anybody without a lawsuit." The career of his great-great-grandmother Anne fascinated and chilled him. Her sincere religious passion, he felt, was in itself no more humane than the destructive fervor of her enemies. Through the whole of the famous Antinomian controversy, which he recounted in a passage of his *History* that is the very essence of the Enlightenment's indictment of bigotry, "the fear of God and love of our neighbor seemed to be laid by and out of the question." At the end, he wrote, Anne no doubt held in reserve "some fine spun distinctions, too commonly made use of in theological controversies, to serve as a subterfuge, if there be occasion; and perhaps, as many other enthusiasts have done, she considered herself divinely commissioned for some great purpose, to obtain which she might think those windings, subtleties, and insinuations lawful which will hardly consist with the rules of morality. No wonder she was immoderately vain when she found magistrates and ministers embracing the novelties advanced by her."

56

A true religious life to Hutchinson meant simply the worship of God and rectitude. He judged the practice of religion by its results, in human terms: "the longer I live the less stress I lay upon modes and forms in religion, and do not love a good man the less because he and I are not just of the same way of thinking." For himself he would have chosen the Anglican Church if he had had the opportunity to choose: "had I been born and bred there," he wrote Bernard in 1771, "I would never have left it for any other communion." Its rational, tolerant views were his own, and he could see no particular objection to the establishment of an American episcopate if its jurisdiction were limited to the spiritual lives of Anglicans. But he felt no need to change formal church affiliations to express his point of view. Most clerics, he believed, of all denominations, were bigots of one sort or another, and his own pastor, Pemberton, though a Calvinist in an erratic way, was at least a "friend of government" and tolerant of other denominations. Besides, it was politically prudent for him to remain in his family's church and share to that extent the religious life of the mass of the people. For he did not think that integrity and virtue ultimately depended on a belief in the supernatural; such a belief, he felt, as often bred stupid superstition and cruel bigotry as it did decency, tolerance, and justice in human dealings.

None of this rationality and circumspection was a strenuous achievement for him. Caution, temperance, and tolerance were natural for him. There is no evidence, as there is for John Adams, of a struggle between nature and nurture, between powerful and erratic impulses and the constraints of culture. Hutchinson did not respond deeply to the physical qualities of life. His sensuous apprehensions were never keen, and he felt no inner promptings, as Adams did, to follow a wayward course. He spoke fearfully to others, especially to the young, of the temptations of dissolute living and of its disastrous consequences. But there is not the slightest shred of evidence, implicit or explicit, that he himself had ever in any way been tempted. He maintained without a struggle a correct and honorable code of conduct.

Virtuous but not stylish, intelligent but didactic, heavy-spirited and self-absorbed, he judged people, and often found them wanting. He had no great admiration for mankind in general. He had found it useful to assume that each man presented to the world not his true self but what he called a "persona" and that it was best therefore to "absolutely suspend all determination upon the real state of his mind" until long acquaintance and a careful matching of external appearances and modes of expression with true motives as they were revealed allowed one to establish the authentic character. For not only were appearances deceiving, but "words you know are arbitrary, a little use would soon cause them to convey quite contrary ideas." This was the way of the world; it had always been so. The great Pompey's friends had said of that man of high character that he "never spake as he thought." Cicero had been a man of even higher character, and he was in addition an incomparable moralist; but a comparison of his writings while Caesar was alive with the orations he delivered after Caesar had been killed shows "what a part he was acting." No doubt some men appeared to be virtuous, wise, and disinterested and in fact were so, but not many. Most lied or at least hid their true intentions as they jostled for position and scrabbled for gain.

The world was a moral tragedy not a human comedy, demanding firmness not subtlety. Hutchinson could see the good and evil in people but seldom their ridiculousness, and so he had no sense of humor. His attempts at humor, almost nonexistent in the mass of his papers, turn for their effect on rather heavy-handed irony, and quickly slip over into moral or political preachments. "I am at Milton," he wrote in 1771 to his recently departed friend Commodore Gambier (one of the few people outside his family with whom he seems to have had a lighthearted relationship).

> You would have made some humorous remarks upon the company if you had been present among us today. About one half had been yesterday at the turtle feast at The Peacock, which they did not quit until between 3 and 4 this morning. . . . Lady William has changed in one evening a tolerably healthy Nova Scotia countenance for the pale, sickly complexion of South Carolina, Mrs. Robinson her natural cheerfulness and fluency for an unusual gravity and taciturnity. Poor Paxton's usual refreshing nap after dinner was turned into a waking coma, more insensible with his eyes open than he used to be when they were shut. In short, there was no need

of a nice discerner to ascertain who had and who had not
been of the party. The physicians, parsons, and sextons may
very well afford to contribute to the support of The Peacock.
I only wish, instead of my good friends, the company might
consist of Otis, Adams, Cooper, Hancock, Molineux, and half
a hundred more of the same cast.

Pale shades of Horace Walpole! Yet this is the gayest, most gossipy
passage Hutchinson left behind, probably that he ever wrote, at least
to anyone outside his family. It marks a partial, passing relaxation of
restraint. But how faint the whole effect. There is no burst of laugh-
ter, no sting of malice. The imagination is austere, local, prosaic. And
so, it seems, was the whole of Hutchinson's mind and sensibility.

Deeply bred—locked tight—in the culture of an intensely Protestant, mercantile province of the British world and heir to its establishment, he felt no elemental discontent, no romantic aspirations.
He sought no conquests in a larger world but steady gains in the one
he knew. Like his ancestors before him, he was an accumulator, a
slow relentless acquisitor, and he remained such, even after his formal
retirement from business in the early 1760s. But though the desire
for gain was an essential part of his nature, he was never crudely
avaricious—he was too intelligent and too much a neo-Puritan ascetic
for that. His lifelong search for profits, like his quest for power and
influence and status, was never ruthless and never flamboyant, and it
was deeply conservative in that it presumed the structure of life as it
was. Like so many ambitious and modestly creative people, he needed
a stable world within which to work, a hierarchy to ascend, and a
formal, external calibration by which to measure where he was.

His correspondence radiates respect for status and an instinct for
small passages through the complexities of the world. So he wrote
the son of an earl who sought his daughter Peggy's hand, that such a
marriage would do "the greatest honor to me and my family," but "it
cannot be approved of by the noble family to which you belong. In
my station, restrained from respect to My Lord Fitzwilliam, I should
think it my duty to do all in my power to discourage any of his sons
from so unequal a match with any person in the province, and I
should certainly be highly criminal if I should countenance and encourage a match with my own daughter." So too he declined a bar-

onetcy, when it was offered to him in 1774, for prudential reasons, but then—prudence within prudence—he "thought it not amiss, however, to ask His Lordship, [that], if I should be reproached with being slighted in England, whether I might say that I [had] had the *offer* of such a mark of honor." To which Dartmouth, he reported, immediately replied (and one can picture the patronizing smile), " 'Most certainly.' " Just so, a decade earlier, in sending Richard Jackson copies of Volume I of his *History* to distribute where they might do the most good, he specified certain particularly important recipients, and then instructed Jackson to present a half dozen other copies "where you think they may be acceptable, as high up as may be in character for me, and order the binding according to the quality of the person."

Sensitively attuned to a world of status and degree, bland, constrained, realistic, unromantic, ambitious, and acquisitive, he was, for all his hatred of religious zeal, the Puritan *manqué*. For he retained the self-discipline and seriousness of the colony's stern founders and something of their asceticism; but he lacked their passion, their transcendent vision, and above all their inner certainty.

For he was never fully confident of his abilities. He was a good jurist: commentators, even some of his most severe critics, testified to his skill as adjudicator and fair-minded enforcer of the law. But he was keenly sensitive to his lack of formal legal training, worked at self-improvement, and readily confessed his own inadequacy. When he visited the great chief justice, Lord Mansfield, and fell into a discussion of the Somerset case and the laws governing slavery, he wished, he confessed to his diary, "to have entered into a free colloquium and to have discovered, if I am capable of it, the nice distinctions he must have had in his mind . . . but I imagined such an altercation would rather be disliked and forebore." He was a genuine if modest intellectual, with a true feeling for history—any history—the history of England, which he knew well; the history of continental Europe, which he studied partly from French sources; the history of Japan, which he came upon by accident and read with interest; above all, the history of his native Massachusetts, which he knew better than any man alive, which he chronicled in full, and whose historical documents he carefully preserved, edited, and published. His mind was remarkably historicist. When the famous Scottish historian William Robertson told him he had put aside his history of the English colonies because "there was no knowing what would be the future condition of them," Hutchinson informed him that the future had nothing to do with it: the outcome, he said, "need make no odds in writing the history of what is past." A true account of the history of the colonies ought to be written, Hutchinson said, and handed down to posterity. But he always regretted his lack of deep learning and never ceased belittling the virtues of his *History*.

Weaknesses of health, to some extent perhaps hereditary, added to his uncertainties. Never very robust, he began around 1762 to follow a careful regimen of exercise, walking and riding at regular intervals, controlling his consumption of food and drink, and guarding against excesses in work. But in April 1767, well before the major crisis of his career had developed, he suffered what appears to have been a nervous breakdown—he was, as he put it, "paralytic" for six or seven weeks—and only gradually regained his health. He was never thereafter free of worry, about himself as well as about the world. Night after night as governor he lay awake struggling to find the proper path for the authority he represented, worrying if he had the wisdom and the physical and psychic strength to guide the colony to peace. Repeatedly, in the ordeals of the seventies, his energy ebbed, his spirits flagged, and he hovered at the edge of collapse.

His refuge in the increasing turmoil of his life remained what it had always been, his family. He was deeply affectionate with those closest to him, and profoundly involved with their lives. However convenient and inevitable his marriage to Margaret Sanford may have been, it proved to be a relationship of intense intimacy. Only scraps of evidence remain, but they gleam in the bulk of his correspondence. After their marriage in 1734, they were parted only once for any length of time, in 1741, when Hutchinson was in England. His one surviving letter to "My Peggy" from that trip tells of his anxiety at being so long separated from her, begs for news from home, implores her to take care of her health, and expresses the fervent hope that "you will never pass another winter alone as long as I live." They spent in all eighteen years together and she bore him twelve children. Such was his attachment to her, he later wrote, "that she appeared in body and mind something more than human." Her death after childbirth in 1754 was the worst thing that ever happened to Hutchinson, worse even than the political catastrophe that later overwhelmed him. "From the first of her danger I never left my house," he recalled in later years, "and seldom her chamber." Her final words, " 'best of husbands,' " uttered "with her dying voice and eyes fixed on me," tore him to pieces; he could never forget that agony. Her death, he wrote, was the loss of more than half his soul. Neither religion nor philosophy, to which he turned, could help him. The only comfort he could find was Pliny the Younger's austere consolation that acceptance of the inevitable, the lapse of time, and a surfeit of grief would gradually heal the wound. But in fact the wound never healed. For years after her death he withdrew from all social activities and lived, Thomas Pownall recorded in 1757, "retired in the country with his children." She had given him, Hutchinson wrote ten years after her death, "the greatest happiness, too too short, I ever enjoyed." Three months before his own death in 1780, and after twenty-six years without her, he said of her that "of all earthly objects ever known [she was] deservedly the dearest."

He was close to all of the five children who survived infancy, but closest of all to his youngest, a daughter, whose birth had occasioned his wife's death, to whom he gave his wife's name, and whom he called by the same pet name, Peggy. She stayed with him, unmarried, as companion, amanuensis, and hostess until her agonizing death of consumption in London at the age of twenty-three. Of his three sons, the two oldest, bearing the ancestral names Thomas and Elisha, followed their father in trade; only the youngest, Billy, failed to pursue the familiar course, but he could find no other, and remained uncertain—a student from time to time, a dabbler, and a source of worry to his father always.

The family group was extraordinarily close: the force of cohesion that bound them fits no ordinary description. It was not merely that they lived together harmoniously until the older children married; not merely that as adults they gathered to watch together the ship carrying one of them overseas until it passed over the horizon; nor that their family letters over a period of almost fifty years express continuing affection, intimacy, and trust. More than that: they could not bear to break away, and sought to keep the group intact, to tighten the bonds, even in the centrifuge of marriage.

At the height of the family's prosperity, in the early 1770s, the extent of endogamy, already visible in the Foster connection in the previous generation, had become a public phenomenon. For the fact was undeniable, however false—and natural—the political purposes imputed to it, that by successive intermarriages the Hutchinsons had become a large and tight-knit tribe with an extraordinary accumulation of high offices.

The genealogy is important. Three family groups—the Sanfords, the Hutchinsons, and the Olivers—were involved. Margaret Sanford, Thomas Hutchinson's wife (distantly related to him by birth), was the second of three sisters. Her younger sister, Grizell, came to live with the Hutchinsons after Margaret's death, and remained with them, unmarried, ever after, serving as Hutchinson's housekeeper. The older sister, Mary, married Andrew Oliver, who became secretary of Massachusetts when Hutchinson became lieutenant governor, and lieutenant governor when Hutchinson became governor. But that is only the start of the relationships between the Oliver and Hutchinson families. In the year of Hutchinson's accession to the governorship and Oliver's to the lieutenant governorship, their children—Hutchinson's eldest son, Thomas, Jr., and Oliver's daughter Sarah—married. But these two were already related in their own generation, for in the previous year, 1770, another Hutchinson child, Sarah, had married an Oliver, Dr. Peter Oliver, Jr., Andrew's nephew. And then to conclude the series, the families were related yet again in 1772 when a third Hutchinson child, Elisha, married Mary Oliver Watson, Peter Oliver's granddaughter. And political relationships kept pace with the development of kinship ties. Andrew Oliver's brother Peter—brother, that is, of the lieutenant governor and father-in-law of one of the governor's children—had been associate justice of the superior court since 1756, and became chief justice when Hutchinson resigned that post to assume the governorship. Thus, all of the three Hutchinson children who married, married Olivers, and they did so during the first three years of Hutchinson's governorship. And thus, too, three brothers and brothers-in-law occupied simultaneously in the 1770s the governorship, the lieutenant-governorship, and the chief-justiceship of Massachusetts. No one but a Hutchinson or an Oliver had been lieutenant governor of Massachusetts after 1758 or chief justice after 1760.

Hutchinson's children, the Sanfords' business agent David Cheeseborough wrote to him in 1771, "seem to marry just as you could wish."

But why they did—what explanation there might be for such extraordinary inbreeding—is a question that eludes the historian's grasp as it did contemporaries'. Its effects, however, cannot be doubted. It created a family situation of maximum reinforcement for Hutchinson, upon which he relied heavily in the great ordeal he faced. But at the same time it helped isolate him from the community at large and intensified his clashes with other, competing family groups which, like the Otises, the Adamses, and the Bowdoin-Temple-Erving clan, reacted bitterly to the exclusiveness of Hutchinson's family ties. More important, it resulted in an immediate environment of thoroughly like-minded people who would support him in his views without criticism or serious discussion. The importance of this cannot be exaggerated, for nothing in Hutchinson's own range of sensibilities disposed him to understand or equipped him to deal with the new currents that were moving Anglo-American politics in the 1760s.

IV

At the start, in the early 1760s, the changes that were slowly overtaking American politics were far from evident. The outward pattern remained what it had been for fifty years or more: a delicately poised, unsteady balance between, on the one hand, executive authorities equipped with archaic powers theoretically supported by the Crown and, on the other hand, popular assemblies whose members were chosen by a broad electorate and which were relatively unaffected by that "influence" of patronage and corruption that had brought stability to England since the days of Robert Walpole. The governors were felt to be legally too powerful, their opponents politically "overgreat"; the one threatened tyranny, the other anarchy; struggle was the inevitable result. And struggle there had been in most colonies, whenever the two powers were active—yet in the end not lethal struggle, nor ultimate conclusions. For the overall structure of the English government had been too weak, too flexible and manipulable, to sustain ultimate confrontations. The lines of authority from Whitehall to the colonies had been too easily turned aside, too sensitive to pressure from various sources, and too devoid of policy or principle to support conclusive struggles.

This looseness and disjointedness had kept in check the political

passions that lay beneath the surface in America. For while the surface was that of the age of Walpole—hard, cynical, unsentimental,
pragmatic, venal—below were the passions of an age of ideology.
They were not unique to America. Fervent commitment to freedom—of the mind and of the person—and to the possibility of the
betterment of the lives of men freed from the fear of arbitrary force,
had been part of the life of Britain itself at least since the great upheaval of the Civil War. But in Britain, in the eighteenth century,
these flows of doctrine and belief had moved most powerfully not in
the central stream of political life but in its deep undercurrents and
at its wide margins—among radical nonconformists nourishing ancient
sources of anti-authoritarianism; among doctrinaire libertarians guarding the pure principles of liberty; and among disaffected politicians
seeking leverage against the powers that were. But in the colonies
the ideological forces of the age had flowed freely in the mainstream.
For it had been there, in the apprehensions caused by what often
seemed an alien and hostile executive, that they seemed most urgent—it had been there, in the naturally free condition of life, that
they seemed most capable of fulfillment—and it was there consequently that deprivation had been felt to be most galling. The flow
of opposition, libertarian, and nonconformist thought, moving everywhere below the surface of the English-speaking world and capable
of endowing ordinary political events with high moral and ideological
meaning, had entered the colonies in the earliest years of the eighteenth century and had threatened again and again to turn ordinary
political conflicts into passionate confrontations. But each time in the
end accommodation had been reached and the pattern of conflict
blurred. So public men like Hutchinson—hardheaded and pragmatic,
eager for profits, appointments, and influence and versed in the means
of acquiring them—had been able to govern with only passing, usually
dismissive, acknowledgment of the force of political belief.

But in the early 1760s this unstable balance was shifting. The accession of George III transformed the basic conditions of American
politics. The pursuit of colonial revenue introduced new stringencies
and new sanctions in the colonial administrative system. The dismissal not only of Pitt's war ministry but of the pliant Newcastle, who
for a generation as secretary of state had been chief custodian of
colonial patronage, threatened the established network of colonial in-

fluence in England and with it the possibility of breaking the official chain of command, mollifying official rigor, and disengaging the lines of conflict. When policy was added—that the colonists assume responsibility for partial repayment of the burden of their keep; that customs be collected and regulations enforced; and that the settlement of new lands proceed within regulations laid down in Whitehall—the world had truly changed.

In 1760, as these changes began, Thomas Hutchinson was at the height of his powers. Forty-nine years of age, an experienced, successful, and influential public figure who prided himself on his ability to withstand the savagery of politics, he was moving toward the fulfillment of his career at the center of colonial affairs, where it was expected that his abilities would once more gain him success. And so they would have, if times had not changed—if politics had not entered a new phase. Never having felt deep personal discontent—never having passionately aspired—never having longed for some ideal and total betterment—never having found in some utopian vision a compelling and transforming cause, he had never understood the motivations of the miserable, the visionary, and the committed, and he was unprepared to grapple with the politics they shaped.

4

Thomas Paine

"Prepare in Time
an Asylum for Mankind"

I

THOMAS PAINE'S *Common Sense* is the most brilliant pamphlet written during the American Revolution, and one of the most brilliant pamphlets ever written in the English language. How it could have been produced by the bankrupt Quaker corset-maker, the some-time teacher, preacher, and grocer, and twice-dismissed excise officer who happened to catch Benjamin Franklin's attention in England and who arrived in America only fourteen months before *Common Sense* was published is nothing one can explain without explaining genius itself. For it is a work of genius—slapdash as it is, rambling as it is, crude as it is. It "burst from the press," Benjamin Rush wrote, "with an effect which has rarely been produced by types and papers in any age or country." Its effect, Franklin said, was "prodigious." It touched some extraordinarily sensitive nerve in American political awareness in the confusing period in which it appeared.

It was written by an Englishman, not an American. Paine had only the barest acquaintance with American affairs when, with Rush's encouragement, he turned an invitation by Franklin to write a history of the Anglo-American controversy into the occasion for composing a passionate tract for American independence. Yet not only does *Common Sense* voice some of the deepest aspirations of the American people on the eve of the Revolution but it also evokes, with superb vigor and with perfect intonation, longings and aspirations that have remained part of American culture to this day.

What is one to make of this extraordinary document and its author after two hundred years? What questions, in the context of the current understanding of the causes and meaning of the Revolution, should one ask of it?

Not, I think, the traditional one of whether *Common Sense* precipitated the movement for independence. To accomplish that was of course its ostensible purpose, and so powerful a blast, so piercing a cry so widely heard throughout the colonies, could scarcely have failed to move some people some of the way. It undoubtedly caused some of the hesitant and vaguely conservative who had reached no decision to think once more about the future that might be opening up in America.

For it appeared at what was perhaps the perfect moment to have a maximum effect. It was published on January 10, 1776. Nine months before, the first skirmishes of the Revolutionary War had been fought, and seven months before, a bloody battle had taken place on Breed's Hill, across the bay from Boston, which was the headquarters of the British army in America, long since surrounded by provincial troops. Three months after that, in September 1775, a makeshift American army had invaded Canada and taken Montreal. In December its two divisions had joined to attack Quebec, and though that attack, on December 30–31, had failed miserably, the remnants of the American armies still surrounded the city when Paine wrote *Common Sense*, and Montreal was still in American hands.

That a war of some sort was in progress was obvious, but it was not obvious what the objective of the fighting was. There was disagreement in the Continental Congress as to what a military victory, if it came, should be used to achieve. A group of influential and articulate leaders, especially those from Massachusetts, were convinced that only independence from England could properly serve American needs, and Benjamin Franklin, recently returned from London, had reached the same conclusion and had found like-minded people in Philadelphia. But that was *not* the common opinion of the Congress, and it certainly was not the general view of the population at large. Not a single colony had instructed its delegates to work for independence, and not a single step had been taken by the Congress that was incompatible with the idea—which was still the prevailing view—that America's purpose was to force Parliament to acknowledge the liberties it claimed and to redress the grievances that had for so long and in so many different ways been explained to the world. All the most powerful unspoken assumptions of the time—indeed, common sense—ran counter to the notion of independence.

If it is an exaggeration, it is not much of an exaggeration to say that one had to be a fool or a fanatic in early January 1776 to advocate American independence. Militia troops may have been able to defend themselves at certain points and had achieved some limited goals, but the first extended military campaign was ending in a squalid defeat below the walls of Quebec. There was no evidence of an area of agreement among the thirteen separate governments and among the hundreds of conflicting American interests that was broad enough and firm enough to support an effective common government. Everyone knew that England was the most powerful nation on earth, and if its navy had fallen into disrepair, it could be swiftly rebuilt. Anyone in whom common sense outweighed enthusiasm and imagination knew that a string of prosperous but weak communities along the Atlantic coast left uncontrolled and unprotected by England would quickly be pounced on by rival European powers, whose ruling political notions and whose institutions of government were the opposite of what Americans had been struggling to preserve. The most obvious presumption of all was that the liberties Americans sought were British in their nature: they had been achieved by Britain over the centuries and had been embedded in a constitution whose wonderfully contrived balance between the needs of the state and the rights of the individual was thought throughout the Western world to be one of the finest human achievements. It was obvious too, of course, that something had gone wrong recently. It was generally agreed in the colonies that the famous balance of the constitution, in Britain and America, had been thrown off by a gang of ministers greedy for power, and that their attention had been drawn to the colonies by the misrepresentations of certain colonial officeholders who hoped to find an open route to influence and fortune in the enlargement of Crown power in the colonies. But the British constitution had been under attack before, and although at certain junctures in the past drastic action had been necessary to reestablish the balance, no one of importance had ever concluded that the constitution itself was at fault; no one had ever cast doubt on the principle that liberty, as the colonists knew it, rested on—had in fact been created by—the stable balancing of the three essential socio-constitutional orders, the monarchy, the nobility, and the people at large, each with its appropriate organ of government: the Crown, the House of Lords, and the House of Commons. If the balance had momentarily been thrown off, let Americans, like Britishers in former ages, fight to restore it: force the evildoers out, and recover the protection of the only system ever known to guarantee both liberty and order. America had flourished under that benign system, and it was simply common sense to try to restore its balance. Why should one want to destroy the most successful political system in the world, which had been constructed by generations of constitutional architects, each building on and refining the wisdom of his predecessors, simply because its present managers were vicious or criminal? And was it reasonable to think that these ill-coordinated, weak communities along the Atlantic coast could defeat England in war and then construct governments free of the defects that had been revealed in the almost perfect English system?

Since we know how it came out, these seem rather artificial and rhetorical questions. But in early January 1776 they were vital and urgent, and *Common Sense* was written to answer them. There was open warfare between Britain and America, but though confidence in the British government had been severely eroded, the weight of opinion still favored restoration of the situation as it had been before 1764, a position arrived at not by argument so much as by recognition of the obvious sense of the matter, which was rooted in the deepest presuppositions of the time.

In the weeks when *Common Sense* was being written, the future—even the very immediate future—was entirely obscure; the situation was malleable in the extreme. No one then could confidently say which course history would later declare to have been the right course to have followed. No one then could know who would later be seen to have been the heroes and who the villains. No one then could know who would be the winners and who the losers.

But Paine was certain that he knew the answers to all these questions, and the immediate impact that *Common Sense* had was in large part simply the result of the pamphlet's ringing assertiveness, its shrill unwavering declaration that all the right was on the side of independence and all the wrong on the side of loyalty to Britain. History favored Paine, and so the pamphlet became prophetic. But in the strict context of the historical moment of its appearance, its assertiveness seemed to many to be more outrageous than prophetic.

All of this is part of the remarkable history of Paine's pamphlet, part of the extraordinary impact it had upon contemporaries' awareness. Yet I do not think that, at this distance in time and in the context of what we now know about the causes of the Revolution, the question of its influence on the developing movement toward independence is the most useful question that can be asked. We know both too much and too little to determine the degree to which *Common Sense* precipitated the conclusion that Congress reached in early July. We can now depict in detail the stages by which Congress was led to vote for independence—who played what role and how the fundamental, difficult, and divisive problem was resolved. And the closer we look at the details of what happened in Congress in early 1776 the less important *Common Sense* appears to have been. It played a role in the background, no doubt; and many people, in Congress and out, had the memory of reading it as they accepted the final determination to move to independence. But, as John Adams noted, at least as many people were offended by the pamphlet as were persuaded by it—he himself later called it "a poor, ignorant, malicious, short-sighted, crapulous mass"—and we shall never know the proportions on either side with any precision.

What strikes one more forcefully now, at this distance in time, is something quite different from the question of the pamphlet's unmeasurable contribution to the movement toward independence. There is something extraordinary in this pamphlet and in the mind and imagination of the man who wrote it—something bizarre, outsized, unique—and that quality helps us understand, I believe, something essential in the Revolution as a whole.

II

Certainly the language is remarkable. For its prose alone, *Common Sense* would be a notable document—unique among the pamphlets of the American Revolution. Its phraseology is deeply involving—at times clever, at times outrageous, frequently startling in imagery and penetration—and becomes more vivid as the pamphlet progresses.

In the first substantive part of the pamphlet, ostensibly an essay on the principles of government in general and of the English constitution in particular, the ideas are relatively abstract but the imagery is concrete: "Government, like dress, is the badge of lost innocence; the palaces of kings are built upon the ruins of the bowers of paradise." As for the "so much boasted constitution of England," it was "noble for the dark and slavish times in which it was erected"; but that was not really so remarkable, Paine said, for "when the world was overrun with tyranny, the least remove therefrom was a glorious rescue." In fact, Paine wrote, the British constitution is "imperfect, subject to convulsions, and incapable of producing what it seems to promise," all of which could be "easily demonstrated" to anyone who could shake himself loose from the fetters of prejudice. For "as a man who is attached to a prostitute is unfitted to choose or judge of a wife, so any prepossession in favour of a rotten constitution of government will disable us from discerning a good one."

The imagery becomes arresting in Part 2, on monarchy and hereditary succession, institutions which together, Paine wrote, formed "the most prosperous invention the devil ever set on foot for the promotion of idolatry." The heathens, who invented monarchy, at least had had the good sense to grant divinity only to their *dead* kings; "the Christian world hath improved on the plan by doing the same to their living ones. How impious is the title of sacred majesty applied to a worm, who in the midst of his splendor is crumbling into dust!" Hereditary right is ridiculed by nature herself, which so frequently gives "mankind an *ass for a lion.*"

What of the true origins of the present-day monarchs, so exalted by myth and supposedly sanctified by antiquity? In all probability, Paine wrote, the founder of any of the modern royal lines was "nothing better than the principal ruffian of some restless gang, whose savage manners or preeminence in subtilty obtained him the title of chief among plunderers; and who, by increasing in power and extending his depredations, overawed the quiet and defenceless to purchase their safety by frequent contributions." The English monarchs? "No man in his senses can say that their claim under William the Conquerer is a very honourable one. A French bastard, landing with an armed banditti and establishing himself king of England against the consent of the natives, is in plain terms a very paltry rascally original." Why should one even bother to explain the folly of hereditary right? It is said to provide continuity and hence to preserve a nation from civil wars. That, Paine said, is "the most bare-faced falsity ever imposed upon mankind." English history alone disproves it. There had been, Paine confidently declared, "no less than eight civil wars and nineteen rebellions" since the Conquest. The fact is that everywhere hereditary monarchy has "laid . . . the world in blood and ashes." "In England a king hath little more to do than to make war and give away places; which in plain terms is to impoverish the nation and set it together by the ears. A pretty business indeed for a man to be allowed eight hundred thousand sterling a year for, and worshipped into the bargain!" People who are fools enough to believe the claptrap about monarchy, Paine wrote, should be allowed to do so without interference: "let them promiscuously worship the Ass and the Lion, and welcome."

But it is in the third section, "Thoughts on the Present State of American Affairs," that Paine's language becomes most effective and vivid. The emotional level is extremely high throughout these pages and the lyric passages even then must have seemed prophetic:

> The sun never shined on a cause of greater worth. . . . 'Tis not the concern of a day, a year, or an age; posterity are virtually involved in the contest, and will be more or less affected even to the end of time by the proceedings now. Now is the seed-time of continental union, faith, and honour. The least fracture now will be like a name engraved with the point of a pin on the tender rind of a young oak; the wound will enlarge with the tree, and posterity read it in full grown characters.

The arguments in this section, proving the necessity for American independence and the colonies' capacity to achieve it, are elaborately worked out, and they respond to all the objections to independence that Paine had heard. But through all of these pages of argumentation, the prophetic, lyric note of the opening paragraphs continues to be heard, and a sense of urgency keeps the tension high. "Every thing that is right or reasonable," Paine writes, "pleads for separation. The blood of the slain, the weeping voice of nature cries, " 'TIS TIME TO PART." *Now* is the time to act, he insists: "The present winter is worth an age if rightly employed, but if lost or neglected the whole continent will partake of the misfortune." The possibility of a peaceful conclusion to the controversy had vanished, "wherefore, since nothing but blows will do, for God's sake let us come to a final separation, and not leave the next generation to be cutting throats under the violated unmeaning names of parent and child." Not to act now would not eliminate the need for action, he wrote, but only postpone it to the next generation, which would clearly see that "a little more, a little further, would have rendered this continent the glory of the earth." To talk of reconciliation "with those in whom our reason forbids us to have faith, and our affections, wounded thro' a thousand pores, instruct us to detest, is madness and folly." The earlier harmony was irrecoverable: "Can ye give to prostitution its former innocence? Neither can ye reconcile Britain and America. . . . As well can the lover forgive the ravisher of his mistress as the continent forgive the murders of Britain." And the section ends with Paine's greatest peroration:

> O ye that love mankind! Ye that dare to oppose not only the tyranny but the tyrant, stand forth! Every spot of the old world is overrun with oppression. Freedom hath been hunted round the globe. Asia and Africa have long expelled her. Europe regards her like a stranger, and England hath given her warning to depart. O! receive the fugitive, and prepare in time an asylum for mankind.

In the pamphlet literature of the American Revolution there is nothing comparable to this passage for sheer emotional intensity and lyric appeal. Its vividness must have leapt out of the pages to readers used to grayer, more stolid prose.

III

But language does not explain itself. It is a reflection of deeper elements—qualities of mind, styles of thought, a writer's personal culture. There is something unique in the intellectual idiom of the pamphlet.

Common Sense, it must be said, is lacking in close rigor of argumentation. Again and again Paine's logic can be seen to be grossly deficient. His impatience with following through with his arguments at certain points becomes almost amusing. In the fourth and final section, for example, which is on America's ability to achieve and maintain independence, Paine argues that one of America's great advantages is that, unlike the corrupt European powers, it is free of public debt, a burden that was believed to carry with it all sorts of disabling social and political miseries. But then Paine recognizes that mounting a full-scale war and maintaining independence would inevitably force America to create a national debt. He thereupon proceeds to argue, in order, the following: (1) that *such* a debt would be "a glorious memento of our virtue"; (2) that even if it *were* a misery, it would be a cheap price to pay for independence and a new, free constitution—though not, for reasons that are not made entirely clear, a cheap price to pay for simply getting rid of the ministry responsible for all the trouble and returning the situation to what it was in 1764: "such a thought's unworthy a man of honour, and is the true characteristic of a narrow heart and a pidling politician." Having reached that point, he goes the whole way around to make the third point, which is that "no nation ought to be without a debt," though he had started with the idea that the absence of one was an advantage. But this new notion attracts him, and he begins to grasp the idea, which the later federalists would clearly see, that "a national debt is a national bond"; but then, having vaguely approached that idea, he skitters off to the curious thought that a national debt could not be a grievance so long as no interest had to be paid on it; and that in turn leads him into claiming that America could produce a navy twice the size of Britain's for one-twentieth of the British national debt.

Close logic, in these specific arguments, contributes nothing to the force of *Common Sense.* But the intellectual style of the pamphlet is extraordinarily impressive nevertheless, because of a more fundamental characteristic than consistency or cogency. Paine's intellectual force lay not in his close argumentation on specific points but in his reversal of the presumptions that underlay the arguments, a reversal that forced thoughtful readers to consider not so much a point here and a conclusion there as a wholly new way of looking at the entire range of problems involved. For beneath all of the explicit arguments and conclusions against independence, there were underlying, unspoken, even unconceptualized presuppositions, attitudes, and habits of thought that made it extremely difficult for the colonists to break with Britain and find in the prospect of an independent future the security and freedom they sought. The special intellectual quality of *Common Sense*, which goes a long way toward explaining its impact on contemporary readers, derives from its reversal of these underlying presumptions and its shifting of the established perspectives to the point where the received paradigm, within which the Anglo-American controversy had until then proceeded, came into question.

No one set of ideas was more deeply embedded in the British and the British-American mind than the notion, whose genealogy could be traced back to Polybius, that liberty could survive in a world of innately ambitious and selfish, if not brutal, men only where a balance of the contending forces was so institutionalized that no one contestant could monopolize the power of the state and rule without effective opposition. In its application to the Anglo-American world this general belief further presumed that the three main socio-constitutional contestants for power—the monarchy, the nobility, and the people—had an equal right to share in the struggle for power: these were the constituent elements of the political world. And most important of all in this basic set of constitutional notions was the unspoken belief, upon which everything else rested, that complexity in government was good in itself since it made all the rest of the system possible, and that, conversely, simplicity and uncomplicated efficiency in the structure of government were evil in that they led to a monopolization of power, which could only result in brutal state autocracy.

Paine challenged this whole basic constitutional paradigm, and although his conclusions were rejected in America—the American state and national governments are, of course, built on precisely the ideas he opposed—the bland, automatic assumption that all of this made sense could no longer, after the appearance of *Common Sense*, be said to exist, and respect for certain points was permanently destroyed.

The entire set of received ideas on government, Paine wrote, was false. Complexity was not a virtue in government, he said—all that complexity accomplished was to make it impossible to tell where the faults lay when a system fell into disarray. The opposite, he said, was in fact true: "the more simple any thing is, the less liable it is to be disordered and the easier repaired when disordered." Simplicity was embedded in nature itself, and if the British constitution had reversed the natural order of things, it had done so only to serve the unnatural purposes of the nobility and the monarchy, neither of which had a right to share in the power of the state. The nobility was scarcely even worth considering; it was nothing but the dead remains of an ancient "aristocratical tyranny" that had managed to survive under the cover of encrusting mythologies. The monarchical branch was a more serious matter, and Paine devoted pages of the pamphlet to attacking its claim to a share in the constitution.

As the inheritor of some thuggish ancestor's victory in battle, the "royal brute of Great Britain," as he called George III, was no less a ridiculous constitutional figure than his continental equivalents. For though by his constitutional position he was required to know the affairs of his realm thoroughly and to participate in them actively, by virtue of his exalted social position, entirely removed from everyday life—"distinguished like some new species"—he was forever barred from doing just that. In fact, the modern kings of England did nothing at all, Paine wrote, but wage war and hand out gifts to their followers, all the rest of the world's work being handled by the commons. Yet by virtue of the gifts the king had at his disposal, he corrupted the entire constitution, such as it was. The king's only competitor for power was the House of Commons, and this body he was able to buy off with the rewards of office and the intimidation of authority. The whole idea of balance in the British constitution was therefore a fraud, for "the will of the king is as much the law of the land in Britain as in France, with this difference, that instead of proceeding directly from his mouth, it is handed to the people under the formidable shape of an act of Parliament." Yet, was it not true that individuals were safer in England than in France? Yes, Paine said, they are, but not because of the supposed balance of the constitution: "the plain truth is that *it is wholly owing to the constitution of the people and not to the constitution of the government* that the crown is not as oppressive in England as in Turkey."

This was a very potent proposition, no matter how poorly the individual subarguments were presented, for it was well known that even in the best of times formal constitutional theory in England bore only a vague relation to the informal, ordinary operation of the government, and although penetrating minds like David Hume had attempted to reconceive the relationship so as to bring the two into somewhat closer accord, no one had tried to settle the matter by declaring that the whole notion of checks and balances in the English constitution was "farcical" and that two of the three components of the supposed balance had no rightful place in the constitutional forms at all. And no one—at least no one writing in America—had made so straightforward and unqualified a case for the virtues of republican government.

This was Paine's most important challenge to the received wisdom of the day, but it was only the first of a series. In passage after passage in *Common Sense* Paine laid bare one after another of the presuppositions of the day which had disposed the colonists, consciously or unconsciously, to resist independence, and by exposing these inner biases and holding them up to scorn he forced people to think the unthinkable, to ponder the supposedly self-evident, and thus to take the first step in bringing about a radical change.

So the question of independence had always been thought of in filial terms: the colonies had once been children, dependent for their lives on the parent state, but now they had matured, and the question was whether or not they were strong enough to survive and prosper alone in a world of warring states. This whole notion was wrong, Paine declared. On this, as on so many other points, Americans had been misled by "ancient prejudices and . . . superstition." Britain's supposedly protective nurturance of the colonies had only been a form of selfish economic aggrandizement; she would have nurtured Turkey from exactly the same motivations. The fact is, Paine declared, that the colonies had never needed Britain's protection; they had indeed suffered from it. They would have flourished far more if Britain had ignored them, for their prosperity had always been based on a commerce in the necessities of life, and that commerce would have flourished, and would continue to flourish, so long as "eating is the custom of Europe." What in fact Britain's maternal nurture had given America was a burdensome share of the quarrels of European states with whom America, independent of Britain, could have lived in harmony. War was endemic in Europe because of the stupidities of monarchical rivalries, and Britain's involvements had meant that America too was dragged into quarrels in which it had no stake whatever. It was a ridiculous situation even in military terms, for neutrality, Paine wrote, is "a safer convoy than a man of war." The whole concept of Britain's maternal role was rubbish, he wrote, and rubbish, moreover, that had tragically limited America's capacity to see the wider world as it was and to understand the important role America had in fact played in it and could play even more in the future:

> . . . the phrase *parent* or *mother country* hath been jesuitically adopted by the king and his parasites with a low papistical design of gaining an unfair bias on the credulous weakness of our minds. Europe, and not England, is the parent country of America. This new world hath been the asylum for the persecuted lovers of civil and religious liberty from *every part* of Europe. . . . we claim brotherhood with every European Christian, and triumph in the generosity of the sentiment. . . . Not one third of the inhabitants even of this province [Pennsylvania] are of English descent. Wherefore I reprobate the phrase of parent or mother country applied to England only, as being false, selfish, narrow, and ungenerous.

The question, then, of whether America had developed sufficiently under Britain's maternal nurture to be able to live independent of the parent state was mistaken in its premise and needed no answer. What was needed was freedom from the confining imagery of parent and child which had crippled the colonists' ability to see themselves and the world as they truly were.

So too Paine attacked the fears of independence not defensively, by putting down the doubts that had been voiced, but aggressively, by reshaping the premises on which those doubts had rested. It had been said that if left to themselves the colonies would destroy themselves in civil strife. The opposite was true, Paine replied. The civil strife that America had known had flowed from the connection with Britain and was a necessary and inescapable part of the colonial relationship. Similarly, it had been pointed out that there was no common government in America, and doubts had been expressed that

there ever could be one; so Paine sketched one, based on the existing Continental Congress, which he claimed was so fairly representative of the thirteen colonies that anyone who stirred up trouble
"would have joined Lucifer in his revolt." In his projected state, people would worship not some "hardened, sullen-tempered Pharaoh"
like George III, but law itself and the national constitution, "for as in
absolute governments the king is law, so in free countries the law
ought to be king." The question was not whether America could
create a workable free constitution but how, in view of what had
happened, it could afford not to.

So too it had been claimed that America was weak and could not
survive in a war with a European power. Paine commented that only
in America had nature created a perfect combination of limitless resources for naval construction and a vast coastal extension, with the
result that America was not simply capable of self-defense at sea but
was potentially the greatest naval power in the world—if it began to
build its naval strength immediately, for in time the resources would
diminish. So it was argued that America's population was too small
to support an army: a grotesquely mistaken idea, Paine said. History
proved that the larger the population, the *smaller* and *weaker* the armies, for large populations bred prosperity and an excessive involvement in business affairs, both of which had destroyed the military
power of nations in the past. The City of London, where England's
commerce was centered, was the most cowardly community in the
realm: "the rich are in general slaves to fear, and submit to courtly
power with the trembling duplicity of a spaniel." In fact, he concluded, a nation's bravest deeds are always done in its youth. Not
only was America now capable of sustaining a great military effort,
but now was the *only* time it would *ever* be able to do so, for its
commerce was sure to rise, its wealth to increase, and its anxiety for
the safety of its property to become all-engrossing:

> The vast variety of interests, occasioned by an increase of
> trade and population, would create confusion. Colony would
> be against colony. Each being able, would scorn each other's
> assistance: and while the proud and foolish gloried in their
> little distinctions, the wise would lament that the union had
> not been formed before.

So on the major questions Paine performed a task more important than arguing points in favor of independence (though he did that too); he shifted the premises of the questions and forced thoughtful readers to come at them from different angles of vision and hence to open for scrutiny what had previously been considered to be the firm premises of the controversy.

IV

Written in arresting prose—at times wild and fierce prose, at times lyrical and inspirational, but never flat and merely argumentative, and often deeply moving—and directed as a polemic not so much at the conclusions that opponents of independence had reached but at their premises, at their unspoken presumptions, and at their sense of what was obvious and what was not, Paine's pamphlet is unique in the literature of the Revolution. But none of this reaches its most important inner quality. There is something in the pamphlet that goes beyond both of these quite distinguishing characteristics, and while it is less susceptible to proof than the attributes I have already discussed, it is perhaps the most important element of all. It relates to the social aspects of the Revolution.

Much ink has been spilled over the question of the degree to which the American Revolution was a social revolution, and it seems to me that certain points have now been well established. The American Revolution was not the result of intolerable social or economic conditions. The colonies were prosperous communities whose economic condition, recovering from the dislocations of the Seven Years' War, improved during the years when the controversy with England rose in intensity. Nor was the Revolution deliberately undertaken to recast the social order, to destroy the last remnants of the *ancien régime*, such as they were in America. And there were no "dysfunctions" building up that shaped a peculiarly revolutionary frame of mind in the colonies. The Anglo-American political community could have continued to function "dysfunctionally" for ages untold if certain problems had not arisen which were handled clumsily by an insensitive ministry supported by a political population frozen in glacial complacency, and if those problems had not stirred up the intense ideological sensibilities of the American people. Yet in an indirect way there was a social component in the Revolutionary movement, but it is subtle and latent, wound in, at times quite obscurely, among other elements, and difficult to grasp in itself. It finds its most forceful expression in the dilated prose of Paine's *Common Sense*.

The dominant tone of *Common Sense* is that of rage. It was written by an enraged man—not someone who had reasoned doubts about the British constitution and the related establishment in America, but someone who hated them both and who wished to strike back at them in a savage response. The verbal surface of the pamphlet is heated, and it burned into the consciousness of contemporaries because below it was the flaming conviction, not simply that Britain was corrupt and that America should declare its independence, but that the whole of organized society and government was stupid and cruel and that it survived only because the atrocities it systematically imposed on humanity had been papered over with a veneer of mythology and superstition that numbed the mind and kept people from rising against the evils that oppressed them.

The aim of almost every other notable pamphlet of the Revolution—pamphlets written by lawyers, ministers, merchants, and planters—was to probe difficult, urgent, and controversial questions and make appropriate recommendations. Paine's aim was to tear the world apart—the world as it was known and as it was constituted. Paine had nothing of the close logic, scholarship, and rational tone of the best of the American pamphleteers. Paine was an ignoramus, both in ideas and in the practice of politics, next to Adams, Jefferson, Madison, or Wilson. He could not discipline his thoughts; they were sucked off continuously from the sketchy outline he apparently had in mind when he began the pamphlet, into the boiling vortex of his emotions. And he had none of the hard, quizzical, grainy quality of mind that led Madison to probe the deepest questions of republicanism not as an ideal contrast to monarchical corruption but as an operating, practical, everyday process of government capable of containing within it the explosive forces of society. Paine's writing was not meant to probe unknown realities of a future way of life, or to convince, or to explain; it was meant to overwhelm and destroy. In this respect *Common Sense* bears comparison not to the writings of the other American pamphleteers but to those of Jonathan Swift. For Swift too had been a verbal killer in an age when pamphleteering was important to politics. But Swift's chief weapon had been a rapier as sharp as a razor and so finely pointed that it entered its victim unfelt. Paine's writing has none of Swift's marvelously ironic subtlety, just as it has none of the American pamphleteers' learning and logic. Paine's language is violent, slashing, angry, indignant.

This inner voice of anger and indignation had been heard before in Georgian England, in quite special and peculiar forms. It is found in certain of the writings of the extreme left-wing libertarians; and it can be found, too, in the boiling denunciations of English corruption that flowed from the pens of such would-be prophets as Dr. John Brown, whose sulphuric *Estimate of the Manners and Principles of the Times* created such a sensation in 1757. But its most vivid expression is not verbal but graphic: the paintings and engravings of William Hogarth, whose awareness of the world had taken shape in the same squalor of London's and the provinces' demimonde in which Paine had lived and in which he had struggled so unsuccessfully. In Paine's pamphlet all of these strains and sets of attitudes combine: the extreme left-wing political views that had developed during the English Civil War period as revolutionary republicanism and radical democracy and that had survived, though only underground, through the Glorious Revolution and Walpole's complacent regime; the prophetic sectarian moralism that flowed from seventeenth-century Puritan roots and that had been kept alive in the militancy of the radical Baptists and the uncompromising Quakers whom Paine had known so well; and finally, and most important, the indignation and rage of the semi-dispossessed, living at the margins of respectable society and hanging precariously over the abyss of debtors' prison, threatened at every turn with an irrecoverable descent into the hell that Hogarth painted so brilliantly and so compulsively in his savage morality tales— those dramatic "progresses" that depict with fiendish, almost insane intensity the passages people in Paine's circumstances took from marginal prosperity, hope, and decency, through scenes of seduction, cruelty, passion, and greed, into madness, disease, and a squalor that became cosmic and apocalyptic in Hogarth's superb late engraving "The Bathos."

These were English strains and English attitudes—just as *Common Sense* was an English pamphlet written on an American theme—and they were closer in spirit to the viciousness of the Parisian demimonde depicted in the salacious reportage of Restif de La Bretonne than to the Boston of the Adamses and the Philadelphia of Franklin. Yet for all the differences—which help explain why so many American radicals found *Common Sense* so outrageous and unacceptable—there are similarities too. In subdued form something of the same indignation and anger lurks around the edges and under the surface of the American Revolutionary movement. It is not the essential core of the Revolution, but it is an important part of it, and one of the most difficult aspects to depict. One catches a sense of it in John Adams's intense hatred of the Hutchinson-Oliver establishment in Boston, a hatred that any reader of Adams's *Diary* can follow in innumerable blistering passages of that wonderful book, and that led to some of the main triggering events of the Revolution. It can be found too in the denunciations of British corruption that sprang so easily to the lips of the New England preachers, especially those most sunk in provincial remoteness and closest to the original fires of Puritanism which had once burned with equal intensity on both sides of the Atlantic. And it can be found in the resentment of otherwise secure and substantial Americans faced with the brutal arrogance and irrational authority of Crown officials appointed through the tortuous workings of a patronage system utterly remote from America and in no way reflective of the realities of American society.

Common Sense expresses all of this in a magnified form—a form that in its intensity no American could have devised. The pamphlet sparked into flame resentments that had smoldered within the American opposition to Britain for years, and brought into a single focus the lack of confidence in the whole European world that Americans had vaguely felt and the aspirations for a newer, freer, more open world, independent of Britain, which had not, until then, been freely expressed. Paine's pamphlet did not touch off the movement for a formal declaration of independence, and it did not create the Revolutionary leaders' determination to build a better world, more open to human aspirations, than had ever been known before. But it stimulated both; and it exposes in unnaturally vivid dilation the anger—born of resentment, frustration, hurt, and fear—that is an impelling force in every transforming revolution.

5

The Index and Commentaries of Harbottle Dorr

"Oh the Villian!"

WE KNOW WHAT the statesmen, intellectuals, and publicists of the American Revolution wrote, and can infer much of what they thought and something of what they felt. But intimate records of the inner experiences of ordinary active participants in the struggle are rare, especially those that reveal not consciously formulated ideas but widely shared assumptions from which the Revolutionary movement developed. The more ordinary the mind and the more typical the career, the more valuable the documentation, and there is no more ordinary active participant in the Revolution who left behind a revealing record of the inner, personal meaning of the Revolution than a Boston shopkeeper with the unlikely name of Harbottle Dorr.

Harbottle Dorr, *Junior*, to be precise, for his father, a Boston leather-dresser who died in 1746, bore the same improbable name. The father had no property to bequeath to his son—his assets, valued at £306 15s 4d Old Tenor, were consumed by debts. But he evidently left his son something more valuable than property. For despite his poverty, the father must have been a bookish man. The administrators of his estate, a tinplate worker and joiner, listed among his assets not only a rather expensive Bible, but 33 printed books and 44 pamphlets as well, a small library that must have been selected with care. In all likelihood some of the publications were histories, for the sense of history the son acquired is something one learns early or not at all; and somewhere, if not at home, the son became acquainted with the apparatus of book publication—dedications, prefaces, indexes, and the rudiments of scholarly annotation.

Of the son's—our Harbottle's—career very little is known. He enjoyed a modest prosperity from the income of his shop on Union Street, near Dock Square, where he sold hardware, especially nails, dishware, and miscellaneous ship supplies both retail and wholesale, and he was an early and enthusiastic member of the Sons of Liberty, signing one of the earliest nonimportation agreements (March 1768) and dining with the Sons of Liberty at the Liberty Tree in Dorchester on August 14, 1769. Occasionally he wrote letters to the newspapers: in one written in 1773, after Governor Thomas Hutchinson's letters to Thomas Whately had been published as evidence of a pan-Atlantic conspiracy to destroy American liberties, Dorr, writing as "A Consistent Whig," criticized the clergy for their coolness and, well in advance of general opinion, called for the convening of a colonial congress and the forging of a unified intercolonial policy of resistance. But he never became an important political leader in Massachusetts, or even in Boston. He achieved the peak of his eminence in 1777, at the age of forty-seven, when he was elected a town selectman, a post to which he was reelected eleven times thereafter; on the last occasion, in 1791, he led the list.

And he was, apparently, in his private life no moral hero. During the war he did what he could to lay hands on the house and copper foundry of a loyalist who had fled, one Martin Gay, though Gay's property, which adjoined Dorr's, was still occupied by the loyalist's helpless wife. "That republican, N[ew] E[ngland] puritanical Harbottle Dorr," Gay fumed in exile in Nova Scotia, "deserves a particular mark of infamy . . . for his unrighteous conduct in adding to Mrs. Gay's other afflictions." But Dorr's acquisitiveness did him little good. At his death in 1794 he left an estate somewhat more complicated than his father's and evidence of a higher status in the community than his father had enjoyed, but little more in material assets. For while his property included gold buttons and buckles, half a pew in the New North Church, cash, and public securities—the total worth £475 1s 2d—his debts totaled £151 4s 8d. Like his father, he left behind a Bible, a few books (fewer than his father had owned), and a collection of pamphlets, but the whole was no more than an ordinary estate of an ordinary tradesman. Harbottle Dorr had entered into the Revolution enthusiastically, had lived to see the new regime consolidated, and in the war years and after had played a modest role in the government of his home community.

There is nothing remarkable in any of this. Dorr was an ordinary active participant in the Revolution. That is why what he began in 1765 and completed some twelve years later is so extraordinarily revealing.

Why he undertook his great labor is not known. All we know is that on January 7, 1765, in the midst of the Stamp Act controversy, Harbottle Dorr set aside for preservation as a historical document the current issue of the *Boston Evening-Post,* and began collecting copies of each of the succeeding issues either of the *Evening-Post* or of the chief opposition newspaper, the *Boston Gazette,* or occasionally of the *Boston Post-Boy & Advertiser.* And not only did he preserve each week a copy of one or another—sometimes of two—of these newspapers, but he commented on their contents in inked notations in the margins and between the lines, expressing himself pungently on the events of the time, identifying anonymous and pseudonymous authors, clarifying obscure references in the political charges and countercharges, referring possible users of his collection of newspapers backward and forward in a maze of cross-references in his own pagination to documents and stories relevant to particular events and statements that were reported in the news, and in this way revealing inconsistencies and misrepresentations, reinforcing the truth as he saw it, and guiding the reader's thoughts into proper channels.

Three years after he had set aside the first issue he had accumulated 789 pages of newsprint—an unbroken run of annotated Boston newspapers from early 1765 to the end of 1767—and he put that large bundle aside as Volume I. Two years after that, at the end of 1769, he had accumulated another 788 pages, and his ambitions had blossomed. To this second volume he added as appendixes a series of documents in the history of Anglo-American liberty—copies of Magna Carta, the Massachusetts charter, the English Bill of Rights, a "Chronology of Arts and Sciences" (itself apparently a documentary history of British liberty), Governor Bernard's confidential letters to the ministry that had been surreptitiously obtained in England and published as pamphlets in Boston, and two other pamphlets of 1769. These documents he repaginated to follow in order the page numbering he had devised for the newspaper texts, and then he went through the whole of the first two volumes carefully, correcting some of his original notes and cross-references, and adding others. And more than that, he began at that point to *index* the volumes—to index not only people, places, and events but the important topics as he saw them, in categories that express, as nothing else could, his immediate response to and understanding of the events he was recording.*

Indexing caused Dorr, as it has so many others, a great deal of trouble. It is difficult to reconstruct precisely how he went about compiling this first index, but apparently he assumed that if he allowed one column of a three-column page for each letter, omitting J and V, and entered the items in sequence as they occurred, he would have no trouble; and so he ruled off three columns on each of eight pages with the intention of filling each column with entries for a single letter. But one column, he quickly discovered, did not suffice for the A's, and he was obliged to hunt around in later columns for space for the leftover A's, stuffing part of them halfway down the D column and the rest among the G's. The B's were even more troublesome, since he was obliged to continue them under the N's but then discovered that there were more N's than he had anticipated, so the N's that should have been where the homeless B's had come to rest had to be pushed off to the bottom of the X column, which fortunately was otherwise occupied only with a few stray P's. By the time he began the index to Volume II he was a grizzled veteran of the indexing wars and he had learned caution. Now he doubled the allocation for the A's, ruling off two columns for that letter, only to run out of space before he had entered such major items as: "*A*dmiralty, vice, court of, new, first established in America"; "*A*ncestors, our, why they left their country"; and "*A*merican British colonies, always have been

---

*My reconstruction of the process of Dorr's compiling and annotating the papers is based on internal evidence in the jottings. Some of the marginalia seem clearly to have been written several years after the appearance of the papers (e.g., I, 216, at date October 7, 1765: "this piece seems calculated as well for the year 1768 as 1765"). A few jottings in Volume IV suggest that he had continued to add to his annotation for the year 1772 after independence. But there is no doubt that some if not most of the notations were contemporary with the appearance of the papers (e.g., Dorr's reference on II, 308, to "last Monday's paper," and his insertion [II, 963] on *A Letter to . . . Hillsborough* (1769) that stamp duties had been tried before in Massachusetts and given up "about 14 years past," an accurate reference to the provincial stamp act of 1755).

considered as (and are) free independent states." But he had apparently expected real trouble from the B's, ruling off no less than ten columns for that letter, creating thereby not only ample room for those entries but a generally useful catchall for all other leftover entries. If that was his strategy, it worked very well: he ran out of B's in the middle of the fifth of the allocated columns and in the empty columns before the C's he had space enough to put in all the extras that later spilled over from the P, R, T, and W columns as well as the held-over A's.

He had solved these organizational problems reasonably well by the time he turned to the third and fourth volumes, but alphabetizing remained a hardship throughout. It was not so difficult, perhaps, to figure out that the index entry "America will rise, and be a mighty empire, maugre all Great Britain can do to prevent it" should be put under the A's, since after all it was something about America, but how was one to index a story about a man who had a remarkable appetite by virtue of possessing three stomachs? (Dorr decided to put that under the E's for "*E*ater.") And do you put a news item about an *h*erb guaranteed to turn things into *g*old under the H's or the G's? (Dorr took no chances and put it under both.) A rather mysterious entry entitled "Ups and Downs" was no doubt safe enough under the U's, though one would scarcely have had occasion to look for it there, since it referred to a listing in parallel columns of the scandalous state of affairs in England ("The [King] *up* in the nursery . . . The [Princess of Wales] *down* on her knees . . . the Scotch *up* in the world . . . Virtue at [Court] kicked *down*stairs"); and a heat record could be entered under the H's not for "*h*eat" but for "*H*ottest day for 22 years past." But how was one to index the story of a German who was executed for endeavoring to ruin his country? (Under the H's, Dorr decided, for "*H*anged.")

For Volume II, which marks Dorr's emergence as a documentary historian, he composed a title page and a table of contents. He began the title page modestly, presenting his work apologetically with the words: "This has a very deformed Body, but a BEAUTIFUL SOUL," and explaining that on reviewing the marginalia and index he had found various misspellings "which I hope whoever peruses will have candour enough to excuse (especially) as the remarks &c, were made at my SHOP amidst my business, &c when I had not leisure to be exact." Then he turned proudly to the substance of the project. Newspapers, he explained in this remarkable title page, contain not only the passing news of the day but "intelligence of the greatest moment"; they were in fact commonly resorted to as repositories of records, and the information they contained was considered to be more authentic than that found in all but legal documents. Since people commonly threw newspapers away, and since "during the period of the Following Papers, Transactions of the utmost importance respecting Liberty in general have taken place, and are recorded in them," he had thought it worthwhile, despite the "considerable Expence, and very GREAT Trouble" it had cost him, to collect the papers that followed, and to annotate them. He hoped, he wrote—still in this title page—"that in Future they may be of some service, towards Forming a Political History of [this] Country, during the shameful and abandoned Administration of ye Disp[otic] Ministers of George ye 3." And then he signed the page, with a flourish: HARBOTTLE DORR—but still he could not stop. A citation seemed needed to validate on higher authority his claim for the value of the papers he had so carefully preserved. So he tacked on a postscript, quoting the editor of the *Gentleman's Magazine* to the effect that though American affairs may seem "tedious at present, when every News-Paper is full of them, yet they afford Ma[te]rials for an important part of the History of the present Times." And then, in a fine little demonstration of the usefulness of his collection, he concluded: "vid. page [479]."

The title page finished, Dorr turned to the table of contents, and for that he poured out so powerful a stream of prose that it broke through all the barriers of grammar, syntax, and simple order: it scarcely mattered that at one point, in his tumult, he wrote a parenthesis backwards-front. Volume II, Dorr wrote, contains

> a full Account of the Jealousies, great uneasinesses, vast difficulties, and cruel TREATMENT of the COLONIES by the DETESTABLE ACTS of PARLIAMENT, granting duties on Tea, Paper, &c, and Establishing a Board of Commissioners of the Customs, &c, &c: — Together with excellent Essays and Letters. — GOVERNOR'S SPEECHES, Instructions to Representatives, RESOLVES of the House of Rep-

resentatives, curious Anecdotes, &c, relative to the same. Also a full Account of the BRAVE, STRENUOUS, and NOBLE ACTIONS, of the Freeborn British Americans, in opposition to the said Acts and OPPRESSIONS, and in defence of their NATURAL, CONSTITUTIONAL, and CHARTER RIGHTS. — Likewise the remaining Letters of the Farmer, Journal of the Times, Essays against the establishment of Bishops in America, &c, &c, &c: Together with an appendix) containing MAGNA CHARTA, petition of RIGHT, Bill of RIGHTS, Charter of the Massachusetts Bay, Chronology, &c, &c,) And complete Index, with Marginal Notes and Explanations.

And then, still in full flight, he appended two sets of verses:

Our worthy fore Fathers
Thro' Oceans to Deserts for Freedom they came,
And dying bequeath'd us their Freedom and Fame.
All ages shall speak with amaze and APPLAUSE,
At the courage we Show in SUPPORT OF OUR LAWS.
To die we can bear, but to SERVE WE DISDAIN:
For shame is to FREEDOM more dreadful than pain.

—Liberty Song

Is there a Power whose engines are of force
To bend the brave and Virtuous mind to Slavery.
NO! In the Drear and Deadly damp of Dungeons,
The Soul can rear her Sceptre, smile in Anguish,
And Triumph o'er OPPRESSION.

—Gustavus Vasa

Thus the front matter for Volume II was completed. The table of contents seemed a worthy model and Dorr repeated it, with minor changes, in Volume III.

That volume, covering the years 1770–71, contains 642 pages of newsprint and an appendix of four pamphlets, all annotated and cross-referenced. Volume IV (1,061 pages of newsprint, with a title page almost identical to that of Volume II) covers the years from 1772 to the siege of Boston (April 1775) with issues of the *Boston Gazette*, and

Case 12 "10/ as

—— This has a very deformed Body, but a
Beautiful Soul.

N.B. —— On reviewing this Vol, I find some words in the margin's and Ind...
misspelt, which I hope who ever peruses will have candour enough to
excuse (especially) as the remarks &c, were made at my Shop amidst my
Business, &c, when I had not leisure to be exact.

Inasmuch as News-Papers in general contain, not only the News of the Da...
often Intelligence of the greatest Moment, (and in general are look'd upon as
Authentic, being often resorted to as valuable Precords, and perhaps are so, more tha...
any other saving legal ones: —— And as Persons in general are too negligent of
preserving them,) and during the period of the Following Papers, Transaction...
of the utmost importance respecting Liberty in general have taken place, and are
recored in them: —— I have thought it worth while to collect them, tho' ...
considerable Expence, and very GREAT Trouble, in hopes that in Futu...
they may be of some service, towards Forming a Political History of ...
Country, during the shameful and abandoned Administration of y.ᵉ De...
Ministers of George y.ᵉ 3.   Harbottle Dorr

The Editor of the Gent. Mag.ᶻ says " Tho' the American Transactions may seem
" tedious at present, when every News-Paper is full of them, yet they afford Ma...
" rials for an important part of the History of the present Times," vid. page...

Title page of volume II of Harbottle Dorr's collection of annotated newspapers and pamphlets.

Courtesy: Massachusetts Historical Society

News Papers

For the Years, 1768, and 1769 (containing) not only what is common to News Papers in general, but also a full Account of the Jealousies, great uneasinesses, vast difficulties, and cruel Treatment of the Colonies by the

Detestable Acts of Parliament,

granting duties on Tea, Paper, &c. and Establishing a Board of Commissioners of the Customs, &c, &c: Together with excellent Essays and Letters.

Governor's Speeches.

Instructions to Representatives, Resolves of the Houses of Representatives, curious Anecdotes &c, relative to the same: Also a full Account

of the

Brave, Strenuous, and Noble Actions.

of the Freeborn British Americans, in opposition to the said Acts

and Oppressions,

and in defence of their Natural, Constitutional, and

Charter Rights. — Likewise the remaining Letters

of the Farmer. Journal of the Times. Essays against the establishment of Bishops in America, &c, &c, &c: Together with an appendix) containing Magna Charta, petition of Right, Bill of Rights, Charter of the Massachusets Bay, Chronology, &c, &c) And complete Index, with Marginal Notes and Explanations.

Compiled, &c, By Harbottle Dorr. Vol 2.

" Our worthy fore Fathers ————

" Thro' Oceans to Deserts for Freedom they came,

" And dying bequeath'd us their Freedom and Fame.

" All ages shall speak with amaze and Applause,

" At the courage we Show in Support of Our Laws.

" To die we can bear, but to Serve we Disdain:

" For shame is to Freedom more dreadful than pain. " Liberty Song

" Is there a Power whose engines are of force

" To bend the brave and Virtuous mind to Slavery.

" No! In the Dread and Deadly damp of Dungeons,

" The Soul can rear her Sceptre, smile in Anguish,

" And Triumph o'er Oppression. " Gustavus Vasa.

Table of contents of Dorr's second volume of newspapers and pamphlets, covering the years 1768 and 1769.

Courtesy: Massachusetts Historical Society

MONDAY, *June* 26. 1769. [NUMB. 1761.]

The BOSTON Evening-Post.

Containing the freshest & most important Advices, Foreign and Domestick.

JOURNAL of the TIMES.

[*Continued.*]

1769. *April* 28. AT the Superiour Court held at Charlestown, application was made by the Custom-House Officers, for a full supply of Writs of Assistance, which were accordingly granted. By the late acts the officers of the customs are "empowered to enter into any house, warehouse, shop, or other place, in the British colonies, or plantations in America, to search for, or seize prohibitted or uncustomed goods."—A dreadful power indeed! And if we can recollect instances of such a wanton use of this power, even in Boston, as that a magistrate should be threatened and his house rummaged, by an officer in resentment at his being fined for breach of law; what may we not fear at a time when Spanish policy has been so far adopted, as that the most ignorant, hair-brain'd, and extravagant persons in commission on board the ships of war are converted into custom house officers? If we only reflect, that the judges of these American courts, are appointed *during pleasure*, and that one purpose for which money is to be levied upon the colonies by a late act is, that they may have adequate provision made for them, which is to continue, *during their complaisant behaviour*, what an engine of oppression may this authority be in such hands! We are well aware that writs of this kind, for searching houses in England, have been granted under the seal of the Court of Exchequer, according to the statute, which seal is kept by the Chancellor of the Exchequer: It should however be remembered that the custom house officers, at home are under certain checks & restrictions, which they cannot be under here; and therefore the writ of assistance ought to be look'd upon as a different thing there, from what it is here. In England the Exchequer has the power of controuling them in every respect; and even of inflicting corporal punishment upon them for mal-conduct, of which there have been instances; they are the proper officers of that court, and are accountable to it as often as it shall call them to account, and they do in fact account to it for money receiv'd, and for their behaviour, once every week. Do the officers of the customs here account with the superior court, or lodge money received into the hands of that court; or are they *as* officers under any sort of check from it? Will they concede to such powers in the superiour court? Or does this court, notwithstanding these are powers belonging to the Exchequer,—notwithstanding it is said to be vested with all the powers belonging to the Exchequer,—and further notwithstanding this very writ of assistance is to be granted as a power belonging to the Exchequer, will the superior court itself assume the power of calling these officers to account, and punish them for misbehaviour? We know not of one instance of this sort, but on the contrary, have we not seen not long ago, an inferior custom-house officer, who has since swelled into a C—m——r of the B——d of C——s, refusing to account to any power in the province for monies receiv'd by him by virtue of his office, belonging to the province, and which we were then assured by the joint declaration of the three branches of the legislature, was unjustly as well as illegally detain'd by him?

But notwithstanding writs of assistance issued in Britain are guarded with such restrictions, "The greatest assertors of the rights of Englishmen have already strenuously contended that such a power was dangerous to freedom, and expresly contrary to the common law, which ever regarded a man's house as his castle, or a place of perfect security—If such power was in the least degree dangerous there, it must be utterly destructive to Liberty here. For the people of England have two securities; against the undue exercise of this power by the crown, which are wanting with us.——In the first place if any injustice is done there, the person injured may bring his action against the offender, and have it tried before independent judges who were *no parties in committing the injury*.—*Here* he must have it tried before dependent judges, being the men who granted the writ."

April 29. We are well informed, that the officers of the customs applied the last year to the chief justices or bench of judges, in several of the colonies, for granting them writs of assistance but that those justices from a tender regard to the constitution and the rights of American freeholders, did actually refuse a compliance with those demands.——The C—l—r of the port of New-London in Connecticut, has lately applied a second time to the superiour court there for such writs; at the same time laying a letter before them, which he had received from one of the crown lawyers in England in answer to one wrote upon the subject, in which letter, a great compliment was paid to the chief justice of the Massachusetts for the proof he had given of a right understanding of the law, and of his zeal for his Majesty's service, by so readily granting those writs, upon the application made by the custom house officers; and his example was recommended as worthy of their imitation. The court did not however, think proper to show a like complaisance, but chose to refer this request, to the consideration of their general assembly at the approaching session.

April 30. The quartering troops in the body of a town is as ruinous to the soldiery as it is distressing to the inhabitants; every day furnishes out instances of their debaucheries and consequent violences.

As an aged woman at the north part of Boston, was setting the other evening in a lower room, having no person in the house with her: a soldier came in and seeing her have a bible on the table before her; he expressed his approbation of her piety and attempted a kind of exposition upon some parts thereof, but soon dropping this discourse, he acquainted her that he had a bad swelling on his hip, and should be glad of her advice; but while the good woman was attending to his relation, this abandoned wretch, seized her, by this shoulders, threw her upon the floor, and notwithstanding her years, attempted a rape upon her, which was prevented by the resistance and screams occasioned by his brutal behaviour; he thought proper to hurry off, taking with him a bundle of shirts and other linen, which had been just before sent into the house for washing, and ironing; a business which the person followed to obtain a livelihood.

May 1. A captain of a vessel lately arrived from Halifax, passing the streets last evening, in company with two married women, were met by some soldiers, who immediately accosted them in a rude indecent manner; the captain tho't proper to inform them, that those women were married, and also to reprove them for such behaviour; but for taking this liberty, he was presently knocked down, and had like to have lost an eye by a blow receiv'd.

May 2. On the other night past 11 o'clock several officers and one soldier, meeting with two of the towns watchmen, they began to curse and damn them, and soon after the soldier struck one of the watchmen, who returned the blow, which laid him in the gutter, then the two officers came up, and were as free with their blows as the soldier; the noise and racket soon brought other watchmen to the assistance of those who were assaulted, when one of the officers drew a bayonet, and damning them, said stand off, or I will run you through; the watchmen not being intimidated, gave him a stroke on the arm which obliged him to drop the bayonet; when they seized him and carried him off to prison, the watchmen were followed by another officer, with a drawn sword or cutlass under his arm, but being told that if he did not leave them, they would endeavour to secure him also, he thought proper to sheer off. Several officers came at different times, and offered the watchmen drink or money, if they would release the prisoner, but to their honor they refused those offers, & entered a complaint against them, to a magistrate the next morning.

[*To be continued.*]

FIFTY DOLLARS Reward.

On the 15th 16th & 17th Inst.

many Panes of Glass in the Casements of the subscriber's Dwelling House, were by some evil minded Person or Persons broken, to the endangering the Lives of his Family, and to his great Expence; and as it is supposed there were some Accomplices therein. If any Person (even an Accomplice) shall give Information to him, who did it, and that he be Convicted thereof, shall be forgiven, and receive said Reward from *John Box.*

Boston, June 19 1769.

Province of MASSACHUSETTS-BAY, June 22. 1769.

Tuesday last a Committee of the Honorable House of Representatives, in General Court assembled at Cambridge, there waited on his Excellency the Governor with the following Message; being a Reply to his Excellency's Answer to their Message of the 13th Instant, viz.

MAY IT PLEASE YOUR EXCELLENCY,

AS you have not thought proper in your Reply to the Message of this House, of the 13th Instant, to throw any Light on the Subject, or invalidate the Principles we therein advanced, your Excellency will allow us to conclude, that those Principles were well grounded, and that there is no Reason for us to alter our Sentiments on this interesting Point.

You are pleased to intimate that much Time and Treasure has been spent in determining a merely speculative Question: The House regarded a standing Army posted within the Province in a Time of the most profound Peace, and uncontroulable by any Authority in it, as a dangerous Innovation; and a Guard of Soldiers with Cannon planted at the Doors of the State House, while the General Assembly was there held, as the most pointed Insult ever offered to a free People, and its whole Legislative. This, Sir, and not the Question of your Excellency's Authority to remove His Majesty's Ships out of the Harbour, or his Troops out of the Town of *Boston*, was the principal Cause of the "Non-activity of the Assembly." Had your Excellency felt for the Assembly and the People over whom you preside, even though you had supposed yourself not properly authorized, you would have employed your Influence, at least, for the Removal of this Grievance; especially as His Majesty's Council, as well as this House, had before expressed to your Excellency their just Indignation at so unprecedented an Affront. But instead of the least Abatement of this military Parade, the General Assembly has been made to give Way to an armed Force: As the only Means in your Power to remove the Difficulty we justly complained of, your Excellency has ordered a Removal of the General Assembly itself, from its ancient Seat and the Place where the public Business has generally been done with the greatest Convenience, Ease and Dispatch.—It is with Pain that we are obliged here to observe, that the very Night after this Adjournment was made, the Cannon were removed from the Court House, as though it had been designed, that so small a Circumstance of Regard should not be paid to the Assembly, when convened by the Royal Authority, and for His Majesty's Service in the Colony.

You are pleased to pass a Censure upon this House, in saying that, "you cannot sit still and see such a Waste of Time and Treasure to no Purpose."—Those alone are answerable for any Expence of Time and Treasure on this Occasion, who have brought us into such a Situation, as has hitherto rendered our Proceeding to Business incompatible with the Dignity, as well as the Freedom of this House.—No Time can better be employed than in the Preservation of the Rights derived from the British Constitution, and insisting upon Points which, though your Excellency may consider as non-essential, we esteem its best Bulwarks.—No Treasure can be better expended than in securing that true old English Liberty, which gives a Relish to every other Enjoyment. These we have the Satisfaction to believe are the Sentiments of our Constituents, to whom alone we are accountable how we apply their Treasure: And we are fully perswaded, from what we have already heard, that, notwithstanding the apparent Design of your Message to prejudice their Minds against us, what your Excellency is pleased to call our "Non-activity," will receive their Approbation, rather than their Censure; for an entire Fortnight spent in Silence, or a much longer Time, cannot be displeasing to them, when Business could not be even entered upon, but at the Expence of *their* Rights and Liberties, and the Privilege of this House.

On Monday last a Committee was chosen in the House to go to the Board, for any Letters or Papers they had received since the sitting of the last General Assembly; and on Tuesday, the Board sent to the House the Copies of several Letters from his Excellency the Governor, and the Copy of one from General Gage, to the Right Hon. the Earl of Hillsborough, (which Copies the Board received sometime since from England;) together with two Letters from the Council to the Earl of Hillsborough in Vindication of their own Character, and the People of the Province.

To be sold by T. & J. FLEET *and* EDES & GILL,

The Case of *Great Britain* & *America*, Addressed to the KING and both HOUSES of PARLIAMENT.

It is against the liberty of the subject, who hath a true property in his goods, which cannot be taken from him, without his actual or implied consent. Trial of HAMPDEN.

At the same Places may be had,

COPIES of several LETTERS from Governor *Bernard* to the Earl of *Hillsborough*, &c.

A page of Dorr's newspaper collection, with annotations in his hand. Typically, Dorr provides numerous cross-references to other pages and documents in the collection, and abuses Thomas Hutchinson, at one point (marker ¶) by contradicting a compliment to him printed in the *Evening-Post*, at another (marker *) by gratuitously explaining that Hutchinson was the first judge to issue writs of assistance.

Courtesy: Massachusetts Historical Society

An ORATION.

them to find barracks at *Brunfwick* or *Lunenburg*, at *Hano-ver*, or *the commodious hall of Weftminfter ?* Suppofe the laft—Suppofe this army was informed, nay *thought* the parliament in actual rebellion, or only on the *eve* of one againft their King, or againft *thofe who paid and cloathed them*—for there it pinches :—We are *rebels againft parliament*;—we adore the King.

Where, in the cafe I have ftated, would be the value of the boafted *Englifh* Conftitution ?

Who are a free people ? Not thofe who do not fuffer actual oppreffion ; but thofe who have a *conftitutional check* upon the power||to opprefs. *vid on Gov.ͬ Hutchinfons Independancy pa. 576*

We are flaves or freemen ; if, as we are called, the laft, where is our check upon the following powers, *France, Spain,* the *States of Holland,* or *the Britifh Parliament ?* Now if any one of thefe (and it is quite immaterial which) has right to make the two acts in queftion operate within this province, they have right to give us up to an unlimited army, under the fole direction of one *Saracen* Commander.

|| *Therefore if the Gov.ͬ Judges &c are* **Thus** *made independanᵗ of the People, as they are to be by the Tea Act (if a fufficient Fund is raifed)(whenever the King pleafes) where have we the Check ? & vid the Act. pa. 735. Vol. I.*

Page from James Lovell's *An Oration Delivered April 2d, 1771 . . .* (Boston, 1771), one of the numerous pamphlets Dorr pasted into his newspaper collection. The pages are renumbered to fit the pagination of the volume. In the footnote, Dorr specifies Lovell's general definition of freedom with reference to the threat of the Tea Act, and he cross-references Hutchinson's salary, independent of the legislature, to illustrate the evil that could result.

Courtesy: Massachusetts Historical Society

A page of the Index to Dorr's third volume, one of three full pages (nine columns) devoted entirely to references to Hutchinson. Dorr highlights every damaging reference, explicit ("severely censured and called Arch fiend") or implicit ("an Implicit parallel drawn between him and The Traytor Tresilean, a corrupt chief Judge"). "A Tool to Lord Hillsborough" was one of Dorr's favorite accusations.

Courtesy: Massachusetts Historical Society

thereafter to the end of 1776 with other Boston, Salem, and Cambridge newspapers. Eight pamphlets of the same years, four of them Massacre Day orations, were added to form Dorr's fourth appendix.*

It is an astonishing archive, these 3,280 pages of annotated newspapers plus the appended documents and indexes, and it has come down to us almost perfectly intact. There is a slight indication that Dorr at one point contemplated selling the collection: he carefully noted on the last three volumes exactly what the papers had cost him (between £12 and £16 Old Tenor for each volume). But if he had once entertained that idea, he apparently gave it up, for the volumes were still in his possession when he died, eighteen years after he had completed the work. His executors estimated the value of "a number of newspapers, some bound" at £1 16s, but in fact they fetched £7 10s when his property was sold. There is no record of who the original purchaser was, but in 1798 Josiah Quincy, the future mayor of Boston and president of Harvard, presented Volumes II and III to the Massachusetts Historical Society; and in 1888 the Society purchased Volume I from the Dedham Historical Society, to which it had been given by the Sumner family. The fourth volume has strayed rather far from home. By a route I cannot completely trace it has ended up in the Bangor, Maine, Public Library, but it is included in the microfilm edition of the entire collection, which was issued by the Massachusetts Historical Society in 1966.

---

*This fourth appendix is the only one that remains intact, still bound into the original volume. Dorr also inserted into the final pages of the body of Volume IV three additional documents that later became available: the American treaties with France as reprinted in the *Continental Journal, and Weekly Advertiser,* Dec. 17, 1778 (inserted at p. 1018); the Massachusetts Act of 1778 banishing the loyalists, also from the *Continental Journal,* Oct. 22, 1778 (pp. 1067–1068); and the Massachusetts treason act of 1777, which Dorr transcribed by hand (pp. 1063–1065). Such insertions were not a new departure for him. In the earlier volumes too he had occasionally pasted to the pages clippings or transcriptions of documents relevant to matters he found interesting in the newspapers, but these documents were almost entirely contemporary with the papers to which they were attached. At one point (IV, 295) he inserted two dramatic prints which he had cut out of current Boston almanacs; both vividly illustrate his partisan view of politics: "The wicked Statesman, or the Traitor to his Country, at the Hour of DEATH," the cover illustration of Ezra Gleason's *The Massachusetts Calendar; or An Almanack for . . . 1774 . . .* (Boston, 1774); and "The Virtuous PATRIOT at the Hour of Death," the cover illustration for Nathaniel Low's *An Astronomical Diary . . . for . . . 1776* (Worcester, [1776]). The former, which pictures Thomas Hutchinson in his death throes, confronted by the devil holding a tablet enumerating the governor's crimes and surrounded by symbols of his avariciousness and lust for power, is reproduced in Bernard Bailyn, *The Ordeal of Thomas Hutchinson* (Cambridge, 1974).

. . .

One hardly knows where to begin in analyzing Harbottle Dorr's painfully composed indexes, his mass of marginal jottings, and the intricate network of cross-references that links hundreds of documents, statements, ideas, and events in the four volumes to passages that precede and follow them. Perhaps the most useful observation is the most general. Contemplating the whole of the annotated collection, one gets a sense of the decade before independence as a single simultaneous whole, a period in which those who in the outcome of history became villainous can be seen to have been villains from the start and in which the ultimate heroes, from the moment they appear in the pages of the *Gazette,* display the valor, virtue, and understanding they would later acquire. With every episode wired up, so to speak, to every subsequent event, with the outcome implicit at the start, there is no movement, no development, no moment in which events hung in the balance and could have swung one way or another, for if there had been such a moment one would have had to contemplate the possibility that the winners might have been the losers and the advocates of peaceful reconciliation with England might have become the heroes, or if not the heroes then at least the prophets, of an uninterruptedly triumphant empire.

Clearly the governorship of Thomas Hutchinson, 1770–74, was crucial in the origins of the Revolution. If there was one person in America whose actions might have altered the outcome, given the set of circumstances that existed in the early 1770s, it was he. But understanding Hutchinson requires stripping away layer after layer of encrusted mythology, the original deposits of which were made by his political enemies, among whom none were more vociferous, none more violent, in their animosity than Harbottle Dorr. Like John Adams, Dorr—who had grown up in the small provincial world in which Hutchinsons had been accepted leaders time out of mind and who must have seen Thomas Hutchinson frequently, heard him speak, known of his endless public service and his integrity in trade—Dorr seems to have been obsessed by what he took to be the malignity, the ineradicable evil, of the man.

Dorr's index and commentaries catalogue Hutchinson's errors, correct his misstatements, and warn at every turn of his evil intentions.

An anonymous columnist's claim that the colonies "had no *rights* of our own" is identified by Dorr in the margin as "Hutchinsonian doctrine." When Hutchinson's zeal is praised by the British government, Dorr scribbles: "no compliment to him; quite the reverse, as coming from such an infamous ministry or their tools," and he supplies the word "pension" for "p——n" lest the reader mistake the unworthy object of Hutchinson's desire. When a writer in the *Boston Gazette* wonders "if our governor is a *mere tool* of an arbitrary minister of state," Dorr instantly removes the doubt: "He certainly is one!" He footnotes a vague newspaper reference to government advisers known to be "supple eno' to bow the *knee of servility* to the tool of a tool of an haughty Thane" with the explanation: "Hutchinson (governor) is a tool to Lord Hillsborough, Lord Hillsborough a tool to Bute, and the Earl of Bute a tool of the Devil!" Dorr will hear nothing of Hutchinson's professed desire to promote the prosperity of his country: "words," he scribbles in the margin, "are but wind; actions speak louder." When Hutchinson as governor in a message to the House explains his aversion to unwanted innovations, Dorr laughs in the margin: "Hah! Hah!" and to document the contrary, triumphantly cites the governor's letters of 1768 supposedly recommending authoritarian changes in the colony's government. He jubilantly records a report that "Governor Hutchinson attempted to cut his throat"; explodes in the margins when the hated name appears: "vile hypocrite! and slanderer," "arch fiend," "traitor!"; and at one point writes simply, in smoldering indignation: "Oh the villian!"

Hutchinson had assiduously sought the governorship, but after the Boston Massacre, in March 1770, believing that his appointment had not yet been signed by the king, he had written soul-baring, abjectly apologetic letters to his patron, the former governor, Sir Francis Bernard, and to the secretary of state, Lord Hillsborough, begging not to be appointed. "If I had more talents than I have," he had written Bernard, "yet I have not strength of constitution to grapple with burdens which . . . exceed beyond comparison what you met with. . . . [A] person of much greater weight than I" was needed, he had insisted. "I must beg you," he had written, "to make my most humble excuse or resignation from a sense of my utter inability to discharge the trust." News of these letters had quickly leaked to the opposition press, where they were wildly lampooned as overwhelming proof of

Hutchinson's devilish hypocrisy. Among the two columns of entries under "Hutchinson" in the index of Dorr's third volume, following such entries as "Compared to King James" and "Would like to be made a baronet," is the reference: "Wrote home desiring not to be appointed governor but always aiming at the chair." When in 1773 Hutchinson's incriminating letters to Whately were published in an elaborate maneuver by Benjamin Franklin, Dorr tore into his copy of the sensational letters (which he included as a pamphlet in the appendix of Volume IV) with a frantic pen. He scribbled curses all over the margins, interleaved the texts of the letters with refutations, and directed the reader to what he believed was the truth through an infinitely complex series of cross-references to other documents in his monumental collection. His index contains no fewer than thirty references under the entry "Hutchinson, Governor, his original traitorous letters," the last of which is: ". . . an insinuation that he and [Lieutenant] Governor Oliver ought to have been immediately put to death on the receipt of their letters." And to be sure that this remarkable suggestion would not go undetected, he indexed it not only under the H's for *H*utchinson but also under the L's for *L*etters and under the J's for "*J*unius Americanus," the pseudonym of Arthur Lee, whose idea such a summary execution had originally been.

To Dorr, Hutchinson was indubitably and always a villain, one of the very worst of the pack he believed was determined to impose an authoritarian regime on the American colonies. Conversely, Otis and the Adamses, Dickinson, Chatham, and Barré were heroes to him from their first appearance, and in his annotation and indexes he praised their speeches and publications with an intensity equal to that with which he scourged the ministry of George III and its adherents.

Naïve? Simplistic? Perhaps. Two hundred years later we are more judicious—but only retrospectively. Every great movement of history has turned in the end on such black-and-white, absolute convictions. And while one is endlessly fascinated by the innocence and ferocious partisanship of Dorr's notations ("*P*imps and cooks appointed to places in America"), one patronizes Harbottle Dorr at one's peril. For in the unqualified condemnations and lavish praise of his polemical jottings there lie revealed with peculiar clarity the animating spirit of the Revolution and the essence of the public faith that it bequeathed.

What dominated the whole of Dorr's editorial labors and colored his opinions of men and events was, first and primarily, the conviction that the Anglo-American government under which he lived and the establishment that controlled it were corrupt and unworthy of public confidence. Hundreds of personal observations, a multitude of writings, and endless gossip and everyday conversation had convinced Dorr beyond all argument that the public trust had been violated; that officeholding at the highest level had become a form of profiteering, at the lowest mere legalized thuggery; that the administration of law was unjust, and government callous to the needs of the people.

Britain, he wrote in entry after entry, was altogether wicked. The king calls America's legitimate resistance the work of a petty faction; Lord Barrington gives "thanks to the troops who murdered young Allen"; Britain's swarming "pensioners [were] more formidable to a free people than troops"; Lord Bute "schemed . . . to ruin our liberties and introduce the Roman Catholic religion"; "Chancellor York[e] cuts his [own] throat"; the king "sometimes grants pardons before conviction or sentence"; Lord Mayor Beckford was "suspected to have been poisoned"; the "corrupt Parliament [was] profuse of the nation's money"; the House of Commons was so foolish, so encrusted with tradition, that its Speaker "died because the House would not let him go to ease the calls of nature." Britain, he concluded, "instead of preserving her liberty by the *virtue* of America, has lost it by *that* means," for America, to preserve its virtue, "separated from G. Britain, which no doubt in the sequel will ruin her, i.e. G. Britain." It was a situation, in Dorr's view, likely to breed at least another Glorious Revolution—a bloodless revolving and cleansing of the government with constitutional changes aimed at securing improvements for the benefit of future generations.

But Dorr's beliefs, as expressed in his jottings on hundreds of newspaper pages, were positive as well as critical; they were constructive and optimistic. Less directly, perhaps, and more subtly, his annotation conveys the essence of the positive faith that underlay the American Revolutionary movement.

It is a faith based, first, on the belief that power—the capacity, legal or illegal, to coerce, to constrain, to limit unduly the actions of other human beings—is evil and corrupting, and that its abuse must be controlled by the people, using any means available to them— "mobbs or riots," if necessary. ("*A*narchy," he explained in his indexes, was "better than tyranny"; "not so dangerous as tyranny.") Dorr's commentaries are fragmentary and disconnected witnesses—but vivid, immediate, and direct witnesses—of a state of mind hostile to the use of power that more learned men—animated like Dorr by the sense that events in America were "giving a new epocha to the history of the world"—would express in enduring constitutional form.

But Dorr's faith, and that of his contemporaries, was based not only on a belief in the liberating effects of restricting the use of power. It was based too on a hatred of privilege—not wealth as such, not distinction as such, not the differences among men: these were never Dorr's targets. Nor did he seek a social upheaval or the elevation of the masses. Dorr hated anyone identified with what he took to be the arbitrary actions of the British state, but his deepest loathing was reserved for those with power who were privileged by birth—people whose advantages and authority were ascribed, unearned, unnatural, invidious. That is the meaning of his fierce hatred and resentment of Hutchinson, his blistering condemnation of plural officeholding (a practice that was in fact altogether common and accepted in his day), and his endless attacks on an officialdom whose authority seemed arbitrary and unjustified. "A Noble Lord," "His Lordship," "My Lord Bishop" were ironic and condemnatory words in Dorr's usage, and he wrote them, as he must have spoken them, with a sneer.

Embedded in the complex network of cross-references that Dorr wove through the immense documentation of twelve years of political upheaval, in the hundreds of marginal comments he scribbled day after day to warn unwary readers of the clever manipulations of over-ambitious, corrupt, and designing men, and in his wonderfully editorialized indexes lies the simple conviction that power was a gift of the people—not a gift of God, or of fate, or of inheritance—and was to be used for the people's good, not for the benefit of those who happen to control it. And entwined too in his index and commentaries lies the belief that privilege was suspect, corrupting in its nature, and a source of misery for the world at large. No theorist of politics, no draftsman of constitutions, no intellectual, no leader of men—indeed, no hero at all, moral or otherwise, but an ordinary, avaricious, self-righteous tradesman—Harbottle Dorr yet deeply shared the principles so elegantly phrased by Jefferson, so agonized over by Adams, and so profoundly comprehended by Madison.

In 1771 Dorr came on a luminous passage in the *Boston Gazette* attacking the acquittal of the soldiers involved in the town's recent massacre. Power, the pseudonymous author (who was in fact Sam Adams) wrote—power, "especially in times of corruption, makes men wanton; . . . it intoxicates the mind; and unless those with whom it is entrusted are carefully watched, such is the weakness or the perverseness of human nature, they will be apt to *domineer* over the people, instead of governing them according to the known laws of the state." And the writer quoted "a celebrated author" to the effect that laws and the constitution alone are the basis of public tranquillity, the firmest support of public authority, and the sole guarantors of the liberty of the citizens. Dorr marked the passage, and wrote beneath it: "This is orthodox, and is *my* political creed."

6

RELIGION AND
REVOLUTION: THREE
BIOGRAPHICAL
SKETCHES

*I*n what follows I have sought to illuminate, through three brief portraits, aspects of the complex involvement of religion in the American Revolutionary movement. For religion was no isolated force in eighteenth-century American culture—it pervaded it—and it had no singular influence on the Revolutionary movement. It was in itself both a stimulus and a deterrent to revolution, brought to different focuses in different ways by different people. The whole of American culture was "religious" in the sense that common modes of discourse in both ordinary life and high culture were derived from Protestant Christianity, and it is a gross simplification to believe that religion as such, or any of its doctrinaire elements, had a unique political role in the Revolutionary movement. The effective determinants of revolution were political, and though religious ideas in general and the views of specific denominational groups in particular provided significant reinforcement to the Revolutionary movement, that movement was shared equally by the Catholic Charles Carroll of Carrollton, the humanist philosophe Jefferson, the theologically liberal preacher Jonathan Mayhew, and the New Divinity Calvinist Stephen Johnson.*

In the first essay, on Andrew Eliot, I have tried to show how a peculiar cast of temperament kept an enthusiastic liberal and reformer from committing himself to revolution when the climax finally came. In this case the key documents are a series of revealing letters, some long in print, some still in manuscript, written over the decade before Independence; these letters alone, I believe, make Eliot's career comprehensible. In the second piece, I have attempted to explain how in his final tormented months Jonathan Mayhew sought to maintain the balance of social stability and political radicalism that lay at the heart of the Revolution. In this case the key document is a memorandum Mayhew prepared in his own defense summarizing a sermon he had preached which many felt had sparked a destructive riot. In the final essay, on a wonderfully obscure Connecticut parson, I have sought to show, through a juxtaposition of two works written by the same man over the same period of weeks—the one a formal sermon, the other a series of anonymous newspaper articles—the precise role of biblical imagery and mythology in the political thought of the time.

Andrew Eliot

"It Is Possible We May Be Mistaken;
Things May Appear Very Differently to
Others As Upright As Ourselves"

THE CAREER of the Reverend Andrew Eliot was modest and moderate, and his middle-of-the-road, liberal-minded course through the controversies of the day epitomizes common experiences. He shared the inner life, the private fears and doubts, of thousands of reasonable, liberal, but ultimately irresolute and unheroic people who were caught up in the upheaval of the American Revolution, and he recorded these inner experiences in detail in his personal correspondence of the years 1765–75 and in his family letters written from the siege of Boston, all of which have come down to us intact.

Eliot's career, expressive of typical experiences and so uniquely recorded, is in another way significant. Long ignored by historians, he has recently been presented as an illustration of the claim that the Old Light, theologically "liberal," clergy were not the revolutionaries some have said they were, but that they were in fact conservatives during the Revolution, as opposed to the New Light, neo-Calvinists. But if Eliot was a reluctant revolutionary it was not because of the pull of his religious ideas, which in any case were indecisive, or of any tepidness in his political thought, which was based on rigorous Whig principles and, like the political ideas of the most extreme Revolutionary leaders, was transformed after 1765 into an insurrectionary creed. His reluctance to declare for independence was temperamental, the reaction of a reasonable, tolerant, instinctively cautious and indecisive person always able to see both sides of the public issues of his time, ever hesitant to draw his thoughts to thoroughgoing conclusions. Closely examined, his writings and the course of his actions reveal the difficulty of explaining by any simple formula the role of religion in the origins of the American Revolution.

I

That the Revolution would be unkind to Andrew Eliot might have been foretold. While his naturally liberal cast of mind and his deeply ingrained fear of the corruption of power would make him a Whig in sympathy, his instinct for compromise, his lifelong incapacity to accept any absolute conclusion, intellectual or political, his insistence on seeing both sides and refusal to decide flatly and unequivocally on any major issue, would paralyze him as a political force and lead inevitably, and unfairly, to his public caricature as "ANDREW sly."

His "disposition to temporize" (the phrase is that of his friend and parishioner Thomas Hutchinson) could scarcely have been expressed earlier than it was. The son of a Boston shoemaker, he was born in 1718 into a family that had settled in Massachusetts with the original Puritan migration. He entered Harvard College at the age of fifteen, graduated in 1737, received his master's degree there in 1740, and remained in residence in the College until 1742, when he was called to share the pulpit of the New North Church of Boston. He remained the pastor (solely, after 1750) of that leading Congregational society for the remaining thirty-six years of his life, presiding with dignity and broadening liberality over a community distinguished by its social standing and political position. He was twenty-four years old when his first publication appeared, his ordination sermon, *The Faithful Steward* (1742). A standard analysis of the duties and difficulties of the ministry, it reveals, in its indecisive handling of the most controversial issue of the day, the permanent cast of Eliot's mind and personality.

For no minister—no Christian—in that era of the Great Awakening could ignore the question of whether a regenerating experience of God's grace was the sole and absolute qualification for the ministry, or whether and to what degree works—piety, knowledge, conduct— also played a part. But though Eliot introduced the topic boldly in *The Faithful Steward*, in the end he evaded the question. On the one hand, he said, "an unconverted minister cannot be faithful," nor would someone "who has never felt the power of divine truths upon his own soul" be likely to be effective in his major task of bringing souls to a knowledge of God. But on the other hand, it must be possible for God to "make use of an unregenerate minister to convince or even to convert sinners. The sovereign GOD may make use of what instruments he pleases." All one could conclude was that an unconverted minister was not "like" to be successful, nor would God "usually put his honour upon such men."

The Faithful Steward is a fabric of compromises. Detailed knowledge of doctrine, Eliot wrote, is necessary for an orthodox and effective minister; nevertheless the great truths are essentially simple and should be taught "without the mixture of any new-fangled notions." Ministers must discipline their congregations and forcefully prevent the propagation of error—but only "so far as it can be done without external force or the least show of persecution." And they must treat people impartially since all souls are equal in the sight of God—but of course to ignore all social distinctions would be ridiculous: "there is a proper respect due to those who are in an exalted station."

Eliot was young when he wrote this sermon, but maturity merely confirmed the personality it reveals. In his subsequent writings he weighed his equivocations more carefully but never developed greater certainty or firmer resolution. His later efforts, in fact, deepened his dilemmas, hardened his incapacity to follow out the ultimate implications of his own thought. So he condemned the temptations and corruptions of worldly delights, but at the same time gave assurances that the capacity to enjoy life is a divine gift. Similarly, in his one published "jeremiad" he blunted the edge of the ritual attack. For though in prescribed form he bewailed the declension of a once holy people ("Oh *New England,* how art thou fallen! We are not the genuine offspring of the first settlers of this land; we are a spurious race . . . guilty of great apostasy; we have broken the covenant"), and though he enumerated the sins of the land with sulphurous condemnation ("*impiety* towards God . . . neglect of *family religion* . . . profanity . . . *intemperance* . . . gaming, excessive drinking, *uncleanness* . . .

lying or *speaking falsly"*), in the end he assured his listeners that he did not mean *them* ("I am not charging the body of this people with the crimes I have mention'd"); *others* were directly responsible; his auditors' guilt consisted simply in "not bear[ing] suitable testimony against the evils which prevail"—a duty that fell particularly to those in public office. Not, of course, that he meant to equate Massachusetts's leaders with the corrupted leaders of the biblical Jews: "Blessed be God, we have *magistrates* who discountenance vice and with some laudable zeal endeavour to suppress it, and we have *ministers* who preach the pure doctrines and precepts of the Gospel." So what, then, "upon the whole," was he saying? Nothing very urgent, apparently: "It must be own'd," he concluded, that "we are in danger of becoming very soon, *an evil and adulterous generation.*"

Eliot never honed the edge of an argument or followed one through to its ultimate conclusion. Increasingly he found justification for not attempting to do so and counseled his fellow ministers to avoid discussing things "in their nature too sublime for us" (the nature of Christ's divinity "and the like") and to concentrate on "plain practical truths." For ministers given to an excess of "abstract reasoning and metaphysical subtilties," he explained in 1766, can reduce true religion to "some little point which if they understand themselves is beyond the comprehension of most others. . . . Abstract reasoning is seldom of use in the pulpit."

How well he followed his own advice his Dudleian Lecture of 1771, *A Discourse on Natural Religion,* made abundantly clear. Nothing so clearly reveals the sources and texture of ordinary liberal ministerial thought in late colonial New England as this Harvard oration—Eliot's one high-level intellectual effort—nor so neatly illustrates the overlap, indeed the identification, of religious and political thought. The set problems were traditional and imposing, and Eliot stated them boldly. His intention, he announced with a slight and understandable note of alarm, was to prove the existence of God, the existence of religion, and the character of natural religion. The first, fortunately, he was able to dispose of readily by the simple device of stating, with utter candor and perfect accuracy, that everything he had to say on the subject "will easily occur to your minds without any help of mine"— a point especially well taken if his readers happened to have read Samuel Clarke's famous Boyle Lectures of 1704–5, which, together with the same author's letters in answer to his critics, Eliot either quoted at length or silently paraphrased. The other great questions too were expeditiously handled, largely by generous borrowings from just those early-eighteenth-century latitudinarian rationalists (Tillotson and Wollaston, in addition to Clarke) whom George Whitefield, in the days when Eliot was still an undergraduate, had condemned the Harvard students for reading, and by heavy reliance on James Beattie's middlebrow guide for the perplexed, *An Essay on . . . Truth, in Opposition to Sophistry and Scepticism* (1770). The one great issue Eliot did, in the end, attempt to confront is the precise theological analogue of the political struggle that had been raging in America since the Stamp Act crisis. His resolution of this problem, though it was, like the rest of his *Discourse on Natural Religion*, technically derivative, was spoken from the heart. How could one reconcile, Eliot asked, God's sovereignty with man's individual freedom? Of God's overriding power to determine the fate of every individual Eliot had no doubt; this was for him axiomatic. But did that mean, as some claimed, that God irresistibly "determine[d] the will of man to the hatred of his own most blessed self, and then . . . exact[ed] the severest punishments for the offense done"? Such "a black conception of God" and such a denial of men's moral freedom were unthinkable. One simply *knows* he has moral freedom, and one could scarcely accept the cynical claim that such knowledge too was part of the divine plan and hence that God deliberately deceives men by endowing them with a false sense of freedom.

Eliot found the solution that satisfied him in a striking passage in Locke's writings, a passage directed to the theological problem at hand but that perfectly prefigures the solution to the political problem of sovereignty and freedom that Eliot would ultimately arrive at. Locke too had struggled with the problem of God's determination and human freedom, but in the end, he reported in the passage now quoted by Eliot, he had been forced to give it up: he had been unable to reconcile the two, and had simply dismissed the matter: "I cannot make freedom in man consistent with omnipotence and omniscience in God, though I am as fully as persuaded of both as of any truths I most firmly assent to. And therefore I have long since given off the consideration of that question, resolving all into this short conclusion, that if it be possible for God to make a free agent, then man is free, though I see not the way of it."

II

Eliot had thus early acquired in his ministerial work the set of mind and personality that would determine his response to the great public crisis of his time. As the Revolution approached he stood out as a man of genial goodwill, modest, tolerant, willing to concede to the intellectual superiority of others, and naturally indulgent of intellectual ambiguity. He had learned to avoid public polemics, to seek comfortable middle-of-the-road positions on difficult current issues, and, as a consequence as much of natural geniality as of principle, extended the hand of fellowship to those who differed with him. In his last two publications (1774) he wrote his own best testament, reporting that in his thirty-two years in the ministry he had never "meddled with abstruse speculations, and . . . have avoided subjects of controversy. . . . The pulpit was not designed to be a school of disputation"; nor had he ever believed that what one happens to accept as "fundamental doctrine" had by virtue of that belief a claim to a monopoly of absolute truth: "It is possible we may be mistaken; things may appear very differently to others as upright as ourselves, and the same desirable effect may be produced by sentiments not in every respect consonant to our's."

Eliot had also acquired very early in his career the basic political beliefs and attitudes, the latent map of the political world, that would guide his specific understanding of the Anglo-American conflict. They had two closely related expressions: the first—formal, public, and ritualistic—in his notable election sermon of 1765; the second—informal, private, and particularistic—in his decade-long correspondence with Thomas Hollis, Archdeacon William Blackburne, and Thomas Brand Hollis, that was touched off by the reception of the election sermon in England.

Eliot's election sermon, *A Sermon Preached before His Excellency Francis Bernard, Esq., Governor . . . May 29th, 1765*, is a ritualistic statement of the duties and characteristics of the just magistrate. A formulary developed through six generations of preaching in New

England, it may be seen as an American provincial version of that voluminous "mirror-of-the-prince" literature whose roots are medieval, whose flowering took place in Renaissance Italy, and whose ultimate fulfillment—or perversion—is Machiavelli's *The Prince*. But the equivocating Eliot, devoted to the idealistic platitudes of his age and in no way able or anxious to transcend them, was no American Machiavelli (the hard-headed, perversely original Madison may have been that). Eliot's purpose in addressing the assembled magistrates on the occasion of the annual election was not to probe or extend the received tradition but to transmit it intact, with only the most modest embellishments. In structure the sermon could scarcely have been a more rigid embodiment of the inherited formulas: discussion, first, following presentation of the biblical text, of "the character of a good ruler"; second, of "the duty of subjects to their rulers." Under the first, a preface on "the great end of government" followed by a careful enumeration of the major attributes of a good ruler; under the second, two essentials: the duty to obey, with formulaic support from Romans xiii:1–5, and the duty to resist, with due consideration of the problem of "where submission ends and resistance may lawfully take place." The whole concludes with a paean to Great Britain, to its prince, "who accounts it his glory to reign over a free people," and to the glory of its constitution and to that constitution's "little model" in Massachusetts, with a coda—a most cautious coda—on the public difficulties of this year of the Stamp Act, and (formula within formula) on the supposedly greater danger from "our internal vices . . . our luxury, extravagance, and intemperance [that] threaten our ruin."

Platitudinous throughout, Eliot's thought rested on the solid bedrock of the contract theory of government as well as the concepts of the innate corruption of man and of the Hobbesian consequence of unlimited freedom. Society is prudential, government fiduciary, and the obligations of both governors and governed are to fulfill the mutually reinforcing duties of the contract. But there are also less obvious, more personal and more provocative elements in the sermon. There is an unexpected, and altogether unintegrated, paragraph describing the political community as "constituted of a number of little societies, in which there will be different branches of business"—a stillborn interest-group theory of politics not unlike others that appeared in eighteenth-century America only to disappear without a

trace. There is the surprisingly straightforward assumption, empha-
sized rather than discounted by Eliot's strenuous dismissal of it, that
American independence was an ever-present possibility and at the
moment a source of suspicion in England of the colonists' motives in
resisting the Stamp Act. There is Eliot's unexpectedly fierce insistence that when rulers "pervert their power to tyrannical purposes,
submission . . . is a crime . . . an offence against the state . . . an
offence against mankind . . . an offence against God." But these are
matters of emphasis, or are undeveloped peculiarities, within a discourse cut to the standard pattern of Puritan New England's "mirror-
of-the-prince" literature. Its chief importance lies in precisely that fact:
in its fine articulation of a tradition of thought familiar to every New
Englander, if not to every American, exemplifying at the outset of
the Revolutionary era the substratum of belief that underlay the developing rebellion.

I I I

The *substratum* of belief: for generalities like these may shape in a
general way the outer boundaries of political thought but they do
not provide the immediate springs of action. Other considerations—
more superficial, perhaps, more pragmatic and more open to dispute—
dictate the use of such generalities, trigger their transformation from
precepts to programs. The specification and application of these universal political assumptions took place for Eliot after 1765, and of this
process his personal correspondence is graphically illustrative. For if
Eliot's election sermon embodies in classic form the ordinary political
assumptions of the age, his correspondence with the two Hollises and
with Archdeacon Francis Blackburne, initiated by the publication of
the election sermon, expresses with unique clarity the transformation
of election-sermon platitudes into revolutionary imperatives. It is
probably the most vivid expression of this transforming, or triggering,
process in the entire literature of the Revolution.

The correspondence begins mildly enough, with an almost apologetic self-introduction by the famous English philanthropist and radical propagandist Thomas Hollis, who in his eccentric way was
devoting himself heart and soul to the task of disseminating radical
Whig writings throughout the English-speaking world and to stimu-

lating awareness everywhere of the corruption of England and of what he took to be the approaching destruction of liberty in that country. Jonathan Mayhew, Hollis explained, heretofore his main agent in America, having died, he had decided to transfer his correspondence to Eliot, whose "similarity of turn, as appeareth by your [election] sermon, to my late honored friend, the regularity of your education, the fullness of your character, your age, station, power, will to render *public* service, all have concurred with me . . . to take this measure." He was therefore directing the latest shipment of books and tracts, originally intended for Mayhew, to Eliot, and had given instructions to his colleagues in propaganda, especially his devoted friend Archdeacon Blackburne ("the very Whig described in the truly noble Lord Molesworth's glorious preface to his translation of *Franco-Gallia*"), to transfer their correspondence also to Eliot.

Eliot was immensely flattered, and said so, in the first of twenty-eight letters on politics, church affairs, and the state of the world in which he responded to this "token of regard from a gentleman of so distinguished a character and so justly honored among us." From the first, Eliot's letters revealed agreement in general viewpoint with Hollis and the other political radicals, sympathy for their dark and progressively despairing interpretation of the tendency of events in England, and, above all, an extreme susceptibility to their conspiratorial explanation of the underlying causes of the developing crisis. It is clear in the correspondence that Hollis did not teach Eliot anything new: he did not fill an empty mind with unfamiliar notions; he did not transform one disposition to another. He and Blackburne evoked, and helped give specific political form to, what had been generally implied in the election sermon and what Eliot otherwise knew. For like the overwhelming majority of his countrymen, Eliot had developed in himself, simply from the milieu of British political culture, a psychological as well as an intellectual readiness for the claims of the British radicals.

He had himself, indeed, a decade earlier sounded the major themes of what would be fully orchestrated in the Hollis correspondence and what would ultimately become, for the colonies at large, the logic of rebellion. In his thanksgiving sermon of 1759 celebrating the conquest of Canada he had traced the origins of the struggle with France back to the Reformation, and explained that "our popish adversaries have

ever since been forming plots and conspiracies to overthrow our religion and liberties." Their clandestine efforts, he then wrote, had
been ceaseless: in 1605 they had sought to wipe out king, Lords, and
Commons "at one blast, and to make a bloody massacre at the same
time all over the kingdom." A century later Louis XIV had "prevailed
more by secret arts than he could by open force. By his intrigues in
the court of *Great Britain* he had obtained a peace [Utrecht] which
has been the fatal cause of most of the evils we have suffered since."
Liberty had then triumphed, but it was still beset, as it had been
throughout history, by hidden forces stimulated not merely by the
endless corruptibility of men and their insatiable lust for power but
specifically, Eliot believed, by a papal-"Stuartine" combination ever
alert to new advantages.

This theme, which had been current in general in the English-
speaking world for a century and a half and which had acquired in
America in the mid-eighteenth century greater political relevance than
it had had in England since the end of the seventeenth century, was
set forth in the very first of Eliot's letters to Hollis and remained
central to their discussion thereafter. What can one expect to find "in
the present state of things," Eliot asked Hollis in his opening letter,
but *"syndics,* men of contracted minds and mean tools of power"?
Even "the great patriot" William Pitt, "who seemed formed to stem
the torrent of corruption," had sold out to "the northern *Thane"* (the
Earl of Bute), forsaking the Commons for the bauble of an earldom
(may he "yet emerge and save a sinking nation!").

Eliot's fears and suspicions ran deep from the start, but in November 1766 he was still willing to say that the evil the colonies had so
far fought may not have been "designed . . . to enslave" them, but was
likely to have that effect. His correspondents made no such delicate
distinctions. Archdeacon Blackburne introduced himself to Eliot as
"one among many others who think they have discovered the dregs
of the Stuartine and Laudean ecclesiastical politics fermenting afresh
in this country"; he assured his Boston correspondent that he had
never been misled as others had into thinking that "that vile spirit
was evaporated"; and he explained that he considered the condition
of politics in England and America "in a state of connexion and in
many respects within the influence of each other," so that "the scheme
of episcopizing the colonies . . . could not fail, had it taken place, to

have blocked up all prospect of any reformation in this country." No one, he instructed Eliot, "who is acquainted with the features of the master-workman in this Episcopal fabric [presumably Archbishop Secker] can doubt but that he intended by it to lock down upon us at home the hierarchical yoke as well as to bend to it the necks of our brethren, the colonists."

So, at the end of 1766, the correspondence began, and so it continued, interrupted after 1771 when Hollis retired but resumed in 1774 with the philanthropist's heir, Thomas Brand Hollis, and concluded only in May 1775, when Eliot found himself trapped in Boston, a prisoner of the besieged British army. Throughout, one theme remained dominant. England was approaching (had already reached, according to Hollis) just that stage of moral decline that Montesquieu had warned of in a celebrated passage (quoted by Eliot, as by almost every political writer in eighteenth-century America)—the state at which "the legislative power shall be more corrupt than the executive" and England's liberty destroyed. Every sign pointed to the fact that "corruption and luxury like a torrent bear down all before them!!!" The political virtue of the nation, Hollis insisted time and time again, was crumbling, and in the resulting putrefaction a malignant force was working its will to effect the final destruction of liberty in both England and America.

This is the major theme, an almost obsessive theme, that dominates the Eliot-Hollis-Blackburne correspondence. The English writers were instructors, the Bostonian a willing disciple, but the lesson was clear at the start. A plan to overthrow the constitution—the latest manifestation of an age-old effort—was underway, dominated by a singular and determined power. Thus, Hollis wrote, the nation's one potential savior, Pitt, had been bought off by "the skulking corroder of the security and felicity of three noble kingdoms and the colonies, White Rose, the Favorite!" (Bute). Yes, Eliot sympathetically replied, "I tremble for the nation which has so few honest patriots. These few, I fear, will not be able to stem the torrent of ambition, luxury, and venality." Already, he noted, there were rumors that the freedom of the press, "the *palladium* of English liberty," was endangered in Britain; "if this is gone, all is gone."

A rising fear of Catholicism runs through Eliot's correspondence, and is closely woven into his political thought. Impudent Jesuits, he noted, had become so bold as to clamor for toleration: "He must have lost all principles of self-preservation who will take a serpent into his bosom, especially when he has felt his sting and but just escaped with his life." A Catholic bishop had been allowed to return to Canada, and since there was doubtless "a concatenation of causes and effects," one might look forward soon to freedom for Catholics, first in Ireland, then in England; and ultimately some "future *archbishop* [may] . . . again bring on the scheme of uniting the two churches, the popish and the protestant, and become *papa alterius orbis!*" As for the "pernicious designs" to establish bishops in America, the purpose, Eliot wrote, was not merely to subject the American dissenters to episcopacy but to extend the episcopal influence in England, and thus, "as Dr. Blackburne judiciously observes . . . to prevent any reformation at home." Perhaps, Eliot suggested at one point, an appropriate use of the funds of the Society for the Propagation of the Gospel would be the subsidizing of a Protestant counterespionage system in the Catholic countries.

From the start Eliot believed the prospects were dark: managers of public affairs were "governed by private views and the spirit of a party. . . . Men are patriots till they get in place, and then are!!!—anything . . . an invisible *favorite* governs all . . . what cannot a K—g, a m—n—st—r, do that has a Parliament devoted to him, and a standing army to—I dare not write what I think." If, as seemed likely, Parliament succeeded in taxing the colonists, they would become obliged to support "a parcel of pitiful sycophants, court parasites, and hungry dependents in luxury and extravagance, and who will probably be sent over to watch and oppress those who support them." If, as was rumored, councillors in the Massachusetts government were to be appointed rather than elected as the charter provided, "we shall have *strangers, crown officers, pensioners, court dependents,* and what not" running the government. And if, as seemed equally probable, governors' and judges' salaries were placed on the Crown's payroll, the colonial bench would be invaded by "needy, *poor* lawyers from England, *Scotland,* or some tools of power of our own" and the governorships filled with ministerial clients as "reward of their despicable services . . . or . . . some *noble* scoundrel who has spent his fortune in every kind of luxury and debauchery." Events confirmed his fears: troops, he reported to Hollis, were being sent to Boston. "To have a standing army! Good God! what can be worse to a people who have tasted the sweets of liberty!" The people of Massachusetts, he assured his correspondents, were "ripe for almost anything." But "what can we do! Tamely to give up our rights and to suffer ourselves to be taxed at the will of persons at such a distance, and to be under military government, is to consent to be slaves . . . and yet how unable to cope with Great Britain! How dreadful the thought of a contest with the parent country, in whose calamities we have always borne a part and in whose peace we have enjoyed peace." There was little to hope for in a change of ministries. He agreed with Blackburne that such changes were merely "a *transmigration*" in which the soul of a departed minister animates its successor; and so it would continue so long as "each one in place is moved by an external and invisible favorite." "In short, Dear Sir," he confided to Hollis, "we have every thing to fear and scarce any room to hope but in the power and goodness of the Almighty Governor of the world. . . . I am sure this will put you in mind of 1641."

Undoubtedly it did, for though Eliot's fervor grew in intensity and the sense of alarm in his letters rose to an almost hysterical pitch, Hollis remained the leader, insisting always, in his peculiarly self-conscious literary style, that "I, a friend to liberty and King George, like not the times nor their expectancies," that "all things here are tending worse and worse, and to confusion, yet no otherwise than has long been expected by me." Hollis kept up the flow of books, all of them Whiggish tracts, many of them republished on his order, into Eliot's welcoming hands, and through him into the library of Harvard College: Marchamont Nedham's *Excellencies of a Free State* (which Eliot had never heard of before but which he quickly decided "justly gives the author a place among the most noble writers of government"); Algernon Sidney's *Discourses Concerning Government* ("as you justly style him, 'martyr to civil liberty' . . . he was the first who taught me to form any just sentiments on government"); Milton's prose works ("I blush to own that I have never gone through the whole of these prose works . . . perhaps my pleasure is the greater now"); and, most important of all, John Trenchard's "excellent" *History of Standing Armies*, which he referred to directly in commenting on the Boston Massacre.

The Bostonian's ardor, Hollis felt, was admirable, but still it fell short. Against Eliot's comment that if only Parliament would stop stirring up trouble, harmony between England and America might be restored, Hollis wrote: "the business of *White Rose* is to inflame *every where!* Of that A. E. thinks not." When Hollis heard that the Massachusetts Assembly had been convened in Harvard Hall during the winter, he pointed out to the incredulous Eliot the likelihood of a plot behind this to burn the building down again and so once more to destroy the College's "library of liberty" that he had so carefully stocked—an action, he explained, that would be consistent with every other "taken with you and with us since October 25, 1760 [George III's accession], and the influence of one person." And he continued to advise him on how best to influence public opinion—how, like Milton, to inject ridicule, irony, and banter into otherwise grave compositions to heighten their effect; what targets to aim at; where best in England to place the politically useful writings that were being published in America.

What Eliot needed most, however, was not reinforcement of his despair, but a way of resolving in his own mind the central constitutional problem of the time and of taking an effective public stand. But his position on Anglo-American constitutional relations remained as ambiguous as his positions on the major questions of church affairs had been throughout his life. On the one hand, he wrote Blackburne in a long letter of December 1767, the original settlers' allegiance to England had been considered by them "a voluntary thing, and it always appear'd to me they judged rightly," for they had been forced to flee England and they therefore had no moral obligation to remain loyal to that country. Only "interest" bound them and their descendants to England—the need, that is, for the protection of some European power and their willingness to subject themselves to England in exchange for this protection. "The moment it ceases to be their interest to be subject, they have a right to set up for themselves." It was simply nonsense to claim that "because our ancestors were born in England six or seven generations ago, that therefore we are obliged in conscience to be subject . . . in all generations to come although that authority be ever so tyrannical and oppressive." But that did not solve the problem. For it was also a fact that the colonies were presently within the jurisdiction of Britain, and therefore Parliament's power must be supreme, for "in every empire there should be some supreme authority to which all branches should be subject." Yet if Parliament were allowed to tax the colonies at will and by definition the colonies could not be represented in that body, "where is their liberty"? The problem, like that of divine determination and individual free will, was simply and tragically insoluble. "The exact line between the power of Parliament and the rights of the colonies cannot be exactly drawn, and therefore the question should have been kept out of sight as long as possible." The only conceivable basis for Anglo-American harmony was the untheoretical, pragmatic, even a-legal *"uti possidetis"* of former years.

Eliot never followed through the implications of his own thought, never agreed that since, as he believed, Britain was hopelessly corrupt, its government run by the "secret influence . . . in favor of the Romish church"; that since "things are hastening fast to a crisis"; that since indeed "it is now plain that if [the ministry] had not had their hands full at home, they would have crushed the colonies, and that if we had not been vigorous in our opposition we had lost all"—despite all of this, Eliot did not conclude, as did so many others, that independence was the only solution. He never ceased insisting, as he had in the election sermon, that no one in his right mind should want independence, that the colonists still "glory in the name of *Englishmen,*" and that independence would usher in "the most terrible convulsions within each government and great contentions with one another." He hoped, he said, never to live to see independence.

Yet the imperatives to rebellion, which he himself recognized as such, continued to mount. In the fall of 1774 he had only a deepening despair to record: "I know not, Dear Sir, from whence deliverance is to come, but if it does not come soon from some quarter or other I fear Great Britain and America are ruined. . . . The least spark will set us all in a blaze and involve us in blood and slaughter." Two months before Lexington he could only attempt to analyze the causes of the mutual intransigence and report the determination of the people to fight. But to fight with whom?

Not with France and Spain, whom we have been used to think our natural enemies, but with Great Britain—our parent country. . . . My heart recoils—my flesh trembles at the thought. . . . I have ever wished for moderate counsels and temperate measures on both sides. But I can have very little influence on men or measures any where. Pride and passion, avarice and a lust of domination have an uncontrolled sway. In a good measure sequestered from the great world, unconnected with parties, I endeavour to attend the duties of my station and enjoy myself never more than when I can find time for reading and contemplation in my own study. I can there wish and pray for better times, which I see no prospect of without some remarkable interposition of divine providence. . . . I am distressed for my country, in which I include Great Britain. I should fear a disconnection with it as one of the greatest evils.

And then, Lexington: "My heart is wounded, deeply wounded, almost to death."

IV

Yet worse was still to come. The climactic episode of Eliot's life took place in 1775–76. It was an episode so vividly expressive of his inner character, so perfectly consistent with the ambiguities of his entire career, and in itself so agonizing, as to form in some classic sense a tragic drama.

Deeply sympathetic with the American cause, yet equally convinced that Parliament's claims to absolute sovereignty were logically compelling and that independence would be a catastrophe for America as well as for England, he hesitated to make the final commitment and leave Boston as the British troops returned from Lexington. Justifying his failure to jettison everything for the American cause by insisting that he could not desert "the inhabitants who were left [in Boston], that they might not be without ordinances and worship in the way which they choose," he sent his family away to safety and settled down in the besieged town of Boston to look after his flock. He was almost the only Congregational minister to do so, and he immediately became suspect to the Revolutionary leaders as he already was to the British. His first letters from the siege described the desperate condition of Boston—depopulated, isolated, its commerce dead, reduced to a mere garrison town of hostile soldiers: "I wish to God the authors of our misery could be witnesses of it." No one can conceivably profit by such a war, he wrote in bitter letters which, fearful of interception, he would soon regret having written. If Britain won and managed to reimpose taxes on the colonies, she could not possibly regain all she had already lost in trade. He could scarcely comprehend the tragedy of it. "Must millions be sacrificed to a mere *punctilio,*" he cried to Hollis, "to a mere point of honor?"

Then came the carnage of Bunker Hill: "men carried through the streets groaning, bleeding, and dying . . . Englishmen destroying one another . . . a town with which we have been so intimately connected all in flames. . . . I cannot stand it long." Yet he was still irresolute. In the same letters he reported to Hollis that he had heard that the governing board of Harvard College, of which he was a member, was meeting: "I wish they may come to no sudden resolutions: it is no time to give offence." It would be best, he felt, if they did nothing at present and simply "wait the issue of things." Perhaps, he concluded, "it will one day be seen that it had been as well if more moderate counsels had been pursued."

Summer brought added miseries—heat, disease, malnutrition. He begged his former parishioners on the other side of the lines to send in needed food, reporting to them the distribution to the sick that he had made of supplies they had already sent. Creditors began dunning him for debts he could not possibly pay; Tories denounced him not only as a rebel but as a cynical rebel, being a latecomer to the insurrection; and it became increasingly difficult for him to perform the services of his church, whose congregation was now a motley crowd drawn from half a dozen former church societies abandoned by their pastors. By the end of July, while "on the whole I cannot say I am sorry I tarried," he began writing to his sons that he had probably done all he could do in Boston and was beginning to feel he should leave. By mid-August he was convinced of it and wished fervently that he were out of the town. Yet he was *still* perplexed. "I am tired of writing about coming out," he said in words that might stand as his epitaph, "but am more tired of being here, and yet am greatly afflicted at the thought of leaving such numbers. I never was so embarrassed in my life."

It was only in September, however, that his embarrassment reached its final depths. It was then that he actually brought himself to apply for a pass to leave Boston—and he was denied it, first by the Mandamus Councillors, before whom, he discovered, he had been secretly denounced as a profiteer, and then, with humiliating brusqueness, by the Town Major. That winter he went through "the most trying scenes that I ever did through my whole life." Deprived of every member of his large family and especially of his wife, the "dearest of all earthly friends," whom he desperately missed; "afraid to speak, to write," he later recalled, "almost to think"; forced to abandon the Thursday Lecture, which had been conducted in Boston for 140 consecutive years, he avoided all contact with the "despots" and withdrew from public affairs, dealing as well as he could with his own immediate problems of survival and, in guarded but frantic correspondence, with those of his scattered family.

The one external concern he sought to attend to through that winter adds a note of poignancy to his frustrations. In the early fall he received word that a memoir of the elder Hollis was being prepared in England and that the compilers would welcome some notice of Hollis's benefactions to Harvard and presumably also of Hollis's friendship with Eliot. In November, Eliot wrote his son Samuel, then in Waltham, to copy from Harvard's Book of Benefactors everything pertaining to Hollis and send the information to him; in December he repeated the instruction; but in February he still had not received the records he needed, and in the end, to his keen disappointment, he was forced to pass up the opportunity of publicly acknowledging Hollis's gifts and of sharing personally in the tribute to this international celebrity.

No one was more greatly relieved than Eliot when the British evacuated Boston. But though at General Washington's personal invitation he renewed the Thursday Lecture and though he was welcomed back into the leadership of the Congregational church and of Harvard College, he never recovered his former reputation. When he died, two years after the declaration of the independence that he had wished never to see, the official funeral ceremonies were elaborate, but the newspapers failed almost entirely to publish the eulogies appropriate to a man of his position. He was remembered by many of his own generation, as he was by John Adams, as "Hutchinson's parish priest and his devoted idolater." He might better be remembered by his own decent, reasonable, tolerant, and fatal words: *"It is possible we may be mistaken; things may appear very differently to others as upright as ourselves, and the same desirable effect may be produced by sentiments not in every respect consonant to our's."*

Jonathan Mayhew

"God Is My Witness, That
from the Bottom of My Heart
I Detest These Proceedings"

I N MAY 1766, two months before he died (of a stroke, at the age of forty-six), Jonathan Mayhew, the famous and controversial Boston minister, composed a political testament and public *apologia* in the form of a thanksgiving sermon on the occasion of the repeal of the Stamp Act. Written in the state of extreme excitement and inner turmoil generated the previous August when he had been caught up in the violence of the Stamp Act protests, the sermon, *The Snare Broken*, not only recapitulates and assesses that crisis, and not only restates the political principles Mayhew had announced in his famous *Discourse Concerning Unlimited Submission* (1750), but points to inner characteristics of politically radical thought that until then had been ignored but that circumstances now starkly revealed. Far from being the expression of a political conservatism characteristic of a status-minded, "rationalist" clergy, Mayhew's final effort, seen in the full context of his career and of the circumstances of the time, marks the struggle of an eighteenth-century radical seeking to maintain, in an explosive situation, a workable balance between political anti-authoritarianism and social stability.

.   .   .

The difficulties of maintaining such a balance were compounded by Mayhew's personality. He was by temperament volatile and enthusiastic. His indignation was intense; he ran to extremes in everything he did. His reputation for radicalism in all the spheres he touched—theology, church affairs, politics—was confirmed in the decade that followed the publication of his classic *Discourse* on resistance to oppressive authority. Before the end of the 1750s his hatred of autocracy had been expressed in a passing condemnation of the whole institution of monarchy and an encomium to the virtues of "the vulgar and middle sorts." Similarly, his belligerent Arminianism, fed by the nourishment he continued to draw from the writings of such Christian rationalists as Samuel Clarke, flowered into a nondoctrinaire Arianism, easily and not incorrectly construed by his horrified Congregational colleagues as a flat repudiation of the divinity of Christ—a charge that Mayhew's impassioned insistence that he had never "denied or treated in a bold or ludicrous manner the divinity of the Son of God, as revealed in scripture" could not dispel. And his early suspicions that the quality of English political life was degenerating, played upon by the English radicals with whom he was regularly corresponding, blazoned into the conviction that England was following the predictable path of other once great and free nations into the state of "infidelity, irreligion, corruption and venality, and almost every kind of vice" that led inevitably to tyranny.

Increasingly belligerent in his views, Mayhew had become increasingly isolated on the outer fringes of politics and religion, increasingly suspicious of the motives of those who attacked him, and increasingly propelled toward still more distant frontiers. His internationally famous controversy with the Anglican Reverend East Apthorp over the role of the Society for the Propagation of the Gospel in America and the threat of an American episcopacy—a struggle that occupied him almost continuously from 1762 to 1764—directed his energies momentarily into universally approved channels. He emerged from that encounter something of a public hero—and even more deeply confirmed than ever in his opposition to hierarchy, authority, and power in all its oppressive forms. He naturally became a protagonist in the Stamp Act controversy. In the summer of 1765, at the climax of the movement toward resistance, despite the long-standing prohibitions on direct clerical participation in politics, he threw himself deliberately into the battle.

Most of the facts of what happened in late August 1765 are not in question. Rumors had long been circulating to the effect that the lieutenant governor, Thomas Hutchinson, and his Oliver kin were not only supporters of the Stamp Act, from which as prospective stamp masters they could expect to profit, but that, for reasons of the narrowest self-interest, they had helped feed the misinformation to England that had shaped the policies of Grenville's administration. On August 14 popular antipathy to the Hutchinson group, stimulated by the partisan animosities of the Otises, burst out in the ceremonial hanging of Andrew Oliver in effigy and a destructive riot against the stamp master's office. Two days later the lieutenant governor himself was threatened with assault. Correctly gauging the mood of the colonies, Mayhew warned his friends in England that the Stamp Act could be enforced only "at the point of the sword, by a large army, or rather by a number of considerable ones"—in effect, by "Great Britain's waging war with her American colonies." And then, in the midst of the growing turmoil, "clear in this point," he wrote Thomas Hollis, "that no people are under a *religious obligation* to be slaves if they are able to set themselves at liberty," he gave notice that on August 25 he would preach "a political discourse" directed to these questions.

The sermon he delivered that day was the fulfillment, according to his enemies, of the destructive implications of the *Discourse Concerning Unlimited Submission* and an object lesson in the disastrous tendencies of radical thought. The remaining nine months of his life, culminating in his testamentary *The Snare Broken,* were consumed with explaining what he had meant and justifying the stand he then took. His exhortation to the crowded audience was based on the text of Galatians v, 12, 13, though exactly how much of those two verses Mayhew used remained a matter of heated controversy. According not only to Hutchinson but to Mayhew's parishioner, the influential merchant Richard Clarke, and other leading Bostonians, Mayhew dwelt exclusively on the theme "I would they were even cut off which trouble you, for brethren ye have been called unto liberty," and he had, they believed, consistent with this text, lent his dignity and the sanction of his office to approval of the "prevailing irregularities," charging his hearers, implicitly or explicitly, with the necessity of taking action in the cause of liberty. When the next day the most destructive mob in Boston's history tore Hutchinson's town house to pieces in a rage so violent that even the most radical did not know how to account for it, some, recalling Mayhew's sermon and knowing of his general reputation for extremism, charged him with a major share in inciting the riot. Direct testimony was soon forthcoming: years later Hutchinson was able to recall the precise words of "one who had a chief hand in the outrages," that he had been "excited to them by this sermon, and that he thought he was doing God service."

Mayhew was sincerely shocked by the riot, and appalled by the accusations leveled against him. His first, instinctive reaction was to publish a disclaimer of some sort in the newspapers, but when he sought to discuss this with Clarke and to get his advice, he was flatly informed that the sermon had indeed been offensive and that no advice would be forthcoming. From this Mayhew concluded, quite correctly, that the influential Clarke had "determined wholly to break with me, and to leave the meeting." By what frantic measures Mayhew sought to right the situation and to bring back into balance a reputation he felt had been grotesquely distorted we do not know. But four documents survive to testify to his efforts in the crowded days that followed the riot, and testify too to the deeper bearing of the episode on his political and social thought. These revealing documents are two letters and a memorandum written almost immediately after the outbreak, and—his final justification and explanation—the thanksgiving sermon he preached nine months later and immediately published, *The Snare Broken*.

The first of the letters, written the day after the riot, was a note of condolence to Hutchinson on "the almost unparalell'd outrages." Admitting his awareness of the charges of complicity that had been hurled by some of his "numerous and causeless enemies," he swore to Hutchinson, "God is my witness, that from the bottom of my heart I detest these proceedings; that I am sincerely grieved for them; and have a deep sympathy with you and your distressed family." Yes, he had expressed himself "strongly in favor of civil and religious liberty, as I hope I shall ever continue to do," and he had spoken of the Stamp Act as a great grievance and detriment to both England and

America—"which I believe is the sense of almost every person of understanding in the plantations," including, he added (accurately), "Your Honor." But he had not only preached in favor of liberty. "I cautioned my hearers very particularly against the abuses of liberty. . . . And, in truth, I had rather lose my hand than be an encourager of such outrages as were committed last night." He begged Hutchinson to believe this protestation—and he begged him also, in a passage that clearly reveals the knife edge he walked, "not to divulge what I now write, so that it may come to the knowledge of those enraged people who have acted such a part, not a single person of whom, or of their advisers, do I know. For it could do no good in the present circumstances and the temper which they are in, and might probably bring their heavy vengeance upon myself."

The second document, Mayhew's letter to his parishioner Clarke, is three or four times as long as the note to Hutchinson, and it is as contrite and self-abusive a letter as anyone in Mayhew's position could possibly have written. For he acknowledged at the start that he had picked "a very unfortunate time to preach a sermon, the chief aim of which was to show the importance of liberty, when people were before so generally apprehensive of the danger of losing it. They certainly needed rather to be moderated and pacified than the contrary." He would gladly give "all that I have in the world rather than have preached that sermon," despite the general approval it had received from the immediate audience. But, he explained, it had not been preached out of a random impulse. He had undertaken it deliberately. The Boston clergy had often in recent times been "blamed for their silence in the cause of liberty, at a time when it was almost universally supposed, as it still is, that our common liberties and rights, as British subjects, were in the most imminent danger. They were called cowards and the like." He had personally been solicited by several people as "a known friend to liberty" and reproached for his inactivity. No doubt the action he finally took had been "ill judged" and inexpedient, given the public temper at the time, "yet candid persons will make some allowance for me if I was too far carried away with the common current." As for the sermon itself, he certainly agreed that "it was composed in a high strain of liberty, tho' I humbly conceive not higher than is warranted by the principles of the Glorious Revolution." From those principles no sensible person could "take encouragement . . . to go to mobbing or to commit such abominable outrages as were lately committed." And in fact in the sermon he had gone out of his way "in the most formal, express manner" to discountenance any such interpretation, a claim he proceeded to prove by a string of quotations from the sermon on the constraints implicit in civil liberty—its clear distinction from the "state of anarchy and confusion" that exists in the state of nature, its presupposition of "the restraint of laws, some persons to govern and some to be governed," its condemnation of those "who cause factions or insurrection against the government under which they live and who rebel against or resist their lawful rulers in the due discharge of their offices." And he assured Clarke that, while it was true that he had mentioned in the sermon the "suspicions of many" that "for the sake of present gain" some people in the colonies had actually encouraged the obnoxious measures of the ministry and that he had indeed discussed "men who could be so mercinary as to ruin their country for the sake of posts and profits," he also had expressed the hope that these suspicions were not, in the *present* situation, justified; his discussion of that subject, he said, had been "mere hypothetical, for I did not at all give it as my opinion that there were actually any such persons in the colonies."

These final points in his plea to Clarke for understanding were neither judicious nor convincing, and it would not have been surprising if they had served to confirm Clarke's opinion rather than change it. But Mayhew had at least been judicious in the selections he had taken from a detailed summary of the sermon he had prepared for his own use sometime between August 27 and September 3. This memorandum—the third document which is the source for the verbatim quotations in his letter to Clarke and which Mayhew preserved among his personal papers—was probably worked up from the notes Mayhew had actually spoken from. Throughout, it presents the contents of the sermon in terms calculated to dispel the charges against him and to strengthen his claim to be a defender of law and order. Yet long passages in even this obviously slanted interpretation of what he had said shows the continuing, fresh enthusiasm of his political beliefs.

The sermon of August 25—as it appears in this private memorandum—had consisted of four topics in explanation of the scriptural text. The first two were relatively inconsequential; in them Mayhew had merely defined the "troublers" referred to in verse 12 of Galatians v as ceremonialists who insisted on retaining the "yoke of bondage" of the past; and he had explained the phrase "cut off" as indicating simply the judgment of God or at most the excommunication of the church, and not the political actions of men. And while it is true, he recalled, that under the fourth heading he had warned of the dangers of excess, under the third he had expatiated at length on the meaning of liberty and its force in the present situation. The main emphasis of the sermon, he wrote, lay in this third section.

The essence of civil liberty, Mayhew recalled himself saying in this passage of the sermon, is governance by a body of laws to which the governed had consented, and that definition held whether the governor happens to be a single person, such as the monarchs he had discussed in the *Discourse* of 1750, or "a considerable number of persons." A nation can enjoy civil liberty under a single ruler perfectly well, he had explained, "provided it is by their own choice, and they delegate the powers of government to him, still reserving to themselves a right to judge whether he discharges his trust well or ill, to discard him and appoint another in his stead." On the other hand, a nation may suffer a real slavery "tho' governed by many persons" if those persons use their authority "for their own interest, pleasure or profit, contrary to the will of the governed. For the essence of slavery consists in being subjected to the arbitrary pleasure of others, whether many, few, or but one, it matters not."

And then, as if this direct association of the radical Whiggism of his earlier *Discourse* with resistance to Parliament were not clear enough, Mayhew recalled himself making the linkage doubly secure in what must have been the climax of the sermon. Given this definition of civil liberty, he had added, it is possible that different groups within the same nation may find themselves in different situations with respect to it, some enjoying perfect liberty, others under the same jurisdiction being slaves. Take, "for example," he had suggested, with what must have been received as elaborate irony, "a mother country and her colonies. While she is free, it is supposeable that her colonies may be kept in a state of real slavery to her. For if they are to possess no property nor to enjoy the fruits of their own labor but by the mere precarious pleasure of the mother or of a distant legislature in which they neither are nor can be represented, this is really slavery, not civil liberty"—quite without reference to whether or not the colonists in question happen to be treated "with tenderness and humanity." All of which, he concluded in a heavily revised paragraph, agrees with the reasoning of "the most approved English writers on liberty"—writers, he decided after some hesitation, "before as well as since the [Glorious] Revolution." And in the very last passage of the sermon, as reported in the memorandum, Mayhew had returned once again to the theme of the *Discourse* and linked it indissolubly to the present problems by posing and answering in the negative the question of whether passive obedience and nonresistance were the duties of oppressed people, and if they were not, whether opposition to unjust rulers could properly be considered, in the words of his biblical text, "using liberty for an occasion to the flesh."

The sermon had indeed contained a full section warning of the excesses of liberty, and Mayhew's quotations to Clarke and Hutchinson from that section are accurate. But while there is no indication that Mayhew deliberately sought to incite his audience to violence there can also be no question that he had endorsed the most radical line of resistance to Parliament's taxation, and explicitly linked such resistance to the English radical tradition whose public advocate he had become fifteen years earlier. It was perhaps fitting, therefore, that it should have been the victims of Mayhew's earlier political controversies who carried the news of his latest outburst to the highest authorities in England. Within a week of the August 25 sermon Henry Caner, the rector of King's Chapel, Boston, had informed the Archbishop of Canterbury that Mayhew "has distinguished himself in the pulpit . . . in one of the most seditious sermons ever delivered, advising the people to stand up for their rights to the last drop of their blood." A month later Hutchinson informed East Apthorp, Mayhew's enemy in earlier controversies, then back in England, of what had transpired, adding, no doubt on the basis of the letters Mayhew had written immediately after the riot, that the preacher had developed "the deepest concern for his imprudence and I have heard he has promised never to meddle with politicks again." By the end of 1765 Thomas Hollis reported hearing rumors in London that the Archbishop of Canterbury was seeking to have Mayhew brought over to England for examination, an effort that was apparently dropped upon the repeal of the Stamp Act in March 1766 but that Mayhew may have heard of only late in May. In any case, it was then, in the late spring of 1766, with the public crisis resolved on what appeared to be the most favorable terms but with his personal situation still unsettled as a result of the riots, that Mayhew decided to clear the air once and for all and to restate his political views in the light of recent experience. The result is *The Snare Broken*, preached as a thanksgiving sermon before the same audience that had heard the notorious discourse of the previous August 25, and on the same text.

The Snare Broken is as extreme a statement of the social limitations of radical Whig thought as the *Discourse* of 1750 and the sermon of August 25 had been of its politically aggressive thrust. Nothing that Mayhew had previously said was repudiated, but the emphasis now falls on the hitherto unarticulated assumption that a stable social order was the counterpart of political freedom and that a reform of politics need not be associated with social upheaval.

The main theme is struck quickly after the fulsome dedication to Pitt, whose role as savior had been the subject of several of Hollis's letters to Mayhew. The topic of his discourse, he indicates, will be not so much rights as duties. In eight paragraphs he quickly summarizes as universally "taken for granted" those principles of British constitutionalism that had been the central subject of his earlier discourses, and brings the discussion to a sudden turn by explaining that *"in this place"* (i.e., from the pulpit) he cannot be expected to support any forms of resistance to authority, "whatever the general sense of the colonists may be concerning this point," save such strictly legal ones as "humble petitioning." And then, as if to wipe out at a stroke all the ambiguities of his role in the Stamp Act violence, he roundly condemns "the riotous and fellonious proceedings of certain *men of Belial,* as they have been justly called, who had the effrontery to cloke their rapacious violences with the pretext of zeal for liberty," and he explains how the self-correcting mechanisms of the British constitution and the still largely uncorrupted purposes of king and Parliament make recourse to such actions unnecessary and wrong. The Stamp Act had been the work not of the highest authorities but rather of "some evil-minded individuals in Britain who . . . spared no wicked arts, no deceitful, no dishonorable, no dishonest means to push on and obtain, as it were by *surprise*, an act so prejudicial . . . and in some sort to the *ensnaring* of His Majesty and the Parliament, as well as the good people of America." There was little doubt in his mind who these individuals were: machinators, he writes, "not improbably in the interests of the houses of Bourbon and the Pretender, whose cause they meant to serve by bringing about an open rupture between Great Britain and her colonies!" And he then proceeds to give thanks for deliverance from so desperate a danger and to explain his personal resolution of the crisis.

This resolution in his own thought, as he expounds it, is winding and erratic, repeatedly circling back on itself and breaking sharply at several points for what appear to be spontaneous interjections. But the two main points are clear. Both are forms of self-justification; both aim at rebalancing the unintended one-sidedness of his earlier public statements. He explains, first, with the direct implication that he had been misunderstood, the sheer confusion that prevails in a crisis such as that of the previous year and the psychological atmosphere created by it that leads not merely to mutual recrimination but to distortion of opposing views. The colonists spoke, he recalls, with a thousand voices, "according to the diversity of their natural tempers and constitutions, their education, religious principles, or the prudential maxims which they had espoused." Some were melancholy, lethargic, and desperate, others were thrown into a frenzy but without knowing "what, when, where, how, nor having any two rational and consistent ideas about the matter." As to policies, only a few were of the "goodly tribe" of Sibthorpe, Mainwaring, and Filmer, standing pat on the reactionary principles of nonresistance and passive obedience. The great majority "were firmly united in a consistent, however imprudent or desperate a plan, to run all risques, to tempt all hazards, to go all lengths if things were driven to extremity." In this boiling cauldron of opinion, judgments were warped and "*strange* notions and fears prevailed," for "there is no end, you know, to people's *fears* and *jealousies* when once they are thoroughly alarmed." The result was "great animosities, mutual censures, and reproaches: insomuch that it was hardly safe for any man to speak his thoughts on the times unless he could patiently bear to lie under the imputation of being a coward, an incendiary, rebel, or enemy to his country, or to have some other odium cast upon him." It was inevitable in such a situation, "approaching so near to anarchy," that "some profligate people" would take the opportunity of gratifying their private resentments and their greed and commit "abominable excesses and outrages on the persons or property of others."

It is to condemning such outrages, which had so recently and grievously been associated with his name, and to dissociating any such action from his well-known views, that he devotes the central passages of the sermon. Political freedom, he writes, now restored after a crisis that threatened not merely America but also Great Britain, Protestantism, and liberty everywhere, is in no way a natural progenitor of civil upheaval. Its natural complement is not defiance but obedience to constituted authority, to king, Parliament, and the laws of Britain's free constitution. Parliament's right to superintend the colonies, "to direct, check, or controul them," is universally conceded "whatever we may think of the particular right of taxation," especially since it is now obvious that any accidental infringements of the colonists' rights will be corrected upon petition. The "malicious prophecies" circulating in England that America's successful resistance will lead to a habit of insolence and defiance of Parliament must be refuted. The colonists must prove their affection and need for England by a return to their ancient obedience and "not entertain a thought of novelties or innovations or be 'given to change.'" A posture of "humility and moderation on the happy success of our late remonstrances and struggles" is the only appropriate one, he urges, especially for the people of Massachusetts, whose leadership in the resistance is so well known.

But let none of this be misunderstood. No claim to a natural obedience, he makes clear, can or should override a people's "just concern for their own rights or legal, constitutional privileges." For the malignancy of power, its "grasping, encroaching nature," is everywhere, and everywhere it must be resisted—not at some convenient time but immediately: *"obsta principiis,"* stop it at the start. And then, having touched once more on the incandescent theme of liberty, Mayhew's imagination blazes forth in an extraordinary peroration in which he sketches the genealogy of modern liberty, the history of his own passionate involvement with it, and, in an almost mystic reverie, his dream of America as an ultimate refuge for freedom-seeking people driven from a Europe sunk in "luxury, debauchery, venality, intestine quarrels, or other vices." The vision passes, rather dramatically

135

("whither have I been hurried by this enthusiasm or whatever else you will please to call it?"), and Mayhew closes the sermon with a return to the theme of obedience to lawful authority and conciliation of differences. Let us "bury in oblivion what is past, to begin our civil, political life anew." Let there be a return to peace, tolerance, and "the duties of our respective stations," the last being especially relevant, he suddenly adds, to "the poor and labouring part of the community, whom I am very far from despising, [and who] have had so much to say about government and politics in the late times of danger, tumult, and confusion that many of them seemed to forget they had any thing to *do*." They, and all the rest of the long-disturbed population, should "do something more and talk something less, . . . letting things return peaceably into their old channels and natural courses after so long an interruption."

The Snare Broken follows the traditional formulas of the Congregationalist thanksgiving sermon. But its deeper purpose, in the context of the events of the time and of Mayhew's career, is the highly personal one of redressing the balance of the preacher's reputation. In the process it reveals the tension at the heart of American Revolutionary thought.

Stephen Johnson

"There Arose a New King over Egypt,
Which Knew Not Joseph"

IN A SHORT period of weeks late in 1765 Stephen Johnson, then in his twentieth year as pastor of the First Congregational Church of Lyme, Connecticut, broke his accustomed silence on public affairs and dashed off a total of some 31,000 words directed to the problems of political liberty in general and the threat of the Stamp Act in particular. The importance of this outburst, aside from the quality of the writing, flows from the fact that it took two different forms, the first a series of six anonymous newspaper articles, published in the *New London Gazette* from September 6 to November 1, 1765; the second a pamphlet, *Some Important Observations* . . . , originally a fast-day sermon delivered on December 18 and published in Newport the following March. Written in colorful prose, the two publications anticipate almost the entire range of arguments that would be debated in the coming decade, and they anticipate, too, the fear of civil war between England and America. But their significance exceeds that. The six newspaper articles are not identified as the work of a Congregational minister; they take no singularly "Christian" point of view, and they develop purely secular arguments that rest for their effect on the evidence they mobilize, on their cogency, and on the rhetoric of their presentation. The pamphlet, on the other hand, ostensibly celebrates a religious ritual and repeats a variety of specific Protestant formulas in explaining the meaning of the public controversy. The two publications, seen as products of the same clerical mind at almost the same moment, illustrate with rare precision the relationship of religious and secular thought in the ideological history of the Revolution.

The structural relationship is perhaps most obvious. If one draws the six newspaper pieces together and views them as a unit they merge into the familiar form of a Puritan sermon. There is no stated text, it is true, but the general theme is announced in the short opening article (September 6) attacking the Stamp Act and the arguments that had been set forth in the *Connecticut Gazette* by "Civis" (Jared Ingersoll) to defend it. Three major "heads" of discussion are then announced (September 20), followed in the remaining issues by an elaborately subdivided discussion in the stated order of topics. The conclusion at the end of the last number (November 1) is in effect an "Application" characteristic of the sermon form: an exhortation to the audience, applying the principles of the discussion to the immediate situation; it is written in intensely emotive prose, and printed entirely in italics with heavy punctuation. The very last passage is a paean, ending with a prayerful "Amen."

It is doubtful that Johnson deliberately intended the newspaper essays to fit into the pattern of a sermon. For two decades he had cast his weekly or semiweekly compositions in this form, and in all probability his thought simply arranged itself automatically in that way. More important than the similarity in form is the relationship in substance between the articles taken as a group and the sermon-pamphlet. Though the sermon invokes familiar religious formulas, the categories of thought in both the sermon and the articles are secular; they are the presuppositions, the framing notions, shared in some degree by the entire British political community, and most fully by the opposition groups. And while it is true that the Puritan tradition, like the American situation, lent particular emphasis to this widely shared body of beliefs and presumptions, the political ideas themselves, the attitudes, motivations, and goals expressed, are independent of a specifically Puritan, or Congregational tradition. Yet the religious formulas in the sermon made a great difference in the presentation and the effect of these ideas—a difference that emerges unmistakably from a close comparison of the substance of the two works.

Almost all of the contents of the five main articles fall under the first of Johnson's headings, "evils apprehended from the late measures of the British ministry." These evils as they are discussed prove to be secular evils—evils, that is, not so much in the sight of God as in the experience of men, and they are demonstrated to be such, first, rationalistically, in terms of tendencies, probabilities, and logic, and second, empirically, in terms of the record of history. In his preliminary attack (September 6) on the Stamp Act and on the ministry's claim that America was "virtually" represented in Parliament, Johnson states his case primarily by running out the logical implications of the administration's position to the point of absurdity. *Why* are we virtually represented, he asks, and *how?*

> Whether . . . because the British Parliament are an assembly of men and of the same species with us, or because they are Englishmen, as we are, or because they represent the nation from whence we descended, or because we are under the same king, or in what other view, is uncertain. In any of those (views) the burroughs and towns in England are as virtually represented in our General Assemblies as the colonies are in Parliament. And all the Jews scatter'd thro'out the world wou'd be as virtually represented by a meeting of the rabbies of Hungary.

Not one member of Parliament had the consent or vote of one American, and "five hundred noughts can never make an unit." And since America could in no way be represented in England, and in addition, since the colonies "have by royal grant and compact certain privileges," the colonies could not be governed in the same way that England itself was governed. To assume the opposite, Johnson declares, would lead directly to "self-repugnancy"—a concept profoundly involved in the most fundamental and subtle questions of British constitutionalism that had been formulated most notably by the great Chief Justice Coke in *Bonham's Case* (1610) and had recently been revived by James Otis—which served in these essays by the obscure

Lyme pastor as the ultimate form of refutation. For while in the context of English institutions, Parliament's power was a balancing element, contributing to the limitation of the undue use of executive power and to the protection of individual liberties, in America its rule as now asserted would be a limitless, authoritarian power, unrestrained by countervailing forces, and hence by definition anticonstitutional and illegal. If Parliament were free to impose a stamp tax on America, it could also impose

> a poll tax, a land tax, a malt tax, a cyder tax, a window tax, a smoke tax, and why not tax us for the light of the sun, the air we breathe, and the ground we are buried in? If they have right to deny us the privilege of tryals by juries, they have as good a right to deny us any tryals at all, and to vote away our estates and lives at pleasure.

The claim that such a power was in any way constitutional refuted itself, Johnson writes.

The concept of "self-repugnancy" was drawn on in a variety of forms in the *Gazette* articles as Johnson worked through the details of his arguments against the new regulations. If the aim of these measures was to raise a revenue, they would defeat themselves, for the colonists "cannot have money enough but a short time to pay these taxes. . . . And what must be the consequence but [that] their lands, the dear patrimony of their fathers . . . must pass to taskmasters here, or to the men of ease and wealth in Britain who have schemed them away for nought"—an eventuality Americans would never endure " 'till they have lost the British spirit, are scandals to the English name, and deserve to wear an eternal chain." The result would be not only severe opposition in America but powerful resistance in England itself when trade, as it would inevitably, came to a stop, and "the merchant, the husbandmen, and the manufacturer of every sort" realized the cost to themselves. The concession that "Civis" had been obliged to make, that Americans did have "certain rights, powers, and privileges circumscribed within their respective limits," Johnson shows by a carefully drawn argument to be either precisely the rights vacated by the Stamp Act or no rights at all: "if we have not these, we have none"; if they could be rightfully taken from the colonists they would become both "rights and no rights, or our's and not our's at the same time . . . our rights only in name, but their's in reality, which is contrary to the supposition and concession allowed us." The "grand argument" of "Civis" was therefore logically so weak "that it can by no means support itself."

But the argument whose internal contradiction Johnson demonstrates with the greatest zest and originality was the claim that Parliament's power rested on the unitary and exclusive character of sovereignty. As the sovereign power, it was claimed, Parliament had by definition "that supreme jurisdiction which . . . every supreme legislature in every state always must have over every part of the dominion . . . and to suppose the contrary would be at once to destroy the very foundation and principles of all government." It was inevitable, Johnson writes in attempting to reply to this assertion of the meaning of sovereignty—an assertion which the British government would never withdraw, though, as Edmund Burke foresaw, it would cost Britain an empire—it was inevitable, Johnson says, that some such claim would be forthcoming. Whenever in history there had been "extraordinary exertions of power (unsupported by reason and the constitution) to be palm'd upon the people" use had been made of "some favorite court maxim of a specious sound and appearance the fallicy of which few will be at the pains to search out and detect." The concept of Parliamentary sovereignty when applied to the American colonies, he says, contradicted the initial premise of the argument advanced for it: that the colonies had rights subordinate to Parliament's—rights of specific validity even if "circumscribed within their respective limits." Since the purpose of all government was to secure the people in whatever rights they had, what Parliament in its sovereign power was attempting to do was to secure America's rights by destroying them, an action that "savours of contradiction and is plainly self-repugnant." To preserve something by destroying it, Johnson believed, was patently absurd.

His mind instinctively sought circularities, anomalies, and contradictions. Were the new regulations and taxes justifiable as *quid pro quos* for the protection Britain gave the colonies? *What* protection, Johnson asks, "past—or future—or present?" *Past?* "When our forefathers were few and poor and incompassed with innumerable enemies, they greatly needed help and protection, yet then . . . they were left unassisted to their own efforts and the protection of their God." Now that the colonies were numerous and strong, and "scarce an enemy dare lift up his head in all the land"—*now* there was "concern and bustle about it," for now there was wealth "to go into the pockets of placemen and stamp officers." As for Britain's expenses in the recent wars, they had long since been repaid—by the capture of Cape Breton by New Englanders, by direct colonial contributions, and by the vast acquisitions (Canada, Louisiana, Florida) that had accrued to Britain—to *Britain*, "and not a farthing to these colonies." *Protection in the future?* If the colonists' limited money supply is drained off by taxes, "is our protection and security against an invasion better in this situation than with our monies and all the profits of them in our own hands?" It would in fact "expose us to be an easy prey to any inslaving power that may invade us." *For present needs?* What needs? Salaries of governors and common-law judges? "Gross stupidity and superlative nonsense." Conceding that the Crown had a legal right to collect "duties upon navigation," the only visible "need" for the internal taxation of the colonies, he says, was "to support arbitrary courts of admiralty and vice-admiralty and a numerous tribe of stamp officers and taskmasters, all . . . a dead weight upon an honest, industrious community. But is this our better protection?" Or perhaps it was to support the 15,000 regular troops said to have been assigned to the colonies "to awe and keep them in order and make them to submit to these taxes, etc." But even the most craven sycophants of a power-hungry ministry should know that a standing army in time of peace was in flat contradiction to the principles of the British constitution—that it had led to the destruction of the liberties of Rome, France, "and many others"—that it had had catastrophic effects in England in the reigns of Charles I and James II—that it might well give rise to "a Caesar to break off our connection to Great Britain and set up as a protector of the liberties of the colonies"—and finally that it might "plunge us here and at home into a bloody civil war, the damage of which to the nation an hundred thousand hireling scribblers could not countervail."

The evidence of history, Johnson points out, was compelling. Assuming, as almost every writer of the time did, that "human nature [was] the same as in foregoing ages, and that like cause will have like effects," what, he asks, were the likely consequences of the new measures? Throughout history such grievances had caused "the most terrible civil wars and rivers of blood in England." The threat to immemorial rights had caused the Barons' War under King John; the raising of taxes without consent and the creation of "arbitrary courts . . . corruption of trials . . . trampling upon the privileges of royal charters . . . the refusing to hear petitions . . . arbitrary suspense of laws" had resulted in the Glorious Revolution.

The pattern of these crises was only too clear. A ruthless gang of corrupt power-seekers panics a weak but liberty-loving nation with cries, first of nonexistent dangers, then of the immediate need for *"better security and protection";* deliberately misinforms and deludes an essentially right-minded sovereign into building up instruments of power (new offices to buy the allegiance of public people; standing armies to intimidate the private) which it and not the sovereign would know how to use in a crisis; and finally begins its assault on the most vulnerable member of the body politic, gradually working inward to the heart.

So in the present circumstances, Johnson writes, the ministry attempts to panic the nation with unreal dangers, among them the fear that the colonies were secretly plotting to throw off their dependence on Britain; then undertakes new programs—of trade regulation, of tax collection—to multiply the "places" at its disposal and to weaken the capacity to resist; finds excuses to station troops in America; deliberately misinforms the Crown about conditions in the colonies; and step by step moves closer to its ultimate goal, the destruction of liberty everywhere in the British world. For if the liberties of Americans are most immediately affected by the Stamp Act,

> in the conclusion it may equally affect the subjects in Britain and Ireland. If the colonies are inslaved, no doubt Ireland will soon be stamped and inslaved also . . . nothing but inexpediency now restrains from taxing Ireland . . . , and if this succeeds it will be so great an accession to the number of placemen and to the power of the m—y that the inexpediency will soon be got over as to Ireland also; and then I conceive the liberty of Great Britain will be worth very little and cannot long survive.

Parliament, moving gradually at the will of an imperious ministry, "first on the colonies—then upon Ireland—then upon Great Britain itself," could destroy the liberties of Britain. But in the end, the effort, Johnson concludes, was not likely to succeed. For America would rise to its dangers and fight for its freedom—with two possible consequences. If the British people and their government responded wisely to the colonists' resistance, these early efforts of the ministry would be reversed, the chief manipulators cast out, and the country and its empire put back on their former course. If the proper responses were not forthcoming, the result would be not ministerial success but "a very fatal civil war": "such a revolt and wide breach" between Britain and America "as could never be healed"; "a bloody civil war in which, by sending away their men of war and forces against America [the British people] would have every thing to fear—from the sword in their own bowels from the powers of France and Spain and the invasion of the Pretender, who would not fail to improve such an opportunity"; a "most unnatural war with the colonies," resulting not only in "the loss of two millions of the best affected subjects" but also "one third, some say one half, of the profits of the national trade." He hopes, however, "in the mercy of God, things may never be pushed to this bloody! this dreadful issue! which must be attended with infinite ill consequences to the mother country and colonies, and, considering the advantage France and Spain would certainly make of such a crisis, could scarce fail of ending in the ruin of England and America." Americans must prevent it from happening not only by being generally vigilant at this early stage but by launching a specific program of action, which Johnson crisply outlines: investigation of the truth; petition for redress; propaganda to counter the misinformation ("printing and dispensing many thousands of the tracts . . . it can't fail of a great and good effect"); and the organization of resistance on a continental scale.

Johnson's six newspaper articles, written and published in a short period of time in the fall of 1765, encapsulate almost the entire range of arguments and issues that would be discussed in the decade that followed. They bring to bear on the Stamp Act crisis the everyday inheritance of British political thought, and while occasional phrases

and references—"taskmasters," "councellors of Rehoboam's stamp"—
reveal a mind attuned to the language of the Bible, they can in no
significant way be described as derivatives or applications of essentially religious ideas. There is scarcely a notion in the series that is
not squarely compatible with, if not essentially repetitive of, ideas
that had been familiar in opposition writing, including that of the most
un-Puritan Bolingbroke, for half a century, or that would not be advocated in the coming years by Americans of every denomination and
persuasion and by Englishmen as different as Burke and Priestley.

How does Johnson's fast-day sermon, *Some Important Observations*,
preached from the pulpit of Lyme's First Congregational Church and
written at almost the same time as the *New London Gazette* articles,
relate to the six essays?

Johnson's sermon translates the political arguments of the six essays
into a universal and categorical language of the highest moral sanction. Setting out "to arouse and animate" his listeners by laying before
them an ultimate extrapolation of their problems, he associates the
colonists' situation with that of the Jews oppressed in Egypt, not by
explicitly analogizing the two but by conflating themes and episodes;
and he then probes in this cosmically dilated example "the general
nature and consequences" of the category of evil the colonists were
faced with. The four main headings he lists at the start and follows
in the body of the sermon are topics that allow him to examine in
the magnification of the Bible story implications too subtle or too
extravagant for the crude and still unresolved politics of the Stamp
Act crisis, and to do this in a mode of discourse so deeply familiar to
his audience and so much a part of their moral universe as to command their immediate assent.

The conflation of the biblical and secular historical worlds—a process familiar to every eighteenth-century preacher and for which there
existed an authoritative model in Samuel Shuckford's famous *"Connection": The Sacred and Prophane History of the World Connected*
(1728)* —is continuous throughout the sermon, and it results not in
a single sustained identification of images but in a shifting series of

---

* Shuckford's *"Connection,"* which, to judge from a footnote reference on page 16 of the published
sermon, Johnson had at his side as he wrote, was an effort to complete the earlier work of the
orientalist Humphrey Prideaux, who in his *Old and New Testament Connected* . . . (1716–18) had
combined scriptural and secular sources to write the history of the world from the point the Old
Testament leaves off to where the New Testament begins. Shuckford's aim was to write a

overlays—of individuals, events, and statements—the net impact of which is an unspecified yet comprehensive portrayal of seventeenth- and eighteenth-century problems in biblical terms. So, in this costume drama, the Old Testament Jews descended into Egypt in the condition of the Puritans escaping from Archbishop Laud: they were a "free people . . . they had a right to freedom afterwards, as they had done nothing to forfeit it, and no man nor nation had a right to take it from them." Then the image blurs in the confusing identification of Indians and Egyptians, but quickly refocuses on Pharaoh and the Stuarts. The Mosaic confrontation becomes the Exclusion Crisis, with Pharaoh exercising the Stuarts' dispensing power, to his own inevitable doom, as once again "cruel oppressions prove the means of [a free people's] deliverance." The focus shifts ("so it happened in the case of Rehoboam's oppression of the ten tribes"), shifts again ("so also in the oppression of Holland, which brought on the revolution and independency of those high and mighty states"), and shifts again ("and it is possible that sooner or later it may happen to the British colonies"), and yet again (for "Rome fell by corruption"), and settles into one of the great flights of rhetoric on the theme of corruption (the purest milk of eighteenth-century opposition thought) in the literature of the Revolution:

> if the British empire should have filled up the measure of its iniquity and become ripe for ruin; if a proud, arbitrary, selfish, and venal spirit of corruption should ever reign in the British court and diffuse itself through all ranks in the nation; if lucrative posts be multiplied without necessity and pensioners multiplied without bounds; if the policy of governing be by bribery and corruption, and the trade and manufactures of the nation be disregarded and trampled under foot; if all offices be bought and sold at a high and extravagant price, which

---

similarly composite history of the world, conflating biblical and secular sources, from the creation of the world to the point Prideaux picked up the story. The task remained unfinished at his death (1754), but the volumes he did complete were often reprinted in the mid-eighteenth century and became a standard reference work, especially for the clergy. The task that Shuckford originally undertook was completed a century later by Michael Russell, the prolific Bishop of Glasgow and Galloway, in his *Connection . . . To Complete the Works of Shuckford and Prideaux . . .* (3 vols., 1827). Though Shuckford himself had no political goal in writing the book, the information he assembled and even more the method he used proved invaluable for writers like Johnson who did. For other references to Shuckford in the writings of the Revolution, see Bernard Bailyn, *The Ideological Origins of the American Revolution* (Cambridge, Mass., 1967), 33.

in the end must come out of the subject in exorbitant fees of office or lawless exactions; and if, to support these shocking enormities and corruptions, the subjects in all quarters must be hard squeezed with the iron arms of oppression—thence we may prognosticate the fall of the British empire—its glory is departing—the grand pillars of the state tremble, and are ready to fail.

The king is Pharaoh—the king is James II—Charles I—*Ahasuerus*, "when Esther must go in to petition the king (in a time of great calamity, great like ours, yea greater than ours)." The conflation is continuous and infinitely flexible. So "there arose a new king over Egypt, which knew not Joseph"—that is to say, who was "wilfully ignorant, or very ungratefully forgetful, of the eminent services done to the nation by the Jews"—which is to say, ungrateful and forgetful "of the good services the colonists have done for Great Britain . . . services in which the colonists, at a vast expense of blood, toil, and treasure, have greatly contributed to the wealth, power, and glory of the British empire"—though Britain "knew not Joseph."

The fusion, abstraction, and magnification of the immediate, parochial world into a mythic, dilated universe allow Johnson to probe freely the hidden impulses and the ultimate dangers of the problems the colonists faced. Slipping easily from the biblical *Ur*-world to present-day realities, he expounds at length the innocence not only of "our gracious King (whom God forever bless)," but of Parliament and the British people in general, and fixes the blame for the present calamities on those latter-day Hamans, "the late British ministry" and their tools and hangers-on in England and America. Their ambitions are nothing new; such lusts as theirs are immemorial, elemental, racial; and their techniques of corruption are as patterned as the movements of the tides. Inevitably they promote falsehoods calculated to panic the innocent; inevitably they raise the cry that a peaceful subordinate people plans to rise in rebellion. Thus Exodus i, 9, 10, 11: " 'Come on, let us deal wisely with them, least . . . when there falleth out any war, they join also unto our enemies . . . and so get them up out of the land.' " Here, Johnson writes, "here you have the grand, the whole strength of the enslaving cause; nothing can be added to it of any avail." For designers of "enslaving measures" needed then what they need now and always will need: a "colourable show of necessary, deep, refined policy," and they therefore devised the "plausible pretext of danger of Israel's independency." Some such "popular turns" must always be given to efforts of this sort "otherwise they are so abominable to nature they cannot go down with a people of common sense and honesty." And so, educated by this "specimen of what has been commonly practised by arbitrary enslavers in all ages," the colonists must be quick to respond to false accusations of seeking independence from England. They must be quick to point out (as Johnson does at great length) that such dark and false prophecies of colonial independence, if acted upon, will inevitably become self-fulfilling, as they did in the case of the ten tribes, in the oppression of Holland, in the deliverance from Egypt—" 'violent arbitrary oppressions has drove the oppressed into that state of independency which the oppressors feared and the oppressed by no means desired.' " Given a "wise, kind, and gentle administration of the colonies: they have no temptation to independency," but if "there be left to the colonies but this single, this dreadful alternative—slavery or independency—they will not want time to deliberate which to choose." Take warning in time, therefore; forestall the choice of such alternatives, and put to use the ample securities that are part of the "transcendent excellencies of the British constitution," the greatest instrument for the protection of freedom, Johnson writes, ever devised by the wit of man.

The sermon probes motives, explains tendencies, counsels action, not on the basis simply of reason, political theory, and ordinary historical evidence but of what are seen as the profoundest experiences of humanity. It translates political arguments into cosmic imperatives, and, freed thereby from the restraints of ordinary debate, presents a magnified version of present problems that is at once clearer, less tractable, and politically more dangerous than what had appeared in the *Gazette* essays. In this way, and not because of its Calvinist derivation or the ritual "jeremiad" that Johnson includes toward the end, the fast-day sermon—a brilliant performance of its kind—reveals the force of religious ideas in the process by which political arguments became a revolutionary creed.

· · ·

Johnson's publications in the fall of 1765 are the highlights of his public career. Little otherwise is known about him. A graduate in 1743 of Yale College, of which he became a Fellow thirty years later, he married three times, fathered eight children, was appointed pastor of the Lyme church in 1746 at the age of twenty-two, and served there successfully and contentedly until his death forty years later. In theology he was conservative, an adherent of the severely predestinarian New Divinity, publishing in the year of his death a 400-page treatise attacking Universalist heresies and the notion "that the end of the creation of the moral world was the happiness of the creature." His only other publication is an election sermon of 1770, an ordinary performance that follows the formulas of the genre closely and without flair. Legend has it that his remarkable outburst of 1765 was inspired by a neighbor of his, one John McCurdy. It may be more reasonable to suppose that Johnson's mind and imagination simply took fire in the explosive atmosphere of the Stamp Act crisis and burned, briefly, with a hard and brilliant flame.

II

THEMES

7

1776 in Britain and America: A Year of Challenge— A World Transformed

IT STARTED MEEKLY ENOUGH. In London, on New Year's day 1776, Dr. Johnson's friend, the Presbyterian divine James Fordyce, D.D., delivered in the Monkwell Street chapel an elevating discourse in three parts entitled *The Character and Conduct of the Female Sex, and the Other Advantages To Be Derived by Young Men from the Society of Virtuous Women*. But ten days later the first of a yearlong series of blasting challenges to the structure and foundation of Anglo-American life and thought tore through the thin membrane of established civility and began a release of energies that would transform the world.

Thomas Paine's *Common Sense*, published on January 10, is no simple argument for American independence. It is a cry of outrage and a searing indictment of the British political world, with its casually accepted hypocrisies and its revered constitutional myths that papered over the reality of what Paine saw as a brutal oligarchy crushing the human spirit. The pamphlet was a product not of the loosely structured and prosperous Philadelphia in which it appeared but of the marginal gentility of the semi-dispossessed of London, faced with destitution at the edge of squalor—a desperate world from which Paine had personally escaped barely a year before his pamphlet appeared. He challenged not simply the British government for its violation of the law and spirit of the constitution but the constitution itself. It was, he said, a sanctified fraud, with its supposed balances, by which the mass of the people were hoodwinked into compliance with the rule of a gluttonous monarchy and an aristocracy soft with the rot of corruption. Within a month the pamphlet, reprinted by the thousands, circulated wildly through a population three thousand miles removed from the source of Paine's passion yet scandalized and energized by its message.

Paine's theme was the corruption of a once-free people, their brutalization, and the threat of a nation's decline. On February 17 the same theme, worked out on a literary canvas that stretched across half the globe and through nearly a thousand years of tumultuous history, found expression in the first volume of Gibbon's *History of the Decline and Fall of the Roman Empire*. No act of political defiance but a sustained masterpiece of literary elegance and historical narration, the *Decline and Fall* nevertheless—in spite of Gibbon's own belief in the social advantages of religious conformity—challenged, by its irony, its wit, its sardonic deflation of pomposity, the established pieties of the day: the cant and hypocrisy of complacent churchmen and the sanctimoniousness of ordinary Christians who dealt in cruelty and called it Truth.

Every literate mind warmed to Gibbon's book, which explained, as no other work of the time, how ecclesiastical and clerical bigotry combined with barbarism had destroyed a brilliant civilization to which Britain might yet be heir. Though most readers, like the *Monthly Review*, wished its author long life and health to complete the massive work, Gibbon's challenge was nevertheless felt. Before the year was out a clerical phalanx, formed to justify the ways of Christianity to men and to set the record straight, had accepted the challenge. Gibbon responded to the rebuttals, especially to a certain East Apthorp, vicar of Croydon near London and formerly rector of Christ Church in Cambridge, Massachusetts. Always quick off the mark to defend Anglican episcopacy against its challengers, Apthorp produced a high-minded and unctuous book, *Letters on the Prevalence of Christianity before Its Civil Establishment, with Observations on a Late History of the Decline of the Roman Empire*, which Gibbon happily skewered. The learned and pious Reverend Apthorp, Gibbon wrote, had taken on too large a task. So many "collateral and accessory ideas" had crowded in on the valiant rector as he had assembled material for his single-handed defense of Christianity that he had finished his book without ever getting around to discussing the *Decline and Fall*. "I could only consider it," Gibbon wrote demurely, "a mark of his esteem that he has thought proper to begin his approaches at so great a distance from the fortifications which he designed to attack."

Gibbon was the gentlest of challengers, for no one loved the ambience of the establishment more than he, and his *History* was the most graceful of polemics. Neither graceful nor gentle but powerfully challenging and destined to achieve contemporary fame greater than either Gibbon's book or Paine's pamphlet was another London publication of February 1776, Richard Price's *Observations on the Nature of Civil Liberty, the Principles of Government, and the Justice and Policy of the War with America*. . . . The challenge of this 128-page tract, which before the year was out went through thirteen printings in England and ten more in Dublin, Philadelphia, New York, Boston, Charleston, Edinburgh, Leyden, and Paris, lay only in part in its fervent justification of the American cause and its systematic and cogent refutation of every argument that had ever been put forward in defense of Britain's policies. In greater part the force of the book lay in its analysis of the intrinsic nature of liberty and the remarkable conclusions Price reached from this analysis.

There should be, he said, a Congress of Europe, with a senate of representatives of the various nation-states to manage "the *common* concerns of the united states [of Europe]," arbitrate disputes among these states, and enforce their decisions by means of a common European army. Closer to home, the British House of Commons should be completely purged of its gross corruptions. An electorate of only 5,723 people, he pointed out, most of them from the lowest part of the population, elects half of the Members, who in any case, because of patronage, are merely "mock representatives." It is simply, he wrote, "an abuse of language to say that [such a] state possesses liberty." Further, the idea must be eliminated that Parliament, even if purged of its corruptions, had sovereign power in itself. Parliament is nothing but a trustee of power that resides "in the PEOPLE," and it should be held strictly accountable for that trust. Further still, he argued that if a choice had to be made between despotism and anarchy, both equally the opposite of liberty, *anarchy* was to be preferred, since lawless mobs at least create "an animation which is favourable to the human mind and which puts it upon exerting its powers"; and in any case mobs have no system or structure and so cannot survive, while despots have armed force, are persistent, and in time reduce human faculties to "stillness and torpor." Finally, "no one community can have any power over the property or legislation of another community that is not incorporated with it by a just and adequate representation." If it does have such a power, the result is a slavery that is worse than the "slavery of private men to one another," for an imperial power is physically distant from its subjects and "cannot be a witness to the sufferings occasioned by its oppressions or a competent judge of the circumstances and abilities of the people who are governed." There is, consequently, no check to rapacity, no grounds for remorse or pity, and no hope that the subordinate state will ever have the power to throw off the master state. There is *no* situation, he wrote, *none whatever*, in which one state may rightfully impose authority over another. The only acceptable association of peoples or states are *voluntary* assemblages in which no one element rules the other by its own determination.

Price's *Observations* was a blatant challenge to the entire political establishment, and replies poured from the presses. Before the end of the year no fewer than thirty-four books and pamphlets, in addition to a series of fifteen letters in the *Morning Chronicle*, were published to refute Price's tract. Some were written by leading figures—Edmund Burke, Dr. Johnson, Adam Ferguson, James Macpherson, the Archbishop of York, the Bishop of London, the Reverend John Wesley— some by hired hacks led by the notorious libeler and jailbird Dr. Shebbeare. Price received anonymous letters threatening his life; people stared at him in the streets; handbills were circulated charging that he was a foreign agent. "I am become," he wrote, "so marked and obnoxious that prudence requires me to be very cautious," and he gave up corresponding with Benjamin Franklin. But the force of his challenge remained undiminished by the replies. He was celebrated by every dissident and radical in Britain and America; Turgot, Necker, and Condorcet wrote from France to make his acquaintance. And his attack on Parliament seemed to release a torrent of abuse on that core of the governmental system.

Thus Major John Cartwright, a pro-American radical commencing a long career as a political reformer, tossed off a pamphlet of boiling abuse on the existing Parliamentary system. Its title summarized its contents: *Take Your Choice! Representation and Respect: Imposition and Contempt. Annual Parliaments and Liberty: Long Parliaments and Slavery*. He minced no words. The House of Commons, he declared, was "filled with idle school-boys, insignificant coxcombs, led-captains and toad-eaters, profligates, gamblers, bankrupts, beggars, contractors, commissaries, public plunderers, ministerial dependents, hirelings, and wretches that would sell their country, or deny their God, for a guinea." Britain stands, he declared, "at a precipice tremendous to look from," and only a total overhaul of the British government that included the introduction of universal manhood suffrage and annually elected parliaments could save it.

But neither Paine's *Common Sense* nor Gibbon's *History*, nor Price's *Observations*, nor Cartwright's *Take Your Choice!* was the most challenging or most influential publication of that extraordinary year. On March 9, a bare three weeks after Gibbon's first volume was issued and four weeks after Price's tract appeared, Adam Smith's *Wealth of Nations* was published. Its target was the foundations of political economy; its goal was the demolition of government regulations including the structure of mercantilist controls which bound Britain to its colonies; and its presumption was the belief that the release of personal self-interest and unbound economic energies, rather than their regulation and management by the state, would enhance the wealth of nations. Smith's book was recognized from the day of its publication as the voice of a new age and, as opposed to tracts like *Common Sense* or Price's *Observations*, a monument of critical intelligence likely to redirect the course of economic development at home and throughout the British world. Its merit, the *Monthly Review* declared, was of a higher order than that of style and composition. It arises "from the depth and accuracy with which the author has investigated a subject of so complex and intricate a nature, from the truth of the principles which he has established, and from the importance and utility of the conclusions which he has enabled his readers to deduce."

And the challenges continued to mount. On the 18th of April—six weeks after the appearance of the *Wealth of Nations*—Jeremy Bentham's *Fragment on Government* was published, anonymously. Bentham's book was cast deliberately as a challenge—he meant to be destructive. His aim, he wrote, was *"to overthrow,"* and his target was nothing less than the fundamental principles of the British constitution—the famous doctrine of the mixed constitution—as expressed in William Blackstone's revered *Commentaries on the Laws of England*. But the twenty-eight-year-old barrister, whose utilitarian doctrines would ultimately reach beyond jurisprudence to ethics, logic, and political economy, not only pilloried Blackstone but excoriated the profession that administered the legal system and profited by it. The goal of the law, he declared, was the happiness of the people, not the maintenance of outmoded theories for their own sakes or of intricate rules for the convenience and profit of lawyers—lawyers, he wrote, "impotent to every enterprise of improvement," most of them

> a passive and enervate race, ready to swallow any thing, and to acquiesce in any thing: with intellects incapable of distinguishing right from wrong, and with affections alike indifferent to either: insensible, short-sighted, obstinate: lethargic, yet liable to be driven into convulsions by false terrors: deaf to the voice of reason and public utility: obsequious only to the whisper of interest, and to the beck of power.

By the time Bentham's *Fragment* was being widely read, a far greater challenge, destined to transform the course of Western history, had exploded, and its first consequences were being felt throughout the Anglo-American world. In far-off Philadelphia the Second Continental Congress, recognizing the state of war that had existed for over a year and responding to the rising aspirations of Americans from Canada to Florida, not only declared its participating thirteen states to be a separate nation equal to all other nations but gave reasons for doing so that were so utterly idealistic and so rational—and yet so manifestly practical—that they stood as a threat and a challenge to every political system that existed. Government, Jefferson wrote, was self-evidently a mere instrument, more or less useful, by which men, born equal, seek to secure their lives and liberties and their right to pursue happiness; when a government violates these purposes, it is, he said in a phrase that would ring through the palaces of Europe, "the right of the people to alter or to abolish it."

To this challenge, unacceptable to any government that then existed, replies were quickly struck off—in September, *An Answer to the*

Declaration of the American Congress, by Bentham's needy friend, the pamphleteer John Lind, hired by the British government to speak for it (he had earlier been hired to refute Price); in October, *Strictures upon the Declaration of the Congress at Philadelphia,* by the exiled former governor of Massachusetts, Thomas Hutchinson, desperate to prove, by demonstrating the flimsiness of the charges against the king, that the colonists had been determined to break away no matter what Britain (or he) had done. But these and other replies were scarcely heard against the ringing affirmations of the Declaration, which made real an ideal, a pure concept, of rational government never acted on before.

The impetus of the colonies' defiance and challenge to the basis of all existing governments swept across the land. Before the end of the year six American states, having shed like a snake's skin the formal integument of imperial government, wrote and formally adopted new constitutions of government based to some degree on rational principles, and two others drew up preliminary drafts. All of them sought to incorporate into constitutional law the program of reform that had been vainly advocated by English reformers since the time of Walpole, thereby overcoming, it was believed, the errors of the past and effecting by rational design the proper balance between power and liberty. There were no precedents for documents like these, and they varied greatly, forming a spectrum from South Carolina's conservative perpetuation of a magistracy of wealth to Pennsylvania's democratic unicameralism. But all were conceived of as rational, as blueprints by which the everyday actions of government and of men bewitched by power could be judged, constrained, restrained.

The revolution in government, once released, could not be confined. Though the restructuring of government in America embodied neither a triumphant proletarian upheaval nor the success of a peasant *jacquerie* but rather the widely shared aspirations of a reform-minded provincial bourgeoisie and plantation gentry, it nevertheless released a force for change whose direction could not be charted and whose results could not be foreseen. Reformers everywhere were inspired. Though wartime patriotism temporarily dampened their ardor, English radicals found new hope, new proof of the practicality of reform, and new guidelines for the achievements they sought. In America, there were not only soaring expectations but an extraordinary release of imagination that spilled out over the social terrain. Men strained to imagine what might be done, fumbled for expression, groped to formulate ideas they scarcely knew they had.

"You and I, my dear friend," John Adams wrote in his *Thoughts on Government* (published in Philadelphia two days after Bentham's *Fragment* appeared in London) "have been sent into life at a time when the greatest lawgivers of antiquity would have wished to live. . . . When, before the present epocha, had three millions of people full power and a fair opportunity to form and establish the wisest and happiest government that human wisdom can contrive?" For himself, Adams wrote—in the very words of Bentham's hedonistic calculus— the best government is the one that brings "happiness to the greatest number of persons and in the greatest degree." And what form is that? A republic, yes; but not Paine's democratic republic. Then *what* kind of a republic? He ruminated on independent executives and independent judiciaries, on mediating middle branches, and on the danger of their becoming overbearing aristocracies.

The issues were bewildering, as Adams himself admitted, and they were pondered everywhere in America, at all levels of society. So in Virginia, Carter Braxton, contemplating the same problems that Adams had considered, fixed on a different formulation. He wrote off *democratic* republics as the "mere creature of a warm imagination," and argued that in the real world of prosperous America the model must be the constitution of Britain, but purged of all its corruptions according to principles that had long since been explained by British reformers and critics—a line of reasoning that Patrick Henry instantly denounced as "weak, shallow, evasive, and . . . an affront and disgrace to this country." In fact, Henry observed, one particularly sinister expression that Braxton had used called his very Whiggism into serious question.

But there was Whiggism and there was Whiggism—and the varieties multiplied as the problems became clear. In Philadelphia an anonymous writer, attempting *de novo*—as if the problem had never been conceived of before—to define the essential nature and functions of constitutions as such, ended by arguing for unicameralism, not on Paine's ground that simplicity of structure kept government more responsive to the people, but on the more original ground that if interests and factions were confined within a single house they would necessarily become "blended together," and their separate interest would cancel each other out to create a voice for the common good. Two houses, the writer of *Four Letters on Interesting Subjects* calculated, would perpetuate two parties; "the more houses the more parties," and so, if an argument could be made for two houses "the same could be said of twenty houses."

No one could see where the limits would be drawn. Somewhere in the backcountry of New England (no one knows where) a printer (no one knows who) struck off a clumsy, ill-written anonymous pamphlet, *The People the Best Governors*, that out-Paine'd Paine, out-Price'd Price, and exceeded even Cartwright's extremism by designing a "popular or a representative government" in which every officeholder would be elected directly by the people and would be held strictly and continuously accountable for his actions in office. Every voter ("any orderly free male of ordinary capacity and more than 21 years of age") would have the individual right at any time to prefer charges against any public official by personally presenting grievances directly to the legislature. The principle was clear: "The people best know their own wants and necessities, and therefore are best able to rule themselves. . . . The people are now contending for freedom, and would to God they might not only obtain, but likewise keep it in their own hands."

These were challenges of mind and understanding; but there were challenges of force and of statecraft too. Units of the British army, which had conquered the world a mere fifteen years before, were first mauled in battle by a makeshift militia of provincial American farmers and townsmen, then, between March and December 1776, were forced to withdraw from their headquarters in Boston, were evaded in a series of battles on Long Island, Manhattan, and in New Jersey, and were taken by surprise and partly destroyed by ill-organized and exhausted American troops on a freezing Christmas night.

During precisely the same months the Congress, reaching toward an unlimited reformation of the evils that beset mankind, had reconceived the basic principles of international relations, drafted a model of treaties between the United States and the state of Europe based less on the irrationality of power than on the rational self-interest of commerce, and had dispatched as its first ambassador abroad that cynosure of the international Enlightenment, the seventy-year-old Benjamin Franklin. On December 3, Franklin arrived in France to begin his sensational embassy to Versailles, which more than any other single event or circumstance brought the American challenge into the heart of the *ancien régime*.

A year of extraordinary, world-transforming challenges in every sphere of life—in ideology, in politics, in government, in religion, in economics, in law, in the uses of military force, and in the basic principles of international relations. In the annals of Western history there is probably no equivalent *annus mirabilis*, so far-reaching in its challenges and in the range of its ultimate consequences. How can it be explained?

Not by reducing it to a collection of discrete events and limiting its range. Of course, each of the events and publications of 1776 has its own immediate history and its own immediate cause and motivation. *Common Sense* had been commissioned by Franklin and Benjamin Rush in 1775 as a history of the Revolutionary movement; Bentham's *Fragment* was an almost accidental offshoot of a work of much grander design that he had been contemplating for some time; Gibbon had conceived of his *History* twelve years before it appeared; Smith's *Wealth of Nations* had been ten years in the writing; and American independence had been the object of passionate discussion long before the decisive resolution was finally passed. Yet there was an underlying unity in these various events and documents, a general character to these scattered challenges.

The connections among these events and publications must be seen. Adam Smith advocated the release of human self-interest as a means of introducing reason, and through reason prosperity, into the economic relations among men; American merchants, with no help from the Scottish professor, had reached the same conclusions in their own immediate concerns, and Congress did too in redesigning the relations among nation-states. Bentham pleaded for the wholesale rationalization and codification of the formulaic, precedent-bound legal system as a matter of principle; American reformers, led by Jefferson and Wythe, set out to do precisely the same, at the same time as American constitution writers were moving away from the sanctified but half-mythological mixed constitution that Bentham pilloried toward a more utilitarian balance of functioning branches of government. Gibbon, though a conservative supporter of the status quo, nevertheless mocked the Church and its hypocrisy when empowered by the force of the state; Americans so weakened the linkage between church and state that such traditional associations became things of the past even before Jefferson's luminous "Act for Establishing Religious Freedom" enacted into law principles that Gibbon, who despised the American Revolution as the work of barbarous clowns, would have been happy to claim as his own. What happened in America was hoped for elsewhere—not by all, but by some, in Ireland and Scotland as well as in England, who sensed some underlying movement of the world, some latent torque or twist or turn in the foundations of society to which ideas and public institutions had failed to adjust.

Whatever the underlying phenomenon may have been, it was neither local nor simple, and it cannot be explained by mechanical linkages between economic interest and personal motivation. Nothing simple, nothing local, nothing mechanical, can explain the challenges of 1776. Something general and fundamental was at work throughout the Anglo-American world to which men variously responded and over which they variously sought some means of control.

What was this elemental movement of the world, and how was it related to the extraordinary events and the remarkable profusion of challenging and prophetic publications that appeared within the span of a single year? Let us approach the question at a distance, and attempt to locate first its outer boundaries.

There are, to begin with, two sets of particularly striking, and relevant, facts. The first relates to economic growth. Though the beginning of the great breakthrough into self-sustained industrial development did not take place until the 1780s, all the significant indicators had been rising quickly since the mid-1740s. Britain's imports had trebled in the three decades after 1745, its foreign trade as a whole rising by almost 3 percent a year. Industrial production was climbing swiftly. The output of woolen goods was growing 13 or 14 percent each decade before 1776, pig iron production 40 percent. The annual value of cotton exports rose 174 percent in the third quarter of the century; coal production doubled between 1760 and 1780, and most of the metals and mining industries were in the midst of a great surge of expansion which lasted for nearly two decades after 1748. The entire generation that had reached maturity at the end of the Seven Years' War lived all its life in an economy that, despite irregularities and setbacks, was sustaining the highest growth rate that the British economy had ever known. On a base of 100 for 1700, the total real output of the British economy reached 115 in 1740, 147 in 1760, and 167 in 1780.

A significant part of this expansion is accounted for by the spectacular growth of the American markets. England's exports to North America increased almost eightfold from 1700 to 1773; between 1750 and 1773 they rose 120 percent; and in the five years from 1768 through 1772 they rose 43 percent. At the same time American production was growing steadily if irregularly, and its sales to Britain rose proportionately. From 1700 to 1773 North American exports to England almost quadrupled; in the two decades before independence the gain was 64 percent.

Economic growth was everywhere—irregular, to be sure, blocked temporarily by war emergencies, restricted from time to time in certain areas and commodities as the economy lurched through complex passages, but rising steadily despite all the dips and specific variations. There were correlative developments on all sides—in improved communications, for example: 800 turnpike trusts were created in England in the twenty years before 1770, which helped make a cultural nation of a congeries of regional enclaves.

The second set of basic facts—fundamental to economic growth itself—was the growth of the population, and this before the fabulous takeoff of the demographic trajectory of the early industrial era. In 1700 the combined population of the British Isles and mainland North America was an estimated 8.4 million; in 1770 it was 13.3 million. This gross rise of 58 percent masks significant regional variations. In these seven decades the combined English and Welsh population grew only 23 percent, but the Irish population grew 73 percent (4 percent in the '60s alone) and the Scottish 67 percent (6 percent in the '60s). Far greater than any of these increases, however, was the remarkable growth of the North American population. It increased more than eightfold in the years from 1700 to 1770—from 250,000 to 2,150,000; in the single decade of the 1760s the American population rose 35 percent.

These economic and demographic data lie in the background of the concatenation of events of 1776. They are fundamental, but they form only the outer boundaries of the explanation one seeks. One comes closer as one distinguishes certain discrete components and characteristics of the population growth. The differences in the rates of growth of the separate peoples of Great Britain had created a significant redistribution of the population. In 1700 the combined populations of Ireland and Scotland had been 40 percent of the combined populations of England and Wales; by 1770 they had become 56 percent. Further, the increase within the English population alone had not been evenly distributed; it had concentrated almost exclusively in Lancashire and the Midlands, where the new industrial cities of Birmingham, Manchester, and Leeds had risen from insignificance in the course of a single generation, and in the London area, now the largest urban concentration in the Western world with over 750,000 inhabitants (it had been just under 600,000 in 1700).

But this redistribution of population balances was not simply the result of differential growth rates. It was the consequence, too, of the extraordinary mobility of the population throughout the English-speaking world, and this was perhaps the most important fact of all. Large segments of the growing multitude within the British Isles were in motion through these years, and not only from village to village and town to town. People in large numbers were moving across wide spaces, through whole countries, from continent to continent. Indeed, the spatial and demographic magnitudes involved can be fully appreciated only if one conceives of a map of large and peculiar dimensions. It must embrace parts of three continents and be detailed down to individual villages and land units of a few square miles. It must center on the British Isles, but focus not on London or the home counties but somewhere in the Irish Sea, with as much detail on northern Ireland and the Scottish Highlands as on southeastern England or the Midlands. It must extend to the Western Hemisphere and include the North American continent west to the Mississippi. It must reach selectively into the continent of Europe, especially along the Rhine Valley and into northern Switzerland; and it must reach, too, into several deep enclaves on the west coast of Africa.

With such a map before us we can begin to grasp the character of the population movements that were taking place in the early years of the reign of George III. There were two major flows: first, a drift south from northern Britain into quickly growing population centers in England; and second, a drainage west to America and then, within America, a complex dispersal in a myriad of separate streams, moving strongly and quickly along routes of easy access leading to rich new lands, weakly across difficult terrain and into lands contested by the Indians, and in this remarkably diffuse way peopling, thinly, an enormous territory, and forming—at transshipment points, route intersections, and military camp sites—hundreds of small concentrations which in another generation would swell into the towns and cities of the trans-Appalachian West.

In this British, transatlantic, and intra-American migration lie some of the deepest elements of the explosion of 1776, and we must examine it more closely.

Throughout the decade and a half before 1776, while the British government grappled with the problems of Anglo-American relations and while American leaders discovered the logic of their own opposition, there was a heavy, continuous, and, as it proved, uncontrollable flow of transatlantic migration. The magnitudes and the consequences were remarkable. Years later the Anglo-Irish historian W. E. H. Lecky, summarizing contemporary responses to the emigration from northern Ireland, wrote that the loss of so great a number of Irish Protestants to America in the mid-eighteenth century ended forever the hope of balancing the religious communities in the island as a whole and hence destroyed the possibility of ever creating stability and peace in that distracted land. He may well have been right. In the twelve years before American independence about 55,000 Protestant Irish emigrated to America, which is 2 percent of the total Irish population as of 1760. And the Scottish emigration was proportionately even greater. Scots were leaving for America at the rate of 4,000 a year, totaling some 40,000 in the same period, which is 3 percent of the 1760 population of Scotland. In all, an estimated 125,000 people left the British Isles for America during the twelve years before independence, and they were only part of the great mass of Britons in motion over long distances.

The phenomenon had an observer of genius. Dr. Johnson, touring the Scottish Highlands with Boswell late in 1773, found there what he called an "epidemic desire of wandering." The Highlanders in some places, he wrote in the *Journal* of the trip that he published, "threaten a total secession," and the reasons were not hard to find. The causes of the emigration, he explained, lay in the breakdown of the ancient social structure of the clans and in the rapacity of landlords who raised rents "with too much eagerness." And behind that lay the attraction of America. Typically, he explained, a few enterprisers, taking advantage of local discontents, get grants to American land, circulate tales of "fortunate islands," and set in motion a flow of migrants from among the discontented. "Whole neighbourhoods formed parties for removal, so that departure from their native country is no longer exile." Some end happy in their transplanted environment, but others find that they "are dispersed at last upon a sylvan wilderness, where their first years must be spent in toil . . . and that the whole effect of their undertaking is only more fatigue and equal scarcity." Everything possible must be done to stop this depopulation of Scotland, he insisted. If wearing native costumes "might disincline them from coalescing with the Pennsylvanians or people of Connecticut," let them keep their ancient dress; if retaining arms will do it, let them have arms as before; if rents are too high, force landlords to lower them and compensate them for their loss by pensions.

The problem became almost obsessive for Johnson on his two trips to the Isle of Skye. There, contemplating the deserted land, he hammered away at the dangers of migration and developed a deep animosity to all things American, an animosity that within a year would express itself in his most famous political tract. The thousands that leave Britain are lost to the nation, he wrote in a brilliant image, *"for a nation scattered in the boundless regions of America resembles rays diverging from a focus. All the rays remain but the heat is gone. Their power consisted in their concentration: when they are dispersed, they have no effect."*

Johnson's concern was a general one. Observers of the exodus from the Western Isles noted in 1772 that since 1768 £10,000 had left with the migrants to America, and that "unless some speedy remedy is fallen upon by the government and landholders" not only would northern Britain be fatally depleted but "the continual emigrations from Ireland and Scotland will soon render our [American] colonies independent on the mother country." The bard Rob Donn and the poet Donald Matheson bewailed the poverty and disarray of once proud and respectable Highland families "with their heads brought low, servants in the role of landlords, and . . . the land full of distress." The emigrating Scots, said the poet, were like Children of Israel oppressed by "enslaving" landlords. "Oh praise be to Him of highest glory, who opened a way out [of] there and prepared sustenance for them." Their destinations were mainly Nova Scotia, New York, and above all North Carolina. For from North Carolina had come "such favourable accounts . . . setting forth the richness of the county [*sic*], the cheapness of living, and the certain prospect of bettering their fortunes etc. etc. . . . that half the people of [Sutherland] . . . would emigrate if they were able."

Ireland was no different. Belfast newspapers teemed with letters from recent emigrants, warning of the lies and avarice of shipmasters, of the swindling advertisements of American land speculators, and of the myriad difficulties of resettlement; and they lamented the circumstances that had forced tens of thousands from their homes. "How melancholy is the prospect when poverty at home compels honest and industrious families to expose their lives and quit their established settlements to seek, perhaps in an advanced age, that support amongst strangers in a new world which avarice and corruption have denied them in the land of their nativity." America was a dream—"a dream of escape from oppressive landlords," but a dark and frightening dream too. Tales were published of murder and fearful savagery on the wild Indian frontiers, especially on the border lands of "the people called Cracker, who live above Augusta in the province of Georgia." But the dangers posed by savage natives and "associated banditti . . . committing all manner of robberies and violences" could not stay the exodus from an impoverished land drained of over 12 percent of its total rentals by absentee landlords.

It was a national problem, recognized as such throughout the nation. While Lord Selkirk, shocked at the depopulation of his properties on the Isle of Skye, struggled to retain his people (later his son would give up the fight and devote himself to managing Scottish resettlement in Canada), others in various parts of Britain pressed for Parliamentary action. Draft laws were circulated. In December 1773, two weeks after Dr. Johnson returned from the Hebrides, the Treasury ordered the customs officials in every port of England and Scotland not only to submit reports of the number of emigrants but to interview them and record their reasons for leaving. In the year and a half that followed, 16,000 names were entered—men, women, and children of every "quality" and occupation beneath the rank of "gentleman"; nearly 10,000 of them were heading for the Western Hemisphere. They were laborers, craftsmen, small tradespeople, and farmers from all over the British Isles. The results of the interviews were predictable. The emigrants wanted relief from the pinched circumstances they had known, and above all they wanted land and independence.

The most vivid details were provided accidentally. In 1773 the ship *Bachelor,* sailing for North Carolina from the northern county of Caithness with 280 emigrants, was shipwrecked off the Shetland Islands. The stranded survivors were interrogated at length by zealous local officials. Thirty-one of their testimonies, given at leisure and recorded in extraordinary detail, were sent by the customs officers to London, where they remain to this day. They describe a deeply troubled world, changing quickly, and a people in disarray, lacking any means—political, economic, or social—of setting things right.

William Gordon reported that his grandfather had rented the family's farm for eight marks Scots; Gordon himself was now obliged to pay sixty. The lands on which he had lived for all of his sixty years "have often changed masters, and . . . the rents have been raised on every change" by the tacksman (the tenant-in-chief), who himself had been squeezed by the landlords' increasing demands. Two sons in Carolina had urged Gordon to join them, and he had finally decided to do so "for the greater benefit of his [six remaining] children, being himself an old man and lame, so that it was indifferent to him in what country he died." William Sutherland, a tenant of Colonel McKay "of Bighouse" in Caithness, explained the increase in rents as the result of returning soldiers offering more to the landlords than ordinary farmers could afford; but he considered the personal services that McKay exacted at least as serious a problem, and one with no visible solution. Each year he and his servants had been obliged to plow, cut turf, mix dung, make manure heaps, fertilize, and cut and stack ten fathoms of peat for McKay—"all done without so much as a bit of bread or a drink to [the] servants." In America his children could surely earn their bread more comfortably than that, and in the end they could help support him. John Catanoch agreed: not only had crops failed, bread become dear, and his rent raised from two to five pounds sterling, but his ancient pastureland had been handed over to new tenants, a loss that would ultimately make it impossible for him to raise cattle. Above all, "the landlord exacted arbitrary and oppressive services, which took up about 30 or 40 days of his servants and horses each year."

It was unencumbered land that drew multitudes to America from all over the British Isles, multitudes who, precisely as Dr. Johnson said, were quickly *"scattered in the boundless regions of America [like] rays diverging from a focus."* They did not physically disappear, but "their power [had] consisted in their concentration," and when they were dispersed over vast spaces their impact, their social consequence, seemed simply to dissolve.

So in 1773 a group of discontented farmers, tradesmen, artisans, and weavers in the western Scottish Lowlands formed a joint-stock company to support a settlement in America, sent emissaries to buy land, and designed an ideal Scottish village for their future community. The result, after explorations in New York, Pennsylvania, the Shenandoah Valley, the Ohio country, and North Carolina, was the purchase of half of the wilderness town of Ryegate, Vermont, which they obtained from a New Hampshire land operator who had himself just bought the title to the property from one of the hundreds of groups of town proprietors which Governor Benning Wentworth created at the end of the Seven Years' War. The Scottish paradise, glowing on paper, quickly faded away in reality. Many of the prospective settlers never made it to Ryegate, sixty miles from the Canadian border, two hundred miles by river from Hartford, Connecticut, a hundred and fifty miles overland from Portsmouth, New Hampshire; and those who did could not exclude outsiders, especially since they needed their labor to help clear the land. Before the Revolutionary War was over, the settlers in that remote spot, once part of a distinctive cultural concentration, had dispersed, lost their identity as Scots, and become simply a collection of rural New Englanders with families and friends in Scotland.

Of such efforts as these there were tens of thousands of examples in the half billion acres of land that lay east of the Mississippi. The migrations, settlements, and resettlements were so constant, so complex, and so widely dispersed over so vast a territory that it is difficult to conceive of all of the motion as a simultaneous whole. While this one small community of Scots was attempting to transplant itself to Ryegate, Vermont, ninety-four new towns were being established in Maine, peopled largely from Massachusetts. By 1772 a total of 250 families founded 39 towns on the Penobscot and Kennebec rivers. Between 1760 and 1776 some 20,000 people moved north from southern New England, mainly along the Connecticut River, to settle in the "new grants" of New Hampshire and Vermont, spreading east and west in two streams, the more conservative Calvinists remaining close by the river, the more radical sectarians moving deeper into Vermont. In all, during the sixteen years between 1760 and 1776, 264 towns were settled in New Hampshire, Maine, and Vermont.

Immediately after the capture of Canada in 1759 the area around Lake Champlain and the Mohawk River was reopened for settlement, especially to veterans who had preferential claims; but the speculators were there ahead of them. In the area of Pennsylvania opened by the Treaty of Fort Stanwix in 1768 lay the Wyoming Valley, to which the Susquehanna Company of Connecticut promoted "a massive migration" from Connecticut which ultimately led to violent conflicts between the New Englanders and the Pennsylvania settlers and resulted in 1774 in the annexation of the Wyoming settlements by Connecticut. At the same time the colony of Pennsylvania was selling land even farther west, near the sources of the Ohio River where Pittsburgh would eventually be built. On the day the land office was opened, 2,790 applications were filed; within four months, over a million acres were disposed of, and families from Ireland and from the German principalities on the upper Rhine poured in to create overnight towns with names like Armagh, Derry, and Donegal. But all of this was a prelude to more dramatic movements. Settlers in western Pennsylvania joined with survivors of an earlier migration from Virginia and Maryland to begin an encirclement of the whole eastern half of the North American continent. From western Pennsylvania they drifted down the Ohio, then down the Mississippi River to the new province of West Florida. There they were joined by others from the more populous southern colonies moving overland and north up the Mississippi. The result was the first Florida land boom.

There were new frontiers everywhere. The West Florida settlement is an almost perfect parallel to the settlements going on in precisely the same years two thousand miles to the northeast, in the upper Connecticut River valley, and some of the same groups were involved. The largest single contribution to the first peopling of West Florida was made by two Yankee speculators, Rufus Putnam and Phineas Lyman, who brought 400 families from Connecticut to the lower east bank of the Mississippi and to points along the Gulf of Mexico from Pensacola to Mobile. One Amos Ogden, an impoverished sea captain, managed to get a Crown grant to 25,000 acres of land near Natchez, Mississippi, and in 1772 brought in settlers from New Jersey. Shortly after, others from the Pennsylvania backcountry and North Carolina joined them. By 1774 West Florida had a population of 2,500 whites and 600 slaves; and East Florida numbered 3,000, a population drawn in a few years mainly from the farms and plantations of South Carolina and Georgia.

There is no way to convey the simultaneity of population movement, the constant settlement and resettlement, save by enumeration and illustration. In April 1775 Daniel Boone, acting for the Transylvania Company, which only the year before had purchased one hundred square miles of Kentucky land from the Cherokee Indians, founded Boonesborough, opened a land office, disposed of over half a million acres in a few weeks, founded three more settlements, and convened a legislature before the year was out. Most of the Kentucky settlers came from North Carolina, which itself was then being settled, in part from Pennsylvania (Franklin estimated that 10,000 families emigrated from Pennsylvania to North Carolina between 1760 and 1763); in part from western Virginia (itself only opened between 1771 and 1774); in part from Scotland (5,000 Scots arrived in North Carolina in the decade before 1775); and in part from the Rhineland. In the course of the autumn and winter of 1766 an observer in the town of Salisbury in western North Carolina counted one thousand wagons, many of them full of German-speaking families, rumbling through the town to settlements in the newly opened piedmont. They swept in along four heavily traveled routes: south through the Shenandoah Valley; south through Chesapeake Bay and then west along the Virginia–North Carolina border; northwest along river routes from Cape Fear; and due north along trade routes from Charleston, South Carolina. In 1750 the total population of North Carolina was 45,000; in 1775, 275,000. Similarly, while Georgia supplied settlers to the Floridas, it was itself the scene of a speculative land boom. Between 1763 and 1775 six million acres on the upper Savannah River were opened to settlers, who came from North Carolina, South Carolina, Pennsylvania, the West Indies, and Ulster.

What conditions these hundreds of thousands of migrants lived in can only be imagined, but our imaginations may be stimulated by occasional travel accounts and journals, some of them as startlingly vivid as the reports of the Anglican itinerant the Reverend Charles Woodmason, who depicted scenes of utter primitivism in the North Carolina backcountry. Pittsburgh in the 1760s was the riotous headquarters of hard-drinking traders, mule drivers, and pioneer farmers, most of them accompanied by temporary wives, white or Indian. Day and night, drunken Indians reeled and roared through the village; murder was common on the farms that fringed the fort. Perhaps the most vivid and accurate portrayal of the raw southwestern frontier is found not in historical documents but in fiction—in the unforgettable portrait of early Mississippi in Faulkner's *Absalom, Absalom!* But one thing is clear: this massive, infinitely complex movement of people from all over the British Isles and the Rhineland, from every corner of the older American settlements to almost every region of the unorganized, wild cis-Mississippi universe—all of this frantic peopling of half a continent—was beyond the control, indeed the comprehension, of those who managed the British government.

Before 1768 the minister in official charge of American affairs was the secretary of state for the Southern Department, a post that was held in the seven years between 1761 and 1768 by no fewer than six individuals, appointed and dismissed in rapid succession for reasons that had nothing to do with American land policy, or with American affairs at all. No policy emerged—*could* emerge—from the understaffed and ill-informed office of the secretary of state, who was himself endlessly embroiled in Byzantine intrigues to achieve and maintain some shred of power in the splintered ministries of George III. The need for policy was inescapable, but there was no agreement on the principles or guidelines for managing the western lands, and the machinery to enforce policy, even if policy had existed, was in any case unavailable. The Proclamation of 1763 restricting trans-Appalachian settlement was symptomatic: it was hastily imposed, rested on no coherent understanding of long-term Anglo-American interests, was subsequently amended and superseded by other equally inconclusive regulations, and was largely ignored by land-hungry settlers. After 1768 the chief official was the secretary of state for the colonies, first the Earl of Hillsborough (1768–72) and then the Earl of Dartmouth (1772–75). Of Hillsborough, whose role was crucial, we know very little, but that little is revealing of the nature of the general crisis that was overwhelming the Anglo-American world.

Fifty years of age in 1768, a Member of Parliament from the age of twenty-three, Hillsborough had served twice in the '60s as president of the Board of Trade and Plantations. His portrait, by John Downman, shows languidly half-lidded eyes and slightly curled, disdainful lips. He was the soul of aristocratic hauteur—a veritable Hapsburg duke, a Russian prince. He took an imperious line in Anglo-American relations almost from the day he became secretary of state, and in January 1771 had an abusive interview with Franklin, refusing to accept the famous Philadelphian's credentials as agent for Massachusetts and dismissing Franklin's arguments "with something," Franklin wrote, "between a smile and a sneer." He treated the sophisticated scientist and man of letters, twelve years his senior, with "anger and contempt," Franklin said, then bewildered him with lavish hospitality when the Philadelphian unwillingly visited the Hillsborough estates, but thereafter instructed his servants not to let Franklin inside the door. Franklin, by then effectively ambassador-at-large from America, never forgave him, and did everything in his power to blacken his name and undermine his influence in the government. Hillsborough's character, Franklin wrote, was a compound of "conceit, wrong-headedness, obstinacy and passion"; he was "as double and deceitful as any man I ever met with." But it was no one-way affair: Hillsborough warmly reciprocated Franklin's hatred, and it was Hillsborough who held power. He used it, with patience, duplicity, and skill, to destroy the colossal enterprise of the Grand Ohio Company, which, though a profiteering venture of high-flying speculators, attempted to deal with some of the newly opened western lands on an appropriate scale.

The culmination of a series of frustrated land-speculating organizations, the company, which eventually included in its membership every major American and British land operator (including Franklin) and half the British cabinet, sought a grant of twenty million acres just south of the Ohio at its eastern sources for the establishment of a new interior colony. Hillsborough fought the grant at every turn, tried to sabotage it by encouraging the company to inflate its claims to unmanageable proportions, and succeeded in delaying the grant even after his enemies drove him from office. His obstructive tactics, supported by others in power, were enough to keep the ministry, almost paralyzed by inefficiency and lack of leadership, from concluding the grant; it was still pending when the Tea Party put an end to all further Anglo-American enterprises.

Hillsborough's reasoning and motivation in this important maneuver were never mysterious, however devious his tactics may have been. He conceived of the empire in the narrowest mercantilist terms. The value of North America lay strictly and solely, he believed, in the benefit it could provide for the commerce and navigation "of this kingdom," which meant that the colonies' fisheries were of value, as were its naval stores and the lumber and provisions it could send to the sugar islands. As to inland settlements, much of the American seacoast and offshore islands remained thinly populated,

> and therefore in the abstract consideration of colonisation, I cannot conceive that it can ever be sound policy in this kingdom to allow settlements in places where, though the mildness of the climate and the fertility of the soil may invite colonists, yet none of the above mentioned great national objects are attainable and consequently settlement cannot be of that commercial benefit to the state which it would be of in the other places.

Moreover, "colonies in remote situations" would be difficult to keep "in a just subordination to and dependence upon this kingdom." As to controlling the fur trade in the trans-Appalachian West and maintaining British domination there, "the only two methods of attaining this object are each of them accompanied with such objections as leave my judgment in a state of perplexity I am not able to get over."

On one point, however, Hillsborough had no perplexity. The further opening of North American lands to European settlement would only increase what he took to be the depopulation of the British Isles, and that troubled him profoundly. For he was an Anglo-Irish landowner, whose estates, spread throughout northern Ireland but concentrated in County Down, were in the third generation of multiplication and growth. In the 1770s his Irish properties were approaching the 100,000-acre mark they would attain by the time of his death in 1793. It was this vast private property in Ireland, as much as his public responsibility in London, that was Hillsborough's principal interest. It approached being a public concern, however, for by 1801 the Hillsborough estates in County Down alone contained 4,656 separate tenancies and a tenant population of well over 20,000. Like the Earl of Selkirk, troubled by the depopulation of the Isle of Skye, like Dr. Johnson touring the Highlands, Hillsborough was determined to put a stop to the exodus of British inhabitants to the new freehold lands opening up in America; he was, Franklin reported as early as 1766, "terribly afraid of depeopling Ireland." To prevent that eventuality he favored the legal prohibition of emigration, dealt sensibly with his own tenants, even joining an association to reduce rents, and never wavered in his opposition to western settlement.

To nourish the mercantile empire as it had been conceived in the seventeenth century, to stabilize the agricultural population of northern Ireland and keep the tenants there from joining the exodus that seemed to be depopulating northern Britain—that was the policy that mainly guided Hillsborough's actions, and it was that policy principally that led him into conflict with the American spokesmen. Committed to furthering the prosperity of Ireland, he condemned England's rigid restriction of the Irish economy (and by extension Parliament's limitation of American manufactures), but he had little comprehension of the broad movement of the events of his time. In 1778, after the decisive British loss in the battle of Saratoga, he denounced all proposals for conciliation with America, and even after Yorktown he repeated his hope "that the independence of America would never be admitted." American independence, he declared, "must prove the ruin of this country"; he hoped not to live "to see the day when a contrary opinion should prevail." If Britain lost or abandoned America, "every thing valuable which we possessed as a great trading and maritime nation must shortly follow."

Some Britons did sense the movement of history and the demands of the time, but like Thomas Pownall, who struggled in five successive revisions of his *Administration of the Colonies* to work out a new structure of empire, they were incapable of solving the problems and in any case were not in the seats of power. Others, like Chatham, who did have power and whose vision was grand, could not rally the support they needed. Still others, like Burke, who had brains, imagination, and access to power, were too deeply committed to the existing establishment and too eager to gain control of it to want to probe the problems to their foundations.

Perhaps only Franklin saw the issues with absolute clarity. Loving both Britain and America, convinced that British arms were almost invincible, and knowing what kind of men there were in control of the British government, he could only pray for stability. Conflict, for him, was unnecessary, and might be tragic. For in the end, he believed, the power of the American economy and the size and productivity of the population would overwhelm the opposition to America's development and lead to a gradual and peaceful transformation of Anglo-American relations. *Wait,* he counseled the Boston radicals; in time American grievances will inevitably be redressed, for Britain is in debt and when another war comes they will turn to America for financial help. Then "is the time to say, '*Redress our grievances.*' . . . Our claims will then be attended to and our complaints regarded." "By our rapidly increasing strength we shall soon become of so much importance that none of our just claims of privilege will be, as heretofore, unattended to, nor any security we can wish for our rights be denied us." And he concluded these admonitions to the Boston radicals with words of great wisdom: just "as between friends every affront is not worth a duel, between nations every injury not worth a war, so between the governed and the governing every mistake in government, every encroachment on rights, is not worth a rebellion." But in the end, when the violence he had hoped would never erupt had escalated to open warfare, he changed his tune:

> . . . when I consider the extreme corruption prevalent among
> all orders of men in this old rotten state, and the glorious
> public virtue so predominant in our rising country, I cannot
> but apprehend more mischief than benefit from a closer union.
> I fear they will drag us after them in all the plundering wars
> which their desperate circumstances, injustice, and rapacity
> may prompt them to undertake; and their wide-wasting prod-
> igality and profusion is a gulf that will swallow up every aid
> we may distress ourselves to afford them. Here numberless
> and needless places, enormous salaries, pensions, perquisites,
> bribes, groundless quarrels, foolish expeditions, false accounts
> or no accounts, contracts and jobs, devour all revenue and
> produce continual necessity in the midst of natural plenty. I
> apprehend, therefore, that to unite us intimately will only be
> to corrupt and poison us also.

Franklin knew the incapacity of the British government and the
narrowness of its vision, even when it was in the hands of men like
Hillsborough's successor, the Earl of Dartmouth, whose spirits were
generous and attitudes benign. All about him he saw the evidence of
its inability to cope with the problems of the time.

He lived in London almost continuously for seventeen years, from
1757 to 1775, and knew what was happening to that city. It was to
him a triumph of talent and enterprise, a great center of civilization,
of sophistication and gaiety, of art, and science, and creativity of all
kinds. But it was also a fearful wen of intrigue and corruption, a chaos
of brutality and social conflict, and a school of cheap cynicism and
false values. Its growth had been tumorous and shapeless. It had
continued to expand, as Defoe had observed in 1724, "just as the
pleasure of every builder or . . . the convenience of the people directs
. . . and this has spread the face of it in a most straggling, confused
manner, out of all shape, uncompact, and unequal." In the fifty years
that had followed, the inequalities had deepened. Growth continued
in two different styles and directions. In the West End, a series
of elegant, carefully arranged squares—Berkeley, Grosvenor, Caven-
dish, Bloomsbury—straight streets, and handsome, well-built houses
marked new settlements of the fashionable and rich. In the East End—
Cheapside, Houndsditch, Whitechapel—the sprawling slums grew like

a rat's nest, a pell-mell, stinking, squalid jumble of hovels and huts. There, jerry-built extensions filled the empty spaces, closed out the light, and reduced the streets to filthy lanes. The poorest lived in wet, dark cellars; thousands packed into nasty lodging houses from which arose, a magistrate wrote, "such an inconceivable stench . . . that I have hardly been able to bear it the little time that my duty required me to stay." Only in 1774 had an attempt been made to legislate some rules for future construction, but it would be many years before the impact would be felt.

In fact, while efforts had been made to improve London's lighting, paving, and drainage, its bursting growth out of its medieval structure was almost entirely unregulated. Except for the new West End developments, it was a dirty, dangerous, and disorderly city—its population volatile, its social services more vicious than humane, its constabulary so inadequate that army troops had to be kept at the ready to maintain order in times of riot. And rioting was constant, endemic. There were anti-calico riots and anti-Irish riots, impressment riots and tradesmen riots, riots by coal heavers and riots by weavers; above all, there were political riots, which run continuously through the history of Hanoverian London. They could never be prevented and seldom restrained save by bloody repression.

London was ill-regulated and ill-governed; and this mismanagement, this incapacity, in the midst of ballooning growth in all directions, was typical—symbolic—of the basic problem of the time. Every major institution was in some way inadequate to its task. Unexpected, unplanned, and uncomprehended realities had overwhelmed the formal façades of public life. Compromises had been extemporized between formal structures and informal realities, but these compromises could no longer contain the forces that were powerfully at work in the world.

The Church of England was the formal establishment in religion; but though dissenters were legally denied the full rights of citizenship, in fact by common consent they were allowed to enjoy what the law officially denied them. The hold of Anglicanism on the British community was declining rather than growing with the expansion of the population. The disjunction between theory and fact had become too great, and dissenters of all sorts—Presbyterians, Catholics, even Jews—were beginning to demand the abolition of all religious disabilities.

So too in the economy: there were regulations on all sides, a jungle of regulations; but they were the formal constraints of a system quickly being outmoded and inadequate to foster and mold the new industrial forms that increasingly dominated the economy. What Adam Smith attacked was an intricate protective mesh that had originally been woven around a small commercial plant. These regulations had become more and more elaborate, more and more complex as the plant had grown this way and that, and they had finally been torn through completely by the explosive force of the eighteenth-century economy. There could be no more reweaving of that bewilderingly intricate mercantilist network. It could only be eliminated, to clear the way for new forms and new dimensions of growth. And in this the colonies were intimately involved. For the Navigation Acts were no less anachronistic than the rest of the regulatory system; and while they were not as yet grounds for political revolt, they were harassing, suspect, provocative. Nor could the old economic system provide for the real economic needs of the time: a colonial medium of exchange, for example, which had to be extemporized in thirteen different forms in the face of repressive regulations dictated by the narrow considerations of British business interests.

So too the law: it was the product of an earlier world, a smaller, more cohesive world in which human values had been protected by community responsibility. It had once been protective of growth and of privileges and rights considered to be legitimate; but in the course of time it had in many respects become a system of organized brutality that placed the pettiest property values over the most profound human suffering. Such a system could no longer go unchallenged, unchanged, unreformed; without some kind of adaptation or reform it could not serve a modernizing world of high mobility, swift growth, and broadening political participation.

Above all, the famous political institutions of Hanoverian Britain were antiquated and inadequate to their task. In formal terms they had been created, or re-created, in the settlement after the Glorious Revolution to serve the needs of a conservative squirearchy and the landed aristocracy. But the formal constitution of Britain's famous mixed government had never functioned as prescribed. Under Walpole, in response to the sweeping social and economic developments of the time, an underworld of political manipulation, informal arrangements, clientage, and "corruption" had grown into a system that became the effective constitution of the realm. This informal constitution in fact made the government work, and through its intricate adjustments brought into the benefits of power some of the major new economic interests of the early eighteenth century. But by the 1760s its deficiencies were being revealed and its operations not only challenged but showing signs of breaking down. For, first, it *was* a system of corruption, in that it operated by the regular and open violation of the principles it presumed to uphold, and for that reason alone it was open to attack on moral and political grounds. Second, it was incapable of satisfying the needs of the most powerful new interests rising quickly with the developing economy, interests distinct from those whose domination had been unchallenged a short generation before. And third, as the effective national government it was grossly inefficient.

Parliament was no legislative body, though national legislation was badly needed. It was more an antiquated equity court, or a "grand jury of the nation," convened mainly "to ventilate grievances, meet emergencies of state, and to provide means for the king to run essential services by voting him money"—which was just as well, since its schedule would scarcely have permitted it to function more energetically. Parliament convened in November for three to six weeks, a session which many MPs ignored and which was frequently omitted altogether. There followed a month-long Christmas vacation. The main session lasted from late January until Easter, after which most Members returned home for good—a schedule perfectly calculated to frustrate efforts to deal effectively with current problems, especially problems that arose in colonies three thousand miles away. Executive and administrative bodies followed a similar pattern, though occasionally they met in the summer or for serious work in the fall. Dockets were forever overcrowded, lobbyists frustrated, and administrative agencies overwhelmed with business they could not properly handle.

The political system had been under attack for years, but the criticism had been largely ideological and had come principally from the extremes—the extreme left led by the inheritors of the commonwealth tradition, and the extreme right-wing proto-Jacobites, who dreamed of a purer agrarian world unencumbered by the new forces that so complicated British life. In the '60s the criticism mounted and was more and more commonly heard from those who earlier would have accepted the compromised mixed constitution and the ineffectiveness of government. By the '70s the major opposition groups—not only the Chathamites but also the Rockingham Whigs—operating within the core of the existing political system, launched attacks on the foundations of the government while professing to defend it against corruption from within.

The trigger for most of these attacks was, in one way or another, the American question, and not accidentally. For of all the rickety compromises by which the mid-eighteenth century British system had operated and of all the delicate adjustments of half-understood realities, Anglo-American relations was the most vulnerable and the most likely to collapse. There never had been any constitutional theory to explain and shape Britain's relations with its dependencies in the West. Somehow the already deficient theory of domestic political and constitutional relations had been stretched to accommodate this burgeoning new world, and the result was a clumsy and inefficient empire which projected in magnified form all the increasingly unworkable compromises that lay at the heart of British life.

If domestic politics was corrupt, the Anglo-American political system was bizarre, at times paralytic. The patronage system in colonial appointments was so irrational with respect to American needs that occasionally even the incumbents were embarrassed. And while local conditions in the colonies led to an enlargement of access to the "popular" branches of government, the executives held powers that had been considered autocratic in the reign of James II and that had been eliminated in Britain at the turn of the seventeenth century. Anglo-American political problems could not be isolated because they were magnifications of the domestic problems of Britain. So James Otis, in a ringing passage of a pamphlet of 1765, asked what purpose was served by attempting to justify the lack of American representation in Parliament by citing parallel failures at home. If cities like Manchester, Birmingham, and Sheffield are not in fact represented in Parliament, he declared, "they ought to be."

The regulation of the domestic British economy was increasingly seen by critics as inept, inefficient, irrational: even more so was the mercantilist system that bound the colonies to the home country. It was, indeed, so complex it could scarcely be understood, so irrational it contradicted itself, so unenforceable it invited wholesale evasion. If religious multiplicity made the establishment of a national church merely pretentious in Britain, it made such an establishment ludicrous in the colonies. In one colony (New York) which was supposed to have some kind of Anglican establishment, Anglicans were outnumbered by at least fifteen to one; in others (Pennsylvania and Rhode Island) the very concept of establishment was formally rejected; and in still others (North Carolina) no one could make out what was going on in the constantly shifting relations among a variety of religious groups.

In all spheres of public life Britain was approaching a crisis generated by the pressures imposed on compromised institutions by the weight of rapid growth; and the leading edge of the national crisis, the most intensely heated center of the spreading infection, lay in the inflamed question of Anglo-American relations.

There is nothing accidental in the chronology of the events of 1776: American independence lay logically in the mid-point of that tumultuous year. For the question of Anglo-American relations was not some separate problem that led by political accident to war and to American independence. It was part and parcel of the major domestic issues in Britain—economic, demographic, religious, and above all political and constitutional. No major thinker could free himself from its perplexing embrace. The question of Anglo-American relations was the occasion and precipitant of Paine's celebrated assault on the British constitution and government. It provided Gibbon with historical parallels and, as a Member of Parliament, with problems he could not solve. It filled two-thirds of Price's *Observations* and even more of the *Additional Observations* he published in 1777. It is built into the heart of Cartwright's *Take Your Choice!* Adam Smith not only included a 125-page chapter on the subject in his *Wealth of Nations* but delayed publication of the book for over a year in an effort to perfect his original draft of that section, which he correctly believed to be a key to his thinking. For Smith saw clearly the connection between the crisis in Anglo-American relations and the basic internal problems that beset Britain's economy. Like Franklin, he understood the economic power that America would soon create and the political dominance that that would eventually entail, and while his political solution, a consolidated union between the two peoples, was impractical, his economic solution, free trade and the open development of American manufactures, was not. Bentham too was involved in the American controversy, and though at the time he, like Gibbon, opposed the principles of the Revolution, he soon came to see in that event a liberating force entirely consistent with his own principles, and became a leading anti-imperialist. The line of thinking that would lead to his pamphlet *Emancipate Your Colonies!* was already evident in his *Fragment on Government*.

The American question drew in most other major issues in one way or another, it magnified the basic domestic problems, and it was the most dangerous issue because the least controllable of all the problems of the time. It was therefore Anglo-American relations that were transformed first, but the other challenges of 1776 too, in time, would find their responses, as Britain and America groped their way forward to modernity.

8

Political Experience and Radical Ideas in Eighteenth-Century America

T HE POLITICAL IDEAS of eighteenth-century British radicalism have had a peculiar importance in American history. More universally accepted in eighteenth-century America than in Britain, they were more completely and more permanently embodied in the formal arrangements of state and society; and, less controverted, less subject to criticism and dispute, they have lived on more vigorously into later periods, more continuous and more intact. The force of these ideas in America resulted from many causes. But originally, and basically, it resulted from the circumstances of the pre-Revolutionary period and from the bearing of these ideas on the political experience of the American colonists.

What this bearing was—the nature of the relationship between radical ideas and early American political experience—is a major question of historical interpretation, and it relates in interesting ways to a fundamental revision of early American history underway since World War II. By implication if not direct evidence and argument, a flood of writings has placed new and insupportable pressures on a central assumption concerning the political significance of eighteenth-century radical thought and on the interpretative structure in which it is embedded. A brief consideration of the problem as a whole, consequently, a survey from a position far enough above the details to see the outlines of the overall architecture, and an attempt, however tentative, to sketch a line—a principle—of reconstruction would seem to be in order.

A basic, organizing assumption of the group of ideas that long dominated the accepted interpretation of early American history is the belief that previous to the Revolution the political experience of the colonial Americans had been roughly analogous to that of the British. Control of public authority had been firmly held by a native aristocracy—merchants and landlords in the North, planters in the South—allied, commonly, with British officials. By restricting representation in the provincial assemblies, limiting the franchise, and invoking the restrictive power of the British state, this aristocracy, it was believed, had dominated the governmental machinery of the mainland colonies. Their political control, together with legal devices such as primogeniture and entail, had allowed them to dominate the economy as well. Not only were they successful in engrossing landed estates and mercantile fortunes, but they were for the most part able also to fight off the clamor of yeoman debtors for cheap paper currency and of depressed tenants for freehold property. But the control of this colonial counterpart of a traditional aristocracy, with its Old World ideas of privilege and hierarchy, orthodoxy in religious establishment, and economic inequality, was progressively threatened by the growing strength of a native, frontier-bred democracy that expressed itself most forcefully in the lower houses of the "rising" provincial assemblies. A conflict between the two groups and ways of life was building up, and it broke out in fury after 1765.

The outbreak of the Revolution, the argument runs, fundamentally altered the old regime. The Revolution destroyed the power of this traditional aristocracy, for the movement of opposition to Parliamentary taxation, 1760–76, originally controlled by conservative elements, was taken over by extremists nourished on the radical ideas of the Enlightenment, and the once dominant conservative groups had gradually been alienated. The break with England over the question of home rule was part of a general struggle, as Carl Becker put it almost a century ago, over who shall rule at home. Independence gave control to the radicals, who, imposing their advanced doctrines on a traditional society, transformed a rebellious secession into a social revolution. They created a new regime, a reformed society, based on enlightened political and social theory.

But that is not the end of the story; the sequel is important. The success of the enlightened radicals during the early years of the Revolution was notable; but, the argument continues, it was not wholly unqualified. The remnants of the earlier aristocracy, combined now with entrepreneurial capitalists, though defeated, had not been eliminated: they were able to reassert themselves in the postwar years. In the 1780s they gradually regained power until, in what amounted to a counter-revolution, they impressed their views indelibly on history in the new federal Constitution, in the revocation of some of the more enthusiastic actions of the earlier Revolutionary period, and in the Hamiltonian program for the new government. This was not, of course, merely the old regime resurrected. In a new age whose institutions and ideals had been born of Revolutionary radicalism, the conservative elements made adjustments and concessions by which to survive and to flourish as a dominant force in American life.

The importance of this formulation, still alive in new forms in writings of the late twentieth century, derived not merely from its usefulness in interpreting eighteenth-century history. It provided a key also for understanding the entire course of American politics. By its light, politics in America, from the very beginning, could be seen to have been a dialectical process in which an aristocracy or oligarchy of wealth and power struggled with the People, who, ordinarily ill-organized and inarticulate, rose upon provocation armed with powerful ideological weapons derived from eighteenth-century radicalism, to reform a periodically corrupt and oppressive polity. And in its most recent form it reinforces the belief of critics of late-twentieth-century liberalism that the modern capitalist world, with its inequities, dominated by the ethic of possessive individualism, is a repudiation, a reversal, not the fulfillment, of the communitarian idealism of the original, true, American Revolution.

In all of this the underlying assumption is the belief that the reforming ideas of radical thinkers of the Enlightenment had been the effective lever by which native American radicals had turned a dispute on the constitution of the British Empire into a sweeping reformation of public institutions, and thereby laid the basis for the inner struggles of America's liberal democracy.

An impressive formulation—well integrated and cogent. But over the years almost every important point has been challenged in one way or another by historians working from different approaches and on different problems. All arguments concerning politics during the pre-Revolutionary years, for example, have been affected by an exhaustive demonstration for two colonies, which could well be duplicated for others, that the franchise, among freemen, far from having been restricted in behalf of a borough-mongering aristocracy, was widely available for popular use. Indeed, it was more widespread than the desire to use it—a fact which in itself calls into question a whole range of traditional arguments and assumptions. Similarly, the populist terms in which economic elements of pre-Revolutionary history have most often been discussed may no longer be used with the same confidence. It has been shown, for example, that paper money, long believed to have been the inflationary instrument of a depressed and desperate debtor yeomanry, was in most places a fiscally sound and successful means—whether issued directly by the governments or through land banks—not only of providing a medium of exchange but also of creating sources of credit necessary for the growth of an underdeveloped economy and a stable system of public finance for otherwise resourceless governments. Merchants and creditors commonly supported the issuance of paper, and many of the debtors who did so turn out to have been substantial property owners.

Equally, the key writings extending the interpretation into the Revolutionary years have come under question. The first, classic monograph detailing the inner social struggle of the decade before 1776 and relating it to positions on the Revolution—Carl Becker's *History of Political Parties in the Province of New York, 1760–1776* (1909)—has been subjected to sharp criticism on points of validation and consistency, as have many of the more recent studies that have followed Becker's line of interpretation. Nor have the efforts to locate the roots of revolution in progressive impoverishment or working-class protest succeeded. And because studies that seek to associate social movements toward revolution with post-Revolutionary politics rest on a belief in the continuity of "radical" and "conservative" elements, they have been weakened by the fact that such terminology fails to define consistently identifiable groups of people. Thus the "class" characteristic of the merchants in the northern colonies, a presupposition of important studies of the merchants in the Revolutionary movement, has been discounted: the colonial merchants formed, it appears, not a class but a spectrum of social groups engaged in trade, with no interest-group solidarity in politics. And following the demolition of Charles Beard's *Economic Interpretation of the Constitution* (1913) have come doubts about the validity of his "counter-revolutionary" argument in any of its later or more general forms: that the Constitution uniquely embodied the interests if not of public creditors then of other capitalist conservatives, or of classical republicans hoping to perpetuate the rule of patricians—that the Constitution in any of these ways marked the Thermidorian conclusion to the enlightened reformism of the early Revolutionary years.

These critical writings are, of course, of unequal weight and validity; but few of them are completely unsubstantiated, almost all of them have some point and substance, and taken together they are sufficient to raise serious doubts about an interpretation of this crucial passage of history concentrated on the theme of a radical revolution followed by a conservative counter-revolution, the suppression of earlier aspirations, and the establishment of a permanent struggle between conservative forces on the one hand and populist impulses on the other. A full reconsideration of the problem is, of course, out of the question here. But one might make at least an approach to the task and a first approximation to some answers by isolating and examining the central premise concerning the relationship between radical ideas and political experience.

Considering the material at hand, old and new, that bears on this question, one discovers an apparent paradox. There appear to be two primary and contradictory sets of facts. The first and more obvious is the undeniable evidence of the seriousness with which colonial and Revolutionary leaders took ideas, and the deliberateness of their efforts during the Revolution to reshape institutions in their pattern. The more we know about these American provincials, the clearer it is that among them were remarkably well-informed students of contemporary social and political thought. There never was a dark age that destroyed the cultural contacts between Europe and America. The sources of transmission had been numerous in the seventeenth century; they increased in the eighteenth. There were not only the impersonal agencies of newspapers, books, and pamphlets, but also continuous personal contact through travel and correspondence. Above all, there were pan-Atlantic, mainly Anglo-American, interest groups that occasioned a continuous flow of fresh information and ideas between Europe and the mainland colonies in America. Of these, the most important were not conveyed principally by the writings of the great figures of the European Enlightenment but by the opposition publicists in British politics and the religious dissenters in constant touch with their numerous co-denominationalists in America. Located for the most part on the left of the English political spectrum, acutely alive to ideas of reform that might increase their prospects and security in Britain, they were a rich source of political and social theory. It was largely through opposition and nonconformist connections that the commonwealth radicalism of seventeenth-century England continued to flow to the colonists, blending, ultimately, with other strains of thought to form a common body of advanced theory.

In every colony and in every legislature there were some people who knew Locke and Beccaria, Montesquieu and Voltaire; but more important, there was in almost every village of every colony someone who knew such transmitters of English nonconformist thought as Watts, Neal, and Burgh; later Priestley and Price—lesser writers, no doubt, but staunch opponents of traditional authority, and they spoke in a familiar idiom. In the bitterly contentious pamphlet literature of mid-eighteenth-century American politics, the most frequently cited authority on matters of principle and theory was not Locke or even the perennially popular Montesquieu but *Cato's Letters,* a series of radically libertarian essays written in London in 1720–23 by two supporters of the opposition factions, John Trenchard and Thomas Gordon. Through such writers, as well as through the major authors, leading colonists kept contact with a powerful tradition of advanced, enlightened thought.

This body of doctrine fell naturally into play in the controversy over the power of the imperial government. For the Revolutionary leaders it supplied a common vocabulary and a common pattern of thought, and, when the time came, common principles of political reform. That reform was sought and seriously if unevenly undertaken, there can be no doubt. Institutions were remodeled, laws altered, practices questioned, all in accordance with advanced doctrine on the nature of liberty and of the institutions needed to achieve it. The Americans were acutely aware of being innovators, of bringing mankind a long step forward. They believed that they had so far succeeded in their effort to reshape circumstances to conform to enlightened ideas and ideals that they had introduced a new era in human affairs. And they were supported in this by the opinion of informed thinkers in Europe. The contemporary image of the American Revolution at home and abroad was complex; but no one doubted that a revolution that threatened the existing order and portended new social and political arrangements had been made, and made in the name of reason.

Thus, throughout the eighteenth century there were prominent, politically active Americans who were well aware of the development of European, particularly British, thinking, took ideas seriously, and during the Revolution deliberately used them in an effort to reform the institutional basis of society. This much seems obvious. But, paradoxically, and less obviously, it is equally true that many, indeed most, of what these leaders considered to be their greatest achievements during the Revolution—reforms that made America seem to the enlightened world like the veritable heavenly city of the eighteenth-century philosophers—had been matters of fact before they were matters of theory and revolutionary doctrine.

No reform in the entire Revolution appeared of greater importance to Jefferson than the Virginia acts abolishing primogeniture and entail. This action, he later wrote, was part of "a system by which every fibre would be eradicated of antient or future aristocracy; and a foundation laid for a government truly republican." But primogeniture and entail had never taken deep roots in America, not even in tidewater Virginia. Where land was cheap and easily available such legal restrictions proved to be encumbrances profiting few. Often they tended to threaten rather than secure the survival of the family, as Jefferson himself realized when in 1774 he petitioned the Assembly to break an entail on his wife's estate on the very practical, untheoretical, and common ground that to do so would be "greatly to their [the petitioners'] interest and that of their families." The legal abolition of primogeniture and entail during and after the Revolution was of little material consequence. Their demise had been effectively decreed years before by the circumstances of life in a wilderness environment.

Similarly, the disestablishment of religion—a major goal of Revolutionary reform—was carried out, to the extent that it was, in circumstances so favorable to it that one wonders not why it was done but why it was not done more thoroughly. There is no more eloquent, moving testimony to Revolutionary idealism than the Virginia Act for Establishing Religious Freedom: it is the essence of Enlightenment faith. But what did it, and the disestablishment legislation that had preceded it, reform? What had the establishment of religion meant in pre-Revolutionary Virginia? The Church of England was the state church, but dissent was tolerated well beyond the limits of the English Acts of Toleration. The law required nonconformist organizations to be licensed by the government, but dissenters were not barred from their own worship or penalized for failure to attend the Anglican communion, and they were commonly exempted from parish taxes. Nonconformity excluded no one from voting, and only the very few Catholics from enjoying public office. And when the itineracy of revivalist preachers led the establishment to contemplate more restrictive measures, the Baptists and Presbyterians advanced to the point of arguing publicly, and pragmatically, that the toleration they had so far enjoyed was an encumbrance, and that the only proper solution was, if not complete disestablishment, then non-discriminatory pluralism.

Virginia was if anything more conservative than most colonies. The legal establishment of the Church of England was in fact no more rigorous in South Carolina and Georgia: it was considerably weaker in North Carolina. It hardly existed at all in the middle colonies (there was, of course, no vestige of it in Pennsylvania), and where it did, as in four counties of New York, it was either ignored or had become embattled by violent opposition well before the Revolution. Rhode Island had never had an establishment of any kind, and in Massachusetts and Connecticut, where the establishment, being nonconformist according to English law, was legally tenuous to begin with, tolerance in worship and relief from church taxation had been extended to the major dissenting groups early in the eighteenth century, resulting well before the Revolution in what was, in effect if not in law, a multiple establishment. And this had been further weakened by the splintering effect of the Great Awakening. Almost everywhere the Church of England, the established church of the highest state authority, was embattled and defensive—driven to rely more and more on its missionary arm, the Society for the Propagation of the Gospel, to sustain it against the cohorts of dissent.

None of this had resulted from formal doctrine. It had been created by the mundane exigencies of the situation: by the distance that separated Americans from ecclesiastical centers in England and the Continent; by the never-ending need to encourage immigration to the colonies; by the variety, the mere numbers, of religious groups, each by itself a minority, forced to live together; and by the weakness of the coercive powers of the state, its inability to control the social forces within it.

Even more gradual and less contested had been the process by which government in the colonies had become government by the consent of the governed. What has been proved about the franchise in early Massachusetts and Virginia—that it was open for practically the entire free adult male population—can be proved to a lesser or greater extent for all the colonies. But the extraordinary breadth of the franchise in the American colonies had not resulted from popular demands: there had been no cries for universal manhood suffrage, nor were there popular theories claiming, or even justifying, general participation in politics. Nowhere in eighteenth-century America was there "democracy"—middle-class or otherwise—as we use the term. The main reason for the wide franchise was that the traditional English laws limiting suffrage to freeholders of certain competencies proved in the colonies, where freehold property was widespread, to be not restrictive but broadly permissive.

Representation would seem to be different, since before the Revolution complaints had been voiced against the inequity of its apportioning, especially in the Pennsylvania and North Carolina assemblies. But these complaints were based on an assumption that would have seemed unnatural and unreasonable almost anywhere else in the

Western world: the assumption that representation in governing assemblages was a proper and rightful attribute of people as such—of regular units of population, or of populated land—rather than the special privileges of peculiarly favored groups, institutions, or regions. Complaints there were, bitter ones. But they were complaints claiming relative deprivation, not invoking abstract ideals or unfamiliar desires. They assumed from common experience the normalcy of regular and systematic representation. And why should it have been otherwise? The colonial assemblies had not, like ancient parliaments, grown to satisfy a monarch's need for the support of particular groups or individuals or to protect the interests of a social order, and they had not developed insensibly from precedent to precedent. They had been created at a stroke, and it was reasonable to assume that their membership would expand regularly and systematically as the population grew and spread into new territories. Nor did the process, the character, of representation as it was known in the colonies derive from theory. For colonial Americans, representation had little of the symbolic and purely deliberative qualities which, as a result of the Revolutionary debates and of Burke's speeches, would become celebrated as "virtual." To the colonists it was direct and actual: it was, most often, a kind of agency, a delegation of powers, to individuals commonly required to be residents of their constituencies and, at times, bound by instructions from them—with the result that eighteenth-century American legislatures frequently resembled, in spirit if not otherwise, those "ancient assemblies" of New York, composed, the contemporary historian William Smith wrote, "of plain, illiterate husbandmen, whose views seldom extended farther than to the regulation of highways, the destruction of wolves, wild cats, and foxes, and the advancement of the other little interests of the particular counties which they were chosen to represent." There was no theoretical basis for such direct and actual representation. It had been created and was continuously reinforced by the pressure of local politics in the colonies and by the political circumstances in England, to which the colonists had found it necessary to send closely instructed, paid representatives—agents, so called—from the very beginning.

But franchise and representation are mere mechanisms of government by consent. At its heart lies freedom from executive power, from the independent action of state authority, and the concentration of power in representative bodies and elected officials. The greatest achievement of the Revolution was, of course, the repudiation of just such state authority and the transfer of power to popular legislatures. No one will deny that this action was taken in accordance with the highest principles of advanced theory. But the way had been paved by fifty years of grinding factionalism in colonial politics. In the details of pre-Revolutionary American politics, in the complicated maneuverings of provincial politicians seeking the benefits of government, in the patterns of local patronage and the forms of factional groupings, and in the shifting, diminished enforcement of seditious libel, there lies a history of progressive alienation from the state which resulted, at least by the 1750s, in what Professor Robert Palmer has lucidly described as a revolutionary situation: a condition

> . . . in which confidence in the justice or reasonableness of existing authority is undermined; where old loyalties fade, obligations are felt as impositions, law seems arbitrary, and respect for superiors is felt as a form of humiliation; where existing sources of prestige seem undeserved . . . and government is sensed as distant, apart from the governed and not really "representing" them.

Such a situation had developed in mid-eighteenth-century America, not from theories of government or radical ideas but from the factional opposition that had grown up against a succession of legally powerful, but often cynically self-seeking, inept, and above all politically weak officers of state.

Surrounding all of these circumstances and in various ways controlling them is the fact that that great goal of the European revolutions of the late eighteenth century, equality of status before the law—the abolition of legal privilege—had been reached almost everywhere in the free communities of the American colonies at least by the early years of the eighteenth century. Analogies between the upper strata of colonial society and the European aristocracies are misleading. Social stratification existed, of course; but the differences between aristocracies in eighteenth-century Europe and in America are more important than the similarities. So far was legal privilege absent in the colonies that where it existed it was an open sore of festering discontent, leading not merely, as in the case of the Penn family's hereditary claims to tax exemption, to formal protests, but, as in the case of the powers enjoyed by the Hudson River land magnates, to violent opposition as well. More important, the colonial aristocracy, such as it was, had no formal, institutional role in government. No public office or function was legally a prerogative of birth. As there were no social orders in the eyes of the law, so there were no governmental bodies to represent them. The only claim that has been made to the contrary is that, in effect, the governors' Councils constituted political institutions in the service of the aristocracy. But this claim—of dubious value in any case because of the steadily declining political importance of the Councils in the later eighteenth century—cannot be substantiated. It is true that certain families tended to dominate the Councils, but they had less legal claim to places in those bodies than certain royal officials who, though hardly members of an American aristocracy, sat on the Councils by virtue of their office. Councillors could be and were removed by simple political maneuver. Council seats were filled either by appointment or by election: when appointive, they were vulnerable to political pressure in England; when elective, to the vagaries of public opinion at home. Thus, on the one hand, it took William Byrd II five years of maneuvering to get himself appointed to the seat on the Virginia Council vacated by his father's death in 1704, and on the other, when in 1766 the Hutchinson faction's control of the Massachusetts Council proved unpopular, it was simply removed wholesale by being voted out of office at the next election. As there were no special privileges, no peculiar group possessions, manners, or attitudes to distinguish councillors from other affluent Americans, so there were no separate political interests expressed in the Councils as such. Councillors joined as directly as others in the factional disputes of the time, associating with groups of all sorts, from transient American opposition parties to massive Anglo-American political syndicates. A century before the Revolution and not as the result of anti-aristocratic ideas, the colonial aristocracy had become a vaguely defined, fluid group whose power—in no way guaranteed, buttressed, or even recognized in law—was competitively maintained and dependent on continuous popular support.

Other examples could be given. Were written constitutions felt to be particular guarantees of liberty in enlightened states? Americans had known them in the rudimentary but still recognizable form of colonial charters and governors' instructions for a century before the Revolution; and after 1763, seeking a basis for their claims against the constitutionality of specific acts of Parliament, they were driven, out of sheer logical necessity, to generalize that experience. Was the distribution of power between a central government and peripheral bodies—a relationship that would later be known as federalism—considered to be a useful way of preventing undue concentrations of authority? In imperial arrangements, Americans had known precisely such a situation for a century—not as a matter of doctrine (none of the accepted constitutional ideas of the time could support such a construction), but as a matter of custom, sanctified by time. But the point is perhaps clear enough. Major attributes of enlightened polities had developed naturally, spontaneously, early in the history of the American colonies, and they existed as simple matters of social and political fact on the eve of the Revolution.

But if all this is true, of what real significance were the ideals and ideas? What was the bearing of advanced thought on the political experience of eighteenth-century Americans?

Perhaps this much may be said. What had evolved spontaneously from the demands of place and time was not self-justifying, nor was it universally welcomed. New developments, however gradual, were suspect by some, resisted in part, and confined in their effects. If it was true that the establishment of religion was everywhere weak in the colonies and that in some places it was even difficult to know what was orthodoxy and what was not, it was nevertheless also true that faith in the idea of orthodoxy persisted and with it belief in the propriety of a privileged state religion. If, as a matter of fact, the spread of freehold tenure qualified large populations for voting, it did not create new reasons for using that power nor make the victims of its use content with what, in terms of the dominant ideal of balance in the state, seemed a disproportionate influence of "the democracy." If many colonists came naturally to assume that representation should be direct and actual, growing with the population and bearing some relation to its geographical distribution, Crown officials did not, and they had the weight of precedent and theory as well as of authority with them: so, when in 1767 it seemed expedient to do so, the British government simply froze the composition of the colonial assemblies. If state authority was seen increasingly as alien and hostile and was forced to fight for survival within an abrasive, kaleidoscopic faction- alism, the traditional idea nevertheless persisted that the common good was somehow defined by the state and that political parties or factions—organized and vocal opposition to established govern- ment—were suspect, perhaps seditious: so the authorities did what they could to enforce the laws of seditious libel. A traditional aristoc- racy did not in fact exist; but the assumption that superiority was indivisible, that social eminence and political influence had a natural affinity to each other, did. The colonists instinctively conceded to the claims of the well-born and rich to exercise public office, and in this sense politics remained aristocratic. If for a century the colonists had enjoyed the benefits and protections of what was, in effect but not in doctrine, a federalist empire—had enjoyed what the twentieth century would call dominion status—the belief persisted that "states within states" was a conceptual and practical impossibility since it was assumed that sovereignty was, and had to be, indivisible: logically, therefore, Americans, who had lived for generations in a world of pragmatically divided sovereignties, in the end were forced to choose between total subservience and complete independence. Behavior had changed—had had to change—with the circumstances of everyday life; but habits of mind and the sense of rightness lagged behind. Many felt the changes to be *away from*, not *toward*, something: that they represented deviance; that they lacked, in a word, legitimacy.

This divergence between habits of mind and belief on the one hand, and experience and behavior on the other, was ended at the Revolution. A rebellion that destroyed the traditional sources of pub- lic authority called forth the full range of advanced ideas. Long-settled attitudes were jolted and loosened. The grounds of legitimacy sud- denly shifted. What had happened was seen to have been good and proper, steps in the right direction. The glass was half full, not half empty; and to complete the work of fate and nature, further thought must be taken, theories tested, ideas applied.

The problems were many, often unexpected and difficult; some were only gradually perceived. Social and personal privilege, for example, could easily be eliminated—it hardly existed: but what of the privileges of corporate bodies? Legal orders and ranks within free society could be outlawed without creating the slightest tremor, and executive power with equal ease subordinated to the legislative: but how was balance within a polity to be achieved? What were the elements to be balanced and how were they to be separated? It was not even necessary formally to abolish the interest of state as a symbol and determinant of the common good; it simply dissolved: but what was left to keep clashing factions from tearing a government apart? Federalist relations between levels of government were obviously beneficial, and constitutions could be written to institutionalize this division of powers. But how could clashes between constituted authorities be reconciled? The problems were pressing, and the efforts to solve them mark the stages of Revolutionary history.

In behalf of the advanced ideas of eighteenth-century radicals the Revolutionary leaders undertook to complete, formalize, systematize, and symbolize what previously had been only partially realized, confused, and disputed matters of fact. Enlightened ideas were not instruments of a particular social group, nor did they destroy a social order. They did not create new social and political forces in America: they released those that had long existed, and vastly increased their power. This propulsion—this completion, this rationalization, this lifting into consciousness and endowing with high moral purpose inchoate, confused, and hitherto disputed elements of social and political change—marks the impact of ideas on political experience in eighteenth-century America. It is an essential facet of the American Revolution.

9

The Central Themes
of the American
Revolution

T HE AMERICAN REVOLUTION not only created the American political nation but molded permanent characteristics of the culture that would develop within it. The Revolution is an event,
consequently, whose meaning cannot be confined to the past.
Whether we recognize it or not, the sense we make of the history of
our national origins helps to define for us, as it has for generations
before us, the values, purposes, and acceptable characteristics of our
public institutions. The questions must repeatedly be asked, therefore, what the nature of the event was, and what bearing it should
have on our lives. A great many books have been published on the
Revolution in the past fifty years, and a veritable library of documents
has been unearthed. What—that makes any difference—does this
mass of information tell us that an earlier generation did not know?
Where does our knowledge fall away, and myth and wish fulfillment
take over?

I

To grasp fully a central theme that emerges from recent writings one
must step back a full generation and note a striking inconsistency that
lay at the heart of the imposing interpretation, or bundle of interpre-

tations, that then prevailed. On the one hand, there was a general agreement on the importance of what was called "the natural rights philosophy" and of the force of British constitutional ideas. Almost all writers who attempted general assessments of the origins and meaning of the Revolution found it necessary somewhere in their accounts to attribute an elemental power to these abstract ideas of Locke and the great continental reformers and to the principles of British constitutionalism. Somehow, through a process that was not explained, the formal legal precedents and the abstractions propounded in the texts of the *philosophes* were transformed into political and psychological imperatives when certain actions were taken by the British government, and the result was resistance and revolution. The first state governments were presumably constructed in conformity with these beliefs and principles, though in the only work then available that attempted to analyze those new constitutions, Allan Nevins's *The American States During and After the Revolution, 1775–1789* (1924), it was impossible to discover the precise relationship between these overarching ideas and the details of the constitutions that were actually written. In some sense too the federal Constitution embodied these principles and beliefs, though the best descriptions then available of what had actually happened failed to establish with any precision the connections between these ideas and the decisions reached by the Philadelphia convention.

There were some historians who *were* concerned with the problem of how ideas and beliefs relate to what people do, but their presumptions were such that, instead of solving the problem realistically, in the end they destroyed it. For these writers the primary forces at work were social and economic: *they* really determined the outcome of events, though adroit politicians had used the famous ideas of the time to agitate an otherwise inert public opinion. Thus in 1923 Arthur M. Schlesinger, Sr., criticized a book on the causes of the Revolution by deploring the author's lack of emphasis on the truly important things—trade, currency, the impact of new commercial regulations— and above all his lack of recognition of the role of propaganda in the Revolutionary movement. By propaganda, Schlesinger explained, he meant not "the constitutional grievances recited in state papers and the more serious pamphlets"; that sort of thing, he said, should only be touched on "lightly," for, as he had already explained, "the popular view of the Revolution as a great forensic controversy over abstract governmental rights will not bear close scrutiny." It was a mistake to believe "that pamphlets were more potent in shaping colonial opinion than the newspapers." Pamphlets contained sustained arguments, appeals to reason, logic, principles, and intellectual coherence, while what really mattered were "the appeals to passion and prejudice to be found in broadsides, bits of popular doggerel, patriotic songs, caricatures, newspapers, slogans, emblems, etc."

Now, what is centrally important in this is not the surface contradiction between, on the one hand, a belief in the force of abstruse points of constitutional law and of natural rights principles and, on the other, the systematic exclusion of ideas and beliefs from an effective role in affairs except as propagandistic weapons. More important are the differing presumptions upon which the two viewpoints rested. The students of constitutional law and Enlightenment ideas assumed that the force, the effect, of beliefs and ideas is somehow related to their cogency, to the quality of the argumentation that supported them, or to the universality of their appeal. The other writers made the quite opposite assumption that, because they could not see how abstract ideas, reason, belief, indeed the whole realm of intellection, could constitute motives, such elements could not in themselves influence events at all and therefore in themselves could explain nothing about what actually happened and why. Ultimately they assumed, though they did not discuss the point, that there is only material self-interest, and that in turn is shaped by the social and economic forces that determine the external character of people's lives.

All of this is worth recalling because it provides a useful perspective within which to understand a central theme of recent writings on the origins and meaning of the Revolution. We know now that the great classic texts of the Enlightenment, while they formed the deep background and gave a general coloration to the liberal beliefs of the time, were not the immediate sources of the ideas, fears, and beliefs that directly shaped Americans' responses to particular events or guided the specific reforms they undertook, nor were they perceived in the American colonies in quite the same way they were perceived elsewhere. And we know, too, that the vaguely formulated, contested,

and unresolved ideas of constitutional relations between the metropolitan center and the colonial periphery were no help in explaining
why drastic changes were suddenly made in the 1760s, why an age-
old working arrangement was suddenly and heedlessly overthrown,
what lay behind this abrupt assertion of imperial absolutism, what
motivated Britain's leaders, and thus what the future portended. While
the formal discourses of Enlightenment thinkers lay in the background of the minds of the best informed Americans, along with the
principles they believed were embodied in constitutional practice, in
the foreground—in the immediate awareness of the political population at large—was a whole world of more concrete, commonplace,
vivid, and compelling ideas and beliefs which both explained and
shaped political behavior. These were views and patterns of responses that determined the outcome; in the constitutional crisis of
the time, they were the triggers of rebellion.

Part of an elaborate map of social and political reality, part of a
pattern that made the world comprehensible, these ideas have a long
derivation, and though drawn indirectly from the whole of European
political culture, they are directly the products of a series of creative
moments in British political and cultural life. The starting point was
the struggle between king and Commons in the early seventeenth
century, which secured the rule of law and the principle of the consent of the governed expressed through representative institutions as
necessities for legitimate governance. But though these principles remained fundamental in the pattern of British liberal thought and
though the seventeenth-century ideas of consent, individual rights,
and parliamentary privilege were drawn on repeatedly in the eighteenth century by colonial assemblies seeking the legislative auton-
omy enjoyed by the House of Commons, they were overlaid with an
array of new conceptions and concerns that took shape later in the
seventeenth century, in the years surrounding the Exclusion Crisis,
1679 to 1681. These few years of desperate struggle over the effort
to exclude the future James II from the succession to the throne saw
not merely the drafting of Locke's two treatises on government, but
also the forging of clusters of much more specific ideas on the nature
of political freedom and on its social preconditions, illustrated by a
fresh view of English history proving the ancient lineage of the liberal
state and by a vivid portrayal of the destructive political effect of

corruption. And everywhere in this late-seventeenth-century world of ideas there was fear—fear that a free condition of life, the preservation of personal rights against the power of the state, was a precarious thing, ever beset by power-hungry, corrupt enemies who would destroy it.

Most of the ideas and beliefs that shaped the American Revolutionary mind can be found in the voluminous writings of the Exclusion Crisis and in the literature of the Glorious Revolution that in effect brought that upheaval to a peaceful conclusion. But there remains still another decisive moment in the shaping of the Revolutionary mind. The terms of settlement of the Glorious Revolution, based on a broad consensus in English public life, forced the extremists of left and right to the margins of English politics, where they remained, after the rocketing instability of the reigns of William III and Anne, to form the shrill and articulate opposition to the government of that fantastically successful political operator Robert Walpole. It was here, in the writings of the early-eighteenth-century opposition of both left and right—the left carrying forward with embellishments most of the radical notions of the seventeenth century, the right nourishing a nostalgia for a half-mythical rural world of stable hierarchical relations, but the two converging from these opposite poles to blast the bloated Leviathan of government they saw developing before them—it was in this populist cry against what appeared to be a swelling financial–governmental complex fat with corruption, complaisant and power-engrossing—in this shrill alarm of alienated intellectuals, outraged moralists, and frustrated politicians, that English radical thought took on the forms that would most specifically determine the outbreak and character of the American Revolution and that thereafter in vital respects would shape the course of American history.

These notions—derived, as I have suggested, from the early seventeenth century, fundamentally redeveloped in and immediately after the Exclusion Crisis, but now in the early eighteenth century given definitive shape by the political opposition—had great power; they carried great conviction; and they fitted neatly the peculiar circumstances of American social and political life. Bearing into the new, modern age of Walpole the traditional anti-statist convictions of seventeenth-century liberalism, the opposition's program was yet distinct in its insistence that all power—royal or plebiscitarian, autocratic or democratic—was evil: necessary, no doubt, for ordered life, but evil nevertheless in the threat it would always pose to the progress of liberty. The opposition's claims were distinct too in their insistence that the primary wielders of power must be kept apart, sealed off from collusive contact with each other in institutions defined by the principles of "mixed" government. And they were distinct, finally, in their heightened emphasis on the dangers of corruption—the corruption of massed wealth, the corruption of luxury, the corruption of indolence and moral obtuseness, all of which threatened to destroy the free British constitution and the rights it protected.

To Americans in distant provinces, faced with local governments that seemed at times to violate the basic precepts of political freedom; ultimately governed not by visible human beings they could acknowledge as natural leaders but by an unseen capricious, unmanageable, but fortunately quite benignly neglectful sovereign; and bred into a Protestant culture whose deep-lying moralism was repeatedly stirred by waves of evangelical fervor—to such people, all of this made the most profound kind of sense, and it shaped their political awareness. Repeatedly through the middle years of the eighteenth century factional leaders responded to local crises by invoking these ideas—not testing their limits or probing their implications, not even applying them systematically, but drawing on them almost casually, and repeatedly, when it seemed appropriate in attacking the power of the state. Then, in the 1760s and 1770s, when the colonists believed themselves faced, not as heretofore with local threats but with an organized pan-Atlantic effort of highly placed autocrats to profit by reducing the free way of life the colonists had known—a "design" set on foot by manipulators of the colossus "at home"—they were led by the force of these ideas, reinforced by suddenly articulated views of the imperial constitution and by the latest formulations of the English radicals, into resistance and revolution.

The noble ideas of the Enlightenment and the abstracted principles of constitutional law were present in the responses of the colonists, but they do not form the immediate, instrumental grasp of their minds. They do not explain the triggering of the insurrection. That is explicable only in terms of that elaborate pattern of middle-level beliefs and ideas that formed for these colonial Britishers the map of social and political reality—a map, originally formed within early-seventeenth-century English libertarianism, fundamentally reshaped during and just after the Exclusion Crisis, modernized for the eighteenth century by the political opposition, the alienated intelligentsia, and the vigilant moralists of Walpole's time, and diffused by an intricate process of cultural dissemination through the political culture of the American colonies. No simpler genealogy can explain the derivation of America's Revolutionary ideology. There was no singular application of something scholars would later call "civic humanism" or "classical republicanism," nor were these ideas felt to be incompatible with what would later be described as "liberalism." The sanctity of private property and the benefits of commercial expansion, within customary boundaries, were simply assumed—the Revolution was fought in part to protect the individual's right to private property—nor were acquisitiveness, the preservation of private possessions, and reasonable economic development believed to be in necessary conflict with the civic rectitude that free, republican governments required to survive. Later, generations later, such a conflict might be seen to emerge in complex ways, but for the Revolutionary generation and its immediate successors these were harmonious values, implicit in a configuration of ideas that had evolved through critical passages of Anglo-American history.

But how, precisely, did these notions relate to political behavior?

How simple and how unreal were the earlier assumptions either, on the one hand, that formal discourse and articulated belief bear directly on political processes or, on the other hand, that ideas are only epiphenomenal, superstructural, not the shapers of events but their rationalizations, and effectual only when wielded by propagandists whose professions are different from their true intent and whose aim is to manipulate the minds and so direct the actions of ignorant and suggestible masses. Both lead to confusion in interpreting an event like the Revolution. But both are resolvable into the concept of "ideology," which draws formal discourse into maps of reality—shifting patterns of values, attitudes, hopes, fears, and opinions through which people perceive the world and by which they are led to impose themselves upon it. Formal discourse can indeed be powerful in politics, but not because in some simple sense it constitutes motives or is a form of weaponry. Formal discourse becomes politically powerful when it articulates and fuses into effective formulations opinions and attitudes that are otherwise too scattered and vague to be acted upon; when it mobilizes a general mood; when it crystallizes otherwise inchoate social and political discontent and thereby directs it to attainable goals; when it clarifies, symbolizes, and elevates to structured consciousness the mingled urges that stir within us. But its power is not autonomous. It can only formulate, reshape, and direct forward moods, attitudes, ideas, and aspirations, rooted in social reality, that in some form, however crude or incomplete, already exist.

It is in these terms that ideas—not disembodied abstractions of the *philosophes,* or the formal arguments of constitutional lawyers, or the pure principles of "civic humanism" or of "classical republicanism," but the integrated set of values, beliefs, attitudes, and responses that had evolved through a century and a half of Anglo-American history— may be understood to have lain at the heart of the Revolutionary outbreak and to have shaped its outcome and consequences. The colonists—habituated to respond vigorously to acts of arbitrary rule; convinced that the existence of liberty was precarious even in the loosely governed provinces of the British-American world; more uncertain than ever of what the intricate shufflings in the distant corridors of power in England portended; and ever fearful that England's growing corruption would destroy its capacity to resist the aggressions of ruthless power seekers—saw behind the actions of the ministry not merely misgovernment and not merely insensitivity to the reality of life in the British overseas provinces but a deliberate design to destroy the constitutional safeguards of liberty. Only concerted resistance— violent resistance if necessary—could effectively oppose this threat. Within the ideological context of the time and in communities whose overall political structure was fragile and prone to conflict and in which direct, "mob" action against obnoxious authorities was familiar—in this situation forceful resistance became, for many, imperative, as did the effort that followed to build still stronger bastions against the inevitable aggressions of power.

The outbreak of the Revolution was not the result of social discontent, or of economic disturbances in the colonies, or of rising misery. Nor was there a transformation of mob behavior or of the lives of the inarticulate in the pre-Revolutionary years that accounts for the disruption of Anglo-American politics. The rebellion took place in a basically prosperous, if temporarily disordered economy and in communities whose effective social distances, for freemen, remained narrow enough and whose mobility, social and spatial, however it may have slowed from earlier days, was still high enough to absorb most group discontents. Nor was it the consequence simply of the inevitable growth of infant institutions and communities to the point where challenges to the parental authority became inescapable: neither institutions nor communities are doomed to grow through phases of oedipal conflict. There was good sense in the expectation occasionally heard in the eighteenth century that American institutions in time would gradually grow apart from Britain's, peacefully attenuating until the connection became mere friendly cooperation. American resistance in the 1760s and 1770s was a response to acts of imperial power deemed arbitrary, degrading, and uncontrollable—a response that was inflamed to the point of explosion by ideological currents generating fears everywhere in America that irresponsible and self-seeking adventurers—what the twentieth century would call political gangsters—had gained the power of the British government and were turning first to the colonies.

Inflamed sensibilities—exaggerated distrust and fear—surrounded the hard core of the Anglo-American constitutional conflict and gave it distinctive shape. These perceptions and anxieties made accommodation at first difficult and then impossible. By 1773 there was a widespread suspicion, primarily in New England but elsewhere as well, that the source of the conflict could be traced to actions taken by Governor Thomas Hutchinson of Massachusetts and a few of his colleagues in office. This long-respected scion of generations of enterprising New England leaders, it was believed, had deliberately misinformed the British ministry on the intentions and opinions of the colonists in order to advance his personal interests with the venal gang in Whitehall. Conversely, Hutchinson himself and most of the ministry believed that a clique of ruthless colonial demagogues headquartered in Boston was deliberately misinforming the American populace on the ministry's intentions in order to advance their own interests. Perhaps only Benjamin Franklin, who loved England, though somewhat despairingly, and who yet knew himself to be the embodiment to all the world of the hopes and possibilities of America, fully understood not only the substantive issues on both sides of the controversy but also the haze of misunderstandings that surrounded it. Believing that given sufficient time America's natural wealth and power would make its claims to British rights irresistible, he attempted, in one of the most revealing and consequential episodes of the early 1770s, to head off the approaching struggle by manipulating popular fears for what he took to be the general good. By arranging for the circulation of certain of Hutchinson's private letters of the late 1760s, he publicly documented the general suspicions of the governor's "deliberate misrepresentations" and, in thus pinning the blame for the conflict on Hutchinson, sought to exonerate the ministry and gain time for fresh approaches to reconciliation. But though Franklin's calculations were careful and sharp, he failed, in his long sojourn in England, to gauge correctly the intensity of the political and moral passions of the majority of his countrymen. The publication of Hutchinson's letters, bound, in the circumstance, to be considered incriminating, far from easing the conflict, intensified it. The "revelation" gave visible, human, and dramatic form to what previously had only been general, vague, and disputable surmises; it "proved" to an outraged public that purpose, not ignorance, neglect, or miscalculation, lay behind the actions of the British government and that reconciliation was therefore unlikely. Only Franklin, characteristically, landed on his feet. While the publication of Hutchinson's letters destroyed the Massachusetts governor and intensified the growing conflict, it helped transform the hitherto ambiguous Pennsylvanian into a popular Revolutionary hero.

All of which, as an explanation of the primary cause of the Revolution, is no more "intellectual" or "idealist" or "neo-Whig" than locating the origins of World War II in the fear and hatred of Nazism. It does not minimize the long-term background of the conflict but presumes it; it does not drain the Revolution of its internal social struggles, its sectional divisions, and its violence; it does not minimize the social and political changes that the Revolution created; it does not deny— indeed it alone explains—the upsurge of reformist zeal that is so central a part of the Revolution; nor does it rob the military struggle of its importance. It merely explains why at a particular time the colonists rebelled, and establishes the point of departure for the constructive efforts that followed.

II

Such, in my view, is the central theme of the origins of the Revolution. But this is, of course, only a beginning of an understanding of the meaning of the Revolution as a whole and of its role in shaping the course of American history. Yet seeing the origins of the Revolution this way makes it possible to come a bit closer to the stage of maturity in historical interpretation where partisanship is left behind, where historians, without abandoning their moral vision, can find an equal humanity in all the participants, the winners and the losers, where they can embrace the whole of the event, see it from all sides, mark out the latent limitations within which all the actors were obliged to act, and trace the influence of the event until it fades indistinguishably into the flow of history that succeeds it. It makes it possible, I believe, to understand the loyalists.

For a century and a half after the Revolution the loyalists' story was the subject of the fiercest and blindest partisanship that can be found anywhere in American historiography. The earliest patriotic chroniclers of the Revolution saw the loyalists as the worst of all enemies: traitors, betrayers of their own people and homeland. Just as they portrayed the Founding Fathers as flawless paragons commanding the almost universal allegiance of the population, so they saw the leading loyalists as craven sycophants of a vicious oligarchy, parasites of the worst corrupters of the *ancien régime*, and they simply blasted them into oblivion. Conversely, Tory historians in England, followed in a modified way in our own time by certain of the more scholarly "imperialist" historians, saw the loyalists much as the loyalists saw themselves, as sensible embodiments of law and order and of a benign rule against which a deluded and hysterical mass, led by demagogues, threw themselves in a frenzy. In recent years, it is true, the polemics have subsided, and the writing on the loyalists is more informative than it has been before, but this more objective writing is largely descriptive, often enumerative if not quantitative in its approach, and it fails to grasp the central interpretative problem that is posed by the lives of the loyalists. For if we are now able to see the peculiar patterns of fears, beliefs, attitudes, perceptions, and aspirations that underlay the Revolutionary movement, we have not yet made clear why any sensible and well-informed person could possibly have opposed the Revolution. And until that is done, until, that is, we also look deliberately from the point of view of the losers at what later would appear to have been the progressive development, we will not understand what that development was all about; we will not understand the human reality against which the victors struggled, and hence we will not have the story whole or entirely comprehensible.

There are no obvious external characteristics of the loyalist group, aside from the natural fact that it contained many Crown officeholders. A multitude of individual circumstances shaped the decisions that were made to remain loyal to Britain. Nor are the inner characteristics of this large group obvious. The loyalists were neither especially corrupt nor especially stupid nor especially closed to the possibilities of the future. Many of them, aside from the one point in their politics, are indistinguishable from the many obscure patriots whose involvement with events was superficial and who simply drifted marginally one way instead of the other in response to immediate pressures. Yet within the leadership of the loyalist group there appears to have been an essential if rather elusive characteristic, or set of characteristics, which, properly understood, illuminates the affirmative side of the Revolutionary movement that the loyalists resisted at such great cost.

Committed to the moral as well as the political integrity of the Anglo-American system as it existed, the loyalist leaders were insensitive to the moral basis of the protests that arose against it. Habituated for the most part to seek gains through an intricate and closely calibrated world of patronage and status, they did not respond to the aroused moral passion and the meliorative, optimistic, and idealist impulses that gripped the Revolutionaries' minds and that led them to condemn as corrupt and oppressive the whole system by which their world was governed. They did not sense the constrictions that the ruling order imposed on the naturally evolving currents of American life, or the frustration it engendered in those who failed to gain the privileges it could bestow. They could find only persistent irrationality in the arguments of the discontented and hence wrote off all of their efforts as politically pathological. And in a limited sense they were right. For the Revolutionary leaders, in their effort somehow to control a world whose political logic was a product of the system it explained, groped for conceptions that could not exist within the received framework of political ideas. They drew on convictions that ran deeper than logic and mobilized sources of political and social energy that burst the boundaries of received political and social wisdom. All of this is reflected in the loyalists' efforts to come to terms with the developing Revolution. They were outplayed, overtaken, bypassed.

Loyal officials who had risen within the narrow and complex passages of the old political system could not govern a morally aroused populace; they could not assimilate these new forces into the old world they knew so well. Thus Thomas Hutchinson, in refusing to approve a bill of 1771 prohibiting the slave trade in Massachusetts, said he could not believe that the motives of the supporters of the bill were what they said they were, namely, "a scruple . . . of the lawfulness in a merely moral respect of so great a restraint of liberty." After all, he wrote, technically in the eyes of Massachusetts law slaves were no worse off than servants bound "for a term of years exceeding the ordinary term of human life": they could not lawfully be executed by their masters, and it was even conceivable—though he admitted the point had never been determined—that they might own property.

Failing to carry the new, ideologically explosive politics with them by arguments and tactics that were familiar to them, failing often even to comprehend the nature of the forces that opposed them, and lacking both the means and the desire to control the turbulent communities by brute power, the loyalist leaders were forced to become devious simply to survive. Inevitably, therefore, they appeared hypocritical, ultimately conspiratorial, though in fact most of them were neither. As the pressure mounted, their responses narrowed. Their ideas became progressively more rigid, their imagination more limited, until in the end they could only plead for civil order as an absolute end in itself, which not only ignored the sources of the conflict but appeared unavoidably to be self-serving.

There is no better testimony to the newness of the forces that were shaping the Revolutionary movement than the failure of the loyalists to control them.

III

Some such understanding of the loyalists, or at least their leaders, must have a place in a general history of the Revolution consistent with what we now know of its origins. A further and perhaps more difficult challenge lies in interpreting within the same general theme the years that followed independence and that culminated in the permanent construction of the national government. For the developments of those years are of a different order from those of the years that preceded independence. The central and unifying themes shift; the approach that allowed one to understand the main events of the earlier years no longer serves for the later: a different kind of analysis and a different focus of attention are required.

The dominant fact of the earlier years had been the intensification of the ideological passions first ignited by the Stamp Act crisis and their final bursting into open insurrection. Thereafter the ideas, fears, and hopes that had first become decisive in the attacks on the British government were turned to positive uses in the framing of the first state constitutions, in the transforming of regressive social institutions that had been casually accepted in the *ancien régime*, and in directing Americans' efforts to new goals altogether: in education, in law, in religion, and in the distribution of land. But the Revolutionary spirit was changing as the original élan slowly filtered through the ordinary activities of life. The initial outburst, in which in some degree the majority of the colonists shared, could not be sustained, nor could the agreement on essentials that had brought together quite disparate groups. Passions cooled as ordinary life reasserted itself and cultural, sectional, and social differences, some of them newly created by the war and the displacement of the loyalists, became important. In the 1780s and 1790s the essential themes of American history became more complicated than they had been in the years before 1776. The creation of the American republic in the period between 1776 and the end of Washington's administration is the product of a complex interplay between the maturing of Revolutionary ideas and ideals and the involvements of everyday life—in politics, in business, and in a wide range of social activities.

A single characteristic of this later Revolutionary period predominates. Despite depressions, doubts, and fears for the future and despite the universal easing of ideological fervor, the general mood remained high through all of these years. There was a freshness and boldness in the tone of the eighties, a continuing belief that the world was still open, that young, energetic, daring, hopeful, imaginative men had taken charge and were drawing their power directly from the soil of the society they ruled and not from a distant, capricious, unmanageable sovereign. It was not simply that new liberty-protecting forms of government were being devised. A new civilization, it was felt, a civilization whose origins could now be seen to have lain in the earliest years of settlement, was being created, free from the weight of the past, free from the corruption and inflexibility of the tangled old-regime whose toils had so encumbered Americans in the late colonial period. Some sense of this had existed before independence, but unevenly, polemically, and without a generalized sanction. On a few rare occasions writers and preachers like Jonathan Mayhew had sketched a vision of future American grandeur; a sense of American separateness had begun to be felt and expressed and had been reinforced now and then from abroad; and in Congregational circles the sense of special mission that had gripped the minds of the Puritan settlers had in modified form persisted. But these had been scattered responses and expressions, constrained within the limits of a provincial culture whose metropolitan center had lain in the distant and ancient complexity of London.

If the colonists in the 1760s had been a "youthful" people, their mood had surely belied it. Nothing so clearly documents the transforming effect of the Revolution as the elevation of spirit, the sense of enterprise and experimentation, that suddenly emerged with independence and that may be found in every sphere of life in the earliest years of the new republic. This expectant stretching and spirited striving can be found in the systematic and ruthlessly aggressive provisions made for opening up new lands in the west and for settling new governments within them—provisions that ignored the welfare of the native population, already devastated by the Revolutionary War. The aggressive spirit of the age can be found, too, in the surge of people westward, hopefully risking security for new and quite unknown possibilities; in the vast outburst of domestic trade and commercial enterprise, spilling out across state boundaries and overseas, into the once restricted markets of the West Indies and Spanish America, into the continent of Europe, into Alaska, Russia, and even China; in experimental finance and path-breaking forms of banking; in bold if not always successful diplomacy; and above all in continuing experiments in government ranging from the recasting of public institutions and of the forms for recruiting leaders to the elimination or weakening of church establishments, the creation of federal relations among states, and a new concept of citizenship. Those years witnessed a release of American energies that swept forward into every corner of life. But in no simple way. The pattern is a complex one, in which ideological impulses move through the ordinary affairs of life, shape them, and are themselves reshaped by the pressures they meet.

In no area were these pressures more complex than in social organization. The background had been notably complex. For a century and a half conditions of life in these frontier communities had weakened the whole range of social reinforcements of traditional order. Yet, with complicated variations, a quasi-traditional order had existed, as had the sense that a proper social organization was hierarchical, with more or less clearly articulated levels of superiority and inferiority. The Revolution made changes in all of this, but not gross changes and not even immediately visible changes. There was no "leveling" of the social order and no outright destruction of familiar social institutions. "Democracy," in its modern form, was not created, in fact or theory, though the essential groundwork was laid. While the war, like so many wars before and since, transformed the economy and sped up mobility in significant ways, and while the displacement of the loyalists and the confiscation of much of their property created room at the top and sources of profit that had not existed before, no sweeping egalitarianism—in status, in wealth, or in power—was imposed. Newcomers to position and influence arrived more quickly and rose higher than they could have done earlier, but social distances remained much as before: narrow perhaps and rather easily bridgeable by European standards, but in local terms highly visible and palpable. And while the creation of new governments multiplied the available public offices and new men were everywhere seen in seats of power, and while the people as a whole were constitutionally involved in the processes of government as never before, socio-political elites whose origins went back a century persisted, apparently unaffected, in local communities, north and south.

And yet—everything was changing. The pressure of culturally sanctioned expectations had shifted to emphasize the status of free individuals as against the community and the integrity of their rights as against the powers of the state. The quasi-traditional society of the colonial period was not immediately destroyed, but the erosions that circumstance had made were not only multiplied, deepened, and broadened but ideologically reinforced as they had never been before. The effect upon a released society, developing economically, demographically, and institutionally at a remarkable rate, was transforming. The process of America's swift emergence as a distinctive society in the early nineteenth century we have scarcely begun to understand, but it is at least clear that the society Tocqueville found in America was the product of the gradually evolving interplay between a radical ideology and the circumstances of life in an expanding frontier world.

The convention at Philadelphia was a product of the same subtle interplay. The document it produced was neither a repudiation of '76, nor an instrument devised to protect aristocracies threatened in the states, nor an effort to preserve patrician rule, nor the product of a slaveholders' plot. It is a second-generation expression of the original ideological impulses of the Revolution applied to the everyday, practical problems of the late 1780s. Young men, almost none of whom had played a major role in the struggle that had led to independence, took for granted what their predecessors had finally achieved and proceeded far beyond them, in circumstances that no one had foreseen. The old ideas and attitudes are there, but now they are viewed from different angles, in part reformulated, and applied to new problems. The fear of power is there, but so too is the inescapable need to create a government potentially more powerful than any yet known—a government complete with its own independent treasury based on the right to tax, a government equipped with all the apparatus of coercion that had proved so fearful a bane to the subjects of despotic regimes. New safeguards must be built; new possibilities explored in the balance of freedom and power. Consent of the governed and the idea of the actual representation of people are there as fundamental principles of government, but so too is the belief that the subjects of this government were not only people but states as well, whose sovereignty must be both preserved and dissolved in this newer and greater creation. The very concept of sovereignty must therefore be probed, and provision now deliberately made for just that inconceivable monster in politics—*imperium in imperio*, states within a state—that right-minded, liberal men had refused to consider barely a decade before. New, awkward, strange political, economic, and constitutional urgencies are everywhere there, impelling forward to an unknown terrain minds formed in an earlier Revolutionary world and loyal to its basic principles. The results were daring, too daring and too threatening for some, but they gave workable and hopeful solutions to inescapable problems, solutions devised by young minds using old notions in new experimental ways. In this sense the Constitution of 1787 was a typical creation of the age: hopeful, boldly experimental, realistic, and faithful to the urges and beliefs that had led to Revolution.

IV

Such a view of the central themes of the Revolution helps one go beyond the immediate events of the Revolution itself and assess the most general meaning of the event in the broad sweep of eighteenth-century history and to isolate its impact on the overall course of American history.

There had been nothing inevitable in the outbreak of revolution. Deep flows of potentially revolutionary beliefs and apprehensions had moved through the delicate structure of mid-eighteenth-century American politics, but in the constitutional crisis of the 1770s there had been no necessity for these passionate concerns to break through the channels of civility. Even when an explosion in Anglo-American relations was generally expected, some knew ways to avoid it. Burke knew the way; so too, at least in the earlier years of crisis, did the preeminent victim of the Revolution, Thomas Hutchinson. But they, and others like them, lacked the power, and those who had the power lacked the concern and desire to avoid the confrontation. What was inevitable—what no one could have restrained—was America's emergence into the modern world as a liberal, more or less democratic, and capitalist society. That would have happened in any case. But that this emergence took place as it did—that it was impelled forward by a peculiar ideological explosion generated within a society less traditional than any then known in the Western world—this crucial fact has colored the whole of our subsequent history, and not only our own, but the world's.

How different elsewhere the process of modernization has been, and how important the differences are! In France, too, political modernization came through an eighteenth-century revolution, but there the prevailing ideas were radically egalitarian, directed to the destruction of a resistant, highly stratified social order dominated by a deeply entrenched nobility and capable of implementation only through a powerful, revolutionary state. The French Revolution created, at a cost of horrendous suffering and great bloodshed, a new state system more elaborate and more effective than the one it had overthrown, a state justified both by the dominant theories of revolution and by the belief that only such a power could dislodge the privileged world of the French *ancien régime*. In Germany two generations later an attempted liberal revolution failed altogether: its idealistic leaders lacked mass support, and could neither break through the protective barriers of the autocratic princely states nor free themselves from dependence on Prussian arms. Traditionalism thereafter deepened in Germany and produced in the end a dynamic industrial regime politically so paternalistic and socially so regressive that it constituted a threat to liberalism everywhere.

But it is the contrast with Britain that is ultimately most revealing. For Britain's was the parent political culture, and there too, as in America, well before the end of the eighteenth century, social and economic changes had eroded the traditional order and laid the groundwork for a modern liberal state. But the state that in fact resulted in nineteenth-century Britain was profoundly different from the American state; the two societies differed as much in politics as in social organization. The constitutional starting point had been the same: a balance of socio-constitutional forces in a theoretically "mixed" monarchical state. But Britain's political modernization, which eliminated the Crown and reduced the House of Lords as effective political forces while a slowly democratized and increasingly representative

House of Commons rose to greater power, moved gradually, through decades of change. The reformers were the most pragmatic and the least theoretical of politicians; they were more Tory than Whig, and their goal was stability. Burke's and the Rockinghams' "economical reform" and Pitt's fiscal reorganization were pragmatic responses to political pressures and to the urgencies of war. Behind them lay no systematic effort to recast politics or the structure of the state, but they began the destruction of the system of "influence" through which the government for so long had been managed. And that was the merest beginning. Multiplying through the reigns of three weak and feckless kings, consolidated by threats from abroad and stresses at home, increments of change added bit by bit to the transforming of the eighteenth-century constitution. By the time of Peel's ministry of 1841 much was formally the same, but the essential structure had been rebuilt. All the powers of the state—executive, legislative, and administrative—had become concentrated in the majority leadership of the House of Commons, which was increasingly responsive to a broadening political world. The modern constitution, politics, and state had evolved slowly and had gradually reshaped for modern use the system that Walpole had built. Somewhere deep within it there lay scattered elements of the ideas, fears, beliefs, and attitudes that had so engrossed the thoughts and so fired the imagination of opposition groups in eighteenth-century England and America; but they were now antique fragments, cemented haphazardly into the new radicalism of Bentham, the Chartists, and Mill.

In America, however, this earlier opposition ideology survived intact and fundamentally shaped the emerging state. The modernization of American politics and government during and after the Revolution took the form of a sudden realization of the program that had first been fully set forth by the opposition intelligentsia—the political moralists, the uncompromising republicans, the coffeehouse journalists, and the nostalgic Tories—in the reigns of the first two Georges. Where the English opposition of those years, forcing its way against a complacent social and political order, had only striven and dreamed, Americans, driven by the same aspirations but living in a society in many ways modern, and now released politically, could suddenly act. Where the English opposition had vainly agitated for partial reforms in the fierce debates that had raged over the duration of Parliaments, over restraints on the press, over standing armies, and over the force of wealth and patronage in corrupting popular rights, American leaders moved swiftly and with little social disruption to implement systematically the whole range of advanced ideas. In the process they not only built permanently into the modern American state system the specific constitutional and political reforms that had been vainly sought for so long in opposition circles, but also infused into American political culture two inner drives, two central spirits, that would distinguish it ever after.

The first is the belief that power is evil, a necessity perhaps but an evil necessity; that it is infinitely corrupting; and that it must be controlled, limited, restricted in every way compatible with a minimum of civil order. Written constitutions; the separation of powers; bills of rights; limitations on executives, on legislatures, and courts; restrictions on the right to coerce and to wage war—all express the profound distrust of power that lies at the ideological heart of the American Revolution and that has remained a permanent legacy. While in Britain the use of power became more concentrated in the passage to the modern state, and while in France and Germany it became more highly structured and more efficient, in America it became more diffused, more scattered, more open to suspicion, less likely ever to be unchallenged in the conduct of public life.

The distrust of power, generated deep within the ideological origins of the Revolution, runs through the entire course of American history and is a potent element in our national life today, when the instruments of power are so fearfully effective and the actuality of the state so overwhelming and inescapable.

Equally a part of our contemporary struggles is the second great theme that derives from the sources of Revolutionary ideology: the belief that through the ages it had been privilege—artificial, man-made and man-secured privilege, ascribed to some and denied to others mainly at birth—that, more than anything else except the misuse of power, had crushed men's hopes for fulfillment.

Not all of the early-eighteenth-century English opposition had been gripped by this belief. All elements had been concerned with corruption and with power, but this broad populist animus had drawn together quite different groups that shared only their common fear of the swollen politico-financial powers that, they believed, had created the Leviathan state. Some had been socially reactionary, or at least, like Bolingbroke, romantically nostalgic. They had sought not a broadening of the individual's self-determination but a return to a lost society of articulated statuses and elaborated hierarchies in which privilege counted for more rather than for less than it did in the modernizing world of eighteenth-century England. Americans had almost never shared these views, even in the proprietary and plantation colonies where the social reality might have seemed most congruous. When the Revolution moved from the negative, critical phase of the years before independence to the constructive era that followed, this reactionary strand of thought was simply ignored, to be taken up only occasionally thereafter by men who scarcely knew the context from which it was derived. The radical-libertarian impulse swept forward.

The dominant belief struck at the heart of the privileged world. Everywhere in America the principle prevailed that in a free community the purpose of institutions is to liberate people, not to confine them, and to give them the substance and the spirit to stand firm before the forces that would restrict them. To see in the Founders' failure to destroy chattel slavery the opposite belief, or some self-delusive hypocrisy that somehow condemns as false the liberal character of the Revolution—to see in the Declaration of Independence a statement of principles that was meant to apply only to whites and that was ignored even by its author in its application to slavery, and to believe that the purpose of the Constitution was to sustain aristocracy and perpetuate black bondage—is, I believe, to fundamentally misread the history of the time.

To condemn the founders of the Republic for having tolerated and perpetuated a society that rested on slavery is to expect them to have been able to transcend altogether the limitations of their own age. The eighteenth century was a brutal age. Human relations in British society were savage in a hundred different ways. In the placid countryside and sleepy market towns of eighteenth-century England, J. H. Plumb writes,

> the starving poor were run down by the yeomanry, herded
> into jails, strung up on gibbets, transported to the colonies.
> No one cared. This was a part of life like the seasons, like

the deep-drinking, meat-stuffing orgies of the good times and bumper harvests. The wheel turned, some were crushed, some favoured. Life was cheap enough. Boys were urged to fight. Dogs baited bulls and bears. Cocks slaughtered each other for trivial wagers. . . . Death came so easily. A stolen penknife and a boy of ten was strung up at Norwich; a handkerchief, taken secretly by a girl of fourteen, brought her the noose. Every six weeks London gave itself to a raucous fete as men and women were dragged to Tyburn to meet their end at the hangman's hands. The same violence, the same cruelty, the same wild aggressive spirit infused all ranks of society. . . . Young aristocrats—the Macaronis—fantastically and extravagantly dressed, rip-roared through the town, tipping up night watchmen, beating up innocent men and women. Jails and workhouses resembled concentration camps; starvation and cruelty killed the sick, the poor and the guilty. . . . Vile slums in the overcrowded towns bred violent epidemics; typhoid, cholera, smallpox ravaged the land.

Chattel slavery was brutal and degrading, but as far as the colonists knew, slavery in one form or another had always existed, and if it was brutal and degrading, so too was much else of ordinary life at the lower levels of society. Only gradually were people coming to see that this was a *peculiarly* degrading and a *uniquely* brutalizing institution, and to this growing awareness the Revolution made a major contribution. To note only that certain leaders of the Revolution continued to enjoy the profits of so savage an institution and in their reforms failed to obliterate it inverts the proportions of the story. What is significant in the historical context of the time is not that the liberty-loving Revolutionaries allowed slavery to survive, but that they—even those who profited directly from the institution—went so far in condemning it, confining it, and setting in motion the forces that would ultimately destroy it. For they were practical and moderate men, though idealistic and hopeful of human progress. Their mingling of the ideal and the real, their reluctance to allow either element to absorb the other altogether, is one of the Revolution's distinctive features. And of this, as of so much else, Jefferson is the supreme exemplar. In him a ruthless practicality mingled so incongruously with a sublime idealism that his personality seemed to his enemies, as it has seemed to modern historians concentrating on his "darker side," to have been grossly lacking in integrity. All of the Founders hoped to create a free society in America; not all of them could, or would, recognize, as Jefferson did, that this could only end in the destruction of chattel slavery. And those who recognized this and who strove to break the hold of this vicious institution so long before its condemnation became a common moral stance acted within a system of priorities that limited what they could achieve.

The highest priority was reserved for whatever tended to guarantee the survival of the republican nation itself, for in its continuing existence lay all hopes for the future. Most of the Revolutionary leaders hated slavery—not one of them ever publicly praised it—but they valued the preservation of the Union more. A successful and liberty-loving republic might someday destroy the slavery that it had been obliged to tolerate at the start; a weak and fragmented nation would never be able to do so. The haters of slavery were also limited in what they could accomplish by their respect for property, which like personal liberty was also part of the liberal state they sought to create. And they were, finally, fearful of the unforeseeable consequences in race relations that would result if the slaves—to the colonists still mysteriously alien, politically backward, and at least latently hostile people—were suddenly set free. It took a vast leap of the imagination in the eighteenth century to consider integrating into the political community the existing slave population, whose very "nature" was the subject of puzzled inquiry and who had hitherto been politically non-existent. But despite all of this, from the very earliest days of the Revolutionary movement the agonizing contradiction between chattel slavery and the freedom of a liberal state was seen, and the hope was formed that somehow, someday, the abhorrent practice of owning human beings would be destroyed. In the year of Jefferson's death slavery still existed, but it was destroyed in the North, forbidden in the Northwest, compressed deeper and deeper—and more and more explosively—into the South. An institution that had once been assumed and securely established had been challenged, confined, and transformed into an inescapable moral problem. If the Free Soilers of the 1850s, like the Republican platform writers of 1860, exaggerated the Founders' political commitment to the outright abolition of slavery, they correctly sensed the antislavery temper of the Revolutionary age. The ideological continuity between Jefferson and Lincoln is direct. However much their approach to the question of race may have differed, both deeply believed that slavery was wrong and ought to be restricted; both groped for ways of advancing that restriction; neither would destroy the Union to effect it.

The Founding Fathers were mortals, not gods; they could not overcome their own limitations and the complexities of life that kept them from realizing their ideals. But the destruction of privilege and the creation of a political system that demanded of its leaders the responsible and humane use of power were their highest aspirations. To note that the struggle to achieve these goals is still part of our lives—that it is indeed the very essence of the politics of our time— is only to say that the American Revolution, a unique product of the eighteenth century, is still in process. It will continue to be, so long as we seek to create a just and free society.

10

The Ideological Fulfillment
of the American Revolution:
A Commentary on the
Constitution

I THINK IT IS SAFE to say that even before the bicentennial cele-
brations the American Constitution had become the subject of
more elaborate and detailed scrutiny and commentary than has ever
been given to any document except the Bible. And now with the
innumerable new volumes, essays, and speeches published over the
past few years, this exegetical scholarship has reached a state of refinement and exhaustiveness beyond which, it would seem, it would
not be possible to go. I doubt if anyone has mastered all the useful
writings, new and old; I doubt if anyone ever will. There is too much;
there is movement in too many directions at once; too many disparate
issues are alive and flourishing quite independently of each other. The
most up-to-date and comprehensive summary becomes out of date
before it can be digested even by the intrepid band of specialists who
are professionally committed to the subject.

Yet there will never be enough. Partly that is because the subject
deeply matters—matters in the most fundamental sense of shaping
the way we live, what we may do, and how the government may act.
We must get the two-hundred-year-old story straight, in some way,
in order to make sense of our own world. The Constitution, in all its
aspects and ramifications, is profoundly relevant.

But it is more than that. The subject is, quite simply, fascinating:

and it is extraordinarily rich. The issues are subtle, the details are often puzzling and intriguing, the movement of events sometimes halting and involuted. And the actors are remarkable. Madison, Wilson, Ellsworth, Hamilton, Jay, Iredell, the Morrises, Sherman; on the other side, the junta of immensely articulate Pennsylvania antifederalists and their counterparts north and south—Melancton Smith, Luther Martin, James Winthrop, George Mason, Patrick Henry, Elbridge Gerry—the list of truly interesting actors in this drama seems endless. Part of the fascination comes simply from seeing these minds at work, formulating and reformulating, shifting, dodging, lunging.

There can be no ordinary historical characterization of the complicated interplay between the maturing of Revolutionary ideas and ideals and the involvements of everyday life, which is the essence of the history of the Constitution period. To me the most subtle and penetrating depiction of the inner character of the drafting of, and the debate on, the Constitution is not a historical discourse but a poem, a short poem by Richard Wilbur. It is called "Mind."

> Mind in its purest play is like some bat
> That beats about in caverns all alone,
> Contriving by a kind of senseless wit
> Not to conclude against a wall of stone.
>
> It has no need to falter or explore;
> Darkly it knows what obstacles are there,
> And so may weave and flitter, dip and soar
> In perfect courses through the blackest air.
>
> And has this simile a like perfection?
> The mind is like a bat. Precisely. Save
> That in the very happiest intellection
> A graceful error may correct the cave.[1]

They did indeed weave and flitter, dip and soar, and they did indeed correct the cave. But how?*

---

*Notes for this chapter are to be found on pp. 269 ff.

Themes

I

The ideological history of the American Revolution developed in three distinct phases. Each has a voluminous documentation and each has a distinctive focus and emphasis. The first was the years of struggle with Britain before 1776 when, under the pressure of events and the necessity to justify resistance to constituted authority, the colonists developed from their complex heritage of political thought the set of ideas, already in scattered ways familiar to them, that was most illuminating and most appropriate to their needs. Centered on the fear of centralized power and rooted in the belief that free states are fragile and degenerate easily into tyrannies unless vigilantly protected by an independent, free, knowledgeable, and uncorrupted electorate working through institutions that balance and distribute rather than concentrate power, their ideas were critical of, and challenging to, the legal authority they had lived under. In this period, as in the others, they were profuse in their writings, but the most effective form of expression was the pamphlet, a flexible form that accommodated collections of letters, sermons, and debates, and also, and most characteristically, fully developed arguments—essays that were less than formal discourses but yet substantial and comprehensive. The writings of this early period drew together the basic ideas which would flow through all subsequent stages of American political thought, and provided the permanent foundation of the nation's political beliefs.[2]

The second phase saw the constructive application of these ideas and the exploration of their implications, limits, and possibilities in the writing and rewriting of the first state constitutions, from 1776 through the 1780s. Obliged now to construct their own governments at the state level, American leaders were forced to think through the fundamentals of their beliefs, and establish republican polities that expressed the principles they had earlier endorsed. They did not work from clean slates. Constrained by institutions that had long existed and by entrenched leadership groups, they were revisers, amenders, elaborators, and conceptualizers, as they applied fresh ideas to existing structures and brought them as close as possible to their ideal. So they explored the nature of written constitutions and of constituent power; worked through the problems of separating functioning powers of government to form balances within single-order societies; and probed the nature of representation, the operative meaning of sovereignty of the people, and individual rights. Few of their conclusions were applied uniformly or in absolute and complete form. But everywhere the institutional problems of republican government at the state level and the principles on which it was based were probed in this constructive phase of the ideological revolution. And while again pamphlets continued to be vital publications, now, in addition, direct exchanges of ideas in constitutional conventions became crucial, as did the drafts and texts of the resulting constitutions, along with statutes that extended the range of basic law, and community responses to proposed constitutions, amendments, and revisions.[3]

The third phase—the writing, debating, ratifying, and amending of the national constitution—resembles the second phase in that it was constructive and concentrated on constitution writing; many of the ideas that had been developed in the writing and discussion of the state constitutions were applied to the national constitution and further refined and developed. But in its essence this phase was distinct. For now, in the 1780s, under the pressure of rising social tensions, economic confusion pointing to the possible collapse of public credit, frustration in international affairs, and the threat of dissolution of the weak Confederation, the central task was reversed. Now the goal of the initiators of change was the creation, not the destruction, of national power—the construction of what could properly be seen, and feared, as a *Machtstaat*, a central national power that involved armed force, the aggressive management of international relations, and, potentially at least, the regulation of vital aspects of everyday life by a government superior to and dominant over all other, lesser governments. The background experiences of constitution writing in the states were informative—they were constantly referred to in the Philadelphia convention and in the ratifying debates—but the central issue of 1787–88 was different in its nature from the main issues in the forming of the state governments, and diametrically opposite to the goals of the pre-Revolutionary years. Yet the pre-Revolutionary ideology was fundamental to all their beliefs. How could it be reconciled with present needs?

The Founders certainly did not leave the confinement—the cave—

of their own intellectual world and depart for some other. That debate and struggle with Britain was only a decade in the past; they still lived in that same intellectual world. How were the original commitments to be reconciled with the radically new needs and proposals?

What follows is not an account of the ratification debate as a whole, but reflections on this limited but basic question.[4]

Until recently the bulk of the available documentation on the ratification debate had been quite small: four volumes of formal debates in the state ratifying conventions published by Jonathan Elliot in 1836, two volumes of pamphlets and essays published by P. L. Ford in the 1890s, and, above all, the *Federalist* papers, which have engrossed attention at least since the appearance of Beard's *Economic Interpretation* in 1913, together with a few well-known antifederalist publications, chiefly the *Federal Farmer* series.[5] In recent years additions have been made to the available antifederalist publications, first in Cecelia Kenyon's collection, and more comprehensively in Herbert Storing's five volumes of documents, which include antifederalist papers from almost all of the states, and ephemera as well as systematic writings. But it was not until the appearance of the first eight of the projected twenty volumes of *The Documentary History of the Ratification of the Constitution* that it became possible to grasp the full dimensions of the outpouring of 1787–89. The brainchild of Merrill Jensen, at the University of Wisconsin, who edited the first three volumes, and since his death carried forward, with great scholarly rigor, by his former assistants, John Kaminski and Gaspare Saladino, this series now forms the foundation on which all studies of the Constitution must be based. The scholarship is excellent—its only faults, redundancy and complexity of organization, result from an excess of zeal—and the scale is vast. I estimate that the completed twenty letterpress volumes will total well over 10,000 pages—upwards of five million words—and microfiche addenda will greatly increase that total. In addition the editors have traced and identify in their annotation the *reprints*, whole or in part, of every published document, thus providing an index of the circulation of the writings, hence their popularity or importance as judged by contemporaries.[6]

In reading through this immensity of writings, ranging from rather silly lampooning squibs and jingle-jangle verses to scholarly treatises and brilliant polemical exchanges, one easily loses track of any patterns or themes. The sheer bulk is overwhelming, for, as Henry Knox wrote at the time, "The new constitution! The new constitution is the general cry this way. Much paper is spoiled on the subject, and many essays are written which perhaps are not read by either side."[7] Storing's edition of antifederalist writings, said to be "complete," turns out in fact to include only about 15 percent of the total available antifederalist material.[8] And the mass of federalist writings reveals the great range and variety of thinking on that side of the struggle, by no means all represented in the *Federalist* papers.[9] In fact, in the full context of the political writings of 1787–88 the importance of the *Federalist* papers seems diminished. Some contemporaries, of course, immediately saw the merits of that long series (more than quadruple the length of any other). George Washington, a close ally of the authors, wrote prophetically to Hamilton that "when the transient circumstances and fugitive performances which attended this *crisis* shall have disappeared, that work will merit the notice of posterity, because in it are candidly discussed the principles of freedom. . . ." Noah Webster thought the series "one of the most complete dissertations on government that ever has appeared in America, perhaps in Europe." And James Iredell, one of the most penetrating minds among the federalists, called *The Federalist*'s treatment of standing armies "masterly" and hoped the whole work "will soon be in every body's hands."[10]

But in the "transient circumstances" of the time it was not so much the *Federalist* papers that captured most people's imaginations as James Wilson's speech of October 6, 1787, the most famous, to some the most notorious, federalist statement of the time. To this early, brief, and luminous pronouncement there were floods of refutations, confirmations, and miscellaneous responses.[11] Comments on the *Federalist* papers, on the other hand, were few, usually scholarly and technical, and politically unremarkable. Rufus King thought Oliver Ellsworth's "Landholder" essays more effective than the *Federalist* (they are indeed remarkably original pieces), and the federalist Judge A. C. Hanson, formerly Washington's private secretary and soon to be the chancellor of the state of Maryland, while acknowledging that the *Federalist* papers display deep penetration and are ingenious and elaborate, found them sophistical in some places, painfully obvious in others, and throughout prolix and tiresome. He could not get through them, he said: they do not "force the attention, rouze the passions, or thrill the nerves." His own short pamphlet, *Remarks on the Proposed Plan*, dedicated to Washington, might be inferior to the *Federalist* as an abstract treatise on government, he said, but "as an occasional pamphlet" he was confident it was "superiour" and "more serviceable."[12]

Hanson was at least right in thinking that for all their remarkable qualities the *Federalist* papers were not altogether original. Oliver Ellsworth wrote more clearly and fully on judicial review than did the *Federalist* authors, and both he and James Wilson recognized the central importance of that topic before they did. Twenty days before the appearance of *Federalist* X the New Jersey lawyer John Stevens, Jr., anticipated Madison's central argument on republicanism, national size, and self-interest in the first of his "Americanus" essays, an analysis that was independently developed also by an anonymous Connecticut writer seventeen days later. Others went beyond Madison in locating the sources of the problem discussed in *Federalist* X in blockages of thought they discovered in the received tradition, inherited ideas that hitherto had been axiomatic but were now revealed to be anachronistic, distorted, or irrelevant.[13]

For the federalists were obliged to work at that basic level if they were to succeed in their central task. They had no choice if they were to justify the creation of a new nation-state potentially as powerful as any other. The old beliefs of '76 which had served to destroy an imperial power had somehow to be reconciled with nationalist needs. Yet it was obvious that the ideological origins of the American Revolution had been rooted not merely in a general fear of power but specifically in the belief that liberty could not survive where corruptible men wielded the apparatus of a powerful national state. Again and again both federalist and antifederalist commentators on the Constitution thought back to the 1760s and 1770s, the federalists to make progress toward justifying a national power system that would be safe for the people's liberties, the antifederalists to show that such a project could never succeed, that it involved a profound self-contradiction, and that the Constitution, if adopted, would plunge the country into precisely the misery that the received wisdom had always predicted for any powerful centralized regime.

II

The antifederalists have been called, in Cecelia Kenyon's seminal essay, "men of little faith" in that they lacked faith in the safe future that the federalists foresaw under the Constitution.[14] But in the context of the great mass of ratification documents the antifederalists emerge as the ones who *kept* the faith—the ancient faith so fundamental a part of the ideological origins of the Revolution, from which, they argued, the Constitution departed. The antifederalist Judge Thomas Tredwell of New York recalled the old days despairingly: in '76, he declared, "the spirit of liberty ran high, and danger put a curb on ambition. . . . Sir, in this Constitution we have not only neglected—we have done worse—we have openly violated, our faith— that is, our public faith." Still emotionally and intellectually involved in that original struggle against an imperial government that had claimed total power over the American people, the antifederalists were haunted by the dangers that had then been foreseen. Now, faced with what seemed a similar threat, they summoned up the ghosts of those passionate years—and in the most specific, literal terms. The identity between antifederalist thought and that of the most fervent ideologists of '76 is at times astonishing.[15]

Mercy Otis Warren could never clear her mind of the dark vision of her ancient enemy, Thomas Hutchinson, who she never ceased believing had been a tool of absolutism, and a willing servant of his despotic patron, the Earl of Hillsborough. Her widely circulated *Observations on the Constitution* (February 1788) is a boiling polemic, not simply against the federalists, but also—and simultaneously—against the long-dead governor, that "great champion for arbitrary power [with his] machinations to subvert the liberties of this country" and his design to bring down on America "the infernal darkness of Asiatic slavery." The same threat, she believed, had been renewed by the federalists, and her task, she felt, was to rekindle the dying embers of the patriotism and the love of freedom that had burned so brightly in '76, and to demonstrate the direct connection—the political descent—between the loyalists of '76, with their program of arbitrary power, and James Wilson and his neo-Hutchinsonians, with their "many-headed monster," the Constitution. For her, little but the personnel had changed over the years. The dangers were the same. In

1788 as in 1768 she saw the "deep-laid plots, the secret intrigues, [and] the bold effrontery of . . . interested and avaricious adventurers for place, who, intoxicated with the ideas of distinction and preferment, have prostrated every worthy principle beneath the shrine of ambition." She, and other ardent antifederalists, could see a direct line from the loyalists and the wartime profiteers to the federalists; and she was convinced that once again America faced "*dark, secret* and *profound intrigues* of . . . statesmen long practiced in the purlieus of despotism." Just as Hutchinson had urged his master Hillsborough to eliminate annual elections in Massachusetts in favor of triennial, so the Constitution would make Congressional elections biennial.[16]

The fear of a conspiracy against the fragile structure of freedom, the same fear that had lain at the heart of the resistance movement before 1776, pervaded the thought of the antifederalists. No writer of the pre-Revolutionary period was more convinced that he was struggling with a secret plot against liberty than Luther Martin, whose rambling account of the Philadelphia convention, *The Genuine Information*, if extracted from its context, would seem an expression of extreme paranoia. Similarly, Samuel Bryan's eighteen-part "Centinel" series in the *Philadelphia Independent Gazetteer* is a foaming diatribe against those "harpies of power," the criminal conspirators against liberty who shield their secret intentions with "the virtues of a Washington," blatantly lie to the public, and shackle the press to suppress opposition—in fact do anything, no matter how foul and vicious, to fob off on the people "the most odious system of tyranny that was ever projected [i.e., the Constitution], a many headed hydra of despotism, whose complicated and various evils would be infinitely more oppressive and afflictive than the scourge of any single tyrant." Precisely who the instigators of this "deep laid scheme to enslave us" were, Bryan was not sure (another Philadelphian was quite certain that the Society of the Cincinnati was responsible and that Rufus King had inadvertently confessed as much in the Massachusetts convention). But it seemed obvious to Bryan that at the very least Franklin had hoodwinked the innocent Washington "by inducing him to acquiesce in a system of despotism and villainy, at which enlightened patriotism shudders."[17]

But at least Bryan included some reasoned arguments against specific provisions of the Constitution, something Benjamin Workman, an Irish immigrant of 1784, never managed to do in his twelve "Phil-adelphiensis" papers. There is nothing to match the violent rhetoric of those feverish diatribes. The federalists, Workman wrote, were "demagogues despising every sense of order and decency"; they were the "meanest traitors that ever dishonoured the human character," and as "the haughty lordlings of the convention" they were engaged in a "conspiracy against the freedom of America both deep and danger-ous," a conspiracy that could only end in "one *despotic monarchy.*" "Ah my friends," Workman wrote, "the days of a cruel Nero approach fast; the language of a monster, of a Caligula, could not be more imperious" than that of the federalist plotters who "now openly browbeat you with their insolence, and assume majesty."[18]

No doubt Workman, in Tench Coxe's phrase, was simply "bellow-ing and braying like a wild asses colt,"[19] but calmer minds too saw in the federalists' efforts a renewal of the hidden dangers Americans had faced in the years before 1776. They declared again and again—in a great outpouring of newspaper squibs, carefully reasoned essays, and convention speeches—that the old struggle had been renewed, and that the ancient issues confronted them once more.

Examination of the Constitution revealed, they believed, a taxing power in the hands of the proposed national government that would prove to be as unqualified by the restraints of the states as Parlia-ment's had been by the colonial assemblies. With such limitless taxing power, Patrick Henry declared in one of his vast speeches in the Virginia convention—one of those heaving oceans of antifederalist passion whose thundering waves threatened to drown Madison's small, tight cogencies—the Senate would live in splendor and a "great and mighty President" would "be supported in extravagant munificence, so that the whole of our property may be taken by this American government, by laying what taxes they please, giving themselves what salaries they please, and suspending our laws at their pleasure." The New York antifederalist "Brutus" could see an even greater danger, in the federal government's power to "borrow money on the credit of the United States." With this power "the Congress may mortgage any or all of the revenues of the union . . . [and] may borrow of foreign nations a principal sum, the interest of which will be equal to the annual revenues of the country. By this means, they may create a national debt so large as to exceed the ability of the country ever to sink. I can scarcely contemplate a greater calamity that could befal this country than to be loaded with a debt exceeding their ability ever to discharge."[20]

The notion that lesser governmental bodies—the states—could effectively share sovereignty with a central power (the principle of federalism) made no more sense to the antifederalists in 1788 than it had when the colonists had fruitlessly proposed it in the years before 1776 and people like Galloway and Hutchinson had effectively ridiculed its logic. So once again the antifederalists rang the changes on the famous "solecism," *imperium in imperio,* explaining in endless iteration that, as George Mason put it, "two concurrent powers cannot exist long together; the one will destroy the other." "There is a spirit of rivalship in power," "An Old Whig" of Pennsylvania wrote, "which will not suffer two suns to shine in the same firmament; one will speedily darken the other, and the individual states will be as totally eclipsed as the stars in the meridian blaze of the sun." A "mutual concurrence of powers," Patrick Henry declared, "will carry you into endless absurdity."[21]

The federal government, like the British government before 1776, "Brutus" wrote in two of his finest papers, empowered by the "necessary and proper" and the "supreme law of the land" clauses, "would totally destroy all the powers of the individual states," for no "two men, or bodies of men, [can] have unlimited power respecting the same object." It contradicts logic, scripture, even the principles of mechanics. "The legislature of the United States will have a right to exhaust every source of revenue in every state, and to annul all laws of the states which may stand in the way of effecting it." In the end, the national government, through its taxing power, "Brutus" then wrote in a florid peroration that conjures up the horrors of totalitarian states,

> exercised without limitation, will introduce itself into every corner of the city and country. It [the national government] will wait upon the ladies at their toilett, and will not leave them in any of their domestic concerns; it will accompany them to the ball, the play, and the assembly; it will go with them when they visit, and will, on all occasions, sit beside them in their carriages, nor will it desert them even at

church; it will enter the house of every gentleman, watch over his cellar, wait upon his cook in the kitchen, follow the servants into the parlour, preside over the table, and note down all he eats and drinks; it will attend him to his bed-chamber, and watch him while he sleeps; it will take cognizance of the professional man in his office or his study; it will watch the merchant in the counting-house or in his store; it will follow the mechanic to his shop and in his work, and will haunt him in his family and in his bed; it will be a constant companion of the industrious farmer in all his labour, it will be with him in the house and in the field, observe the toil of his hands and the sweat of his brow; it will penetrate into the most obscure cottage; and finally, it will light upon the head of every person in the United States. To all these different classes of people and in all these circumstances in which it will attend them, the language in which it will address them will be, GIVE! GIVE!

"Brutus's" only solution, which was endorsed by other antifederalists, was to go back to the distinction between external and internal taxes and external and internal spheres of power, which had flourished during the Stamp Act struggle twenty-three years earlier and had been endorsed by Franklin in his testimony before Parliament, only to be repudiated in John Dickinson's *Farmer's Letters* and thereafter dropped from serious discussion.[22]

Thus the antifederalists, impelled by the fear of power, saw ancient issues in modern problems. Just as the king in Parliament once had had absolute power over the selection of representatives who collectively might protect the people against excessive exactions by a central power, so, they pointed out, the Constitution, in Article I, Section 4—one of the most hotly debated clauses in the entire ratification struggle—gave Congress the right to alter the times and manner of holding elections for Senators and Representatives. And more than that, Patrick Henry declared, representation in Congress will be not actual but virtual. "We contended with the British about representation," he reminded the Virginia ratifying convention. "They offered us such a representation as Congress now does. They called it virtual representation. If you look at that paper [the Constitution] you will find it so there. . . . Representation is not, therefore, the vital principle of this government. So far it is wrong"—and so far "the tyranny of Philadelphia [the federal convention] may be like the tyranny of George III."[23]

Representation was a basic issue, in 1788 as in 1776; but nothing excited antifederalist passions more than Congress's power, under Article I, Section 8, "to raise and support armies," the curse of which, for most antifederalists, was in no way diminished by the two-year limit on military appropriations. (Britain's Parliament, they immediately pointed out, was limited to *annual* funding; and what would keep Congress from continuing appropriations indefinitely?) There is simply no way to measure the volume and fervor of the antifederalists' denunciation of this provision, which revived for them not simply a general fear of military power but the specific danger of "standing armies," a peculiar and distinctive threat to liberty that had been formulated for all time, they believed, in England in the 1690s, and had been carried forward intact to the colonies. There the danger had been fully realized in 1768, when the first British troops had been stationed in peaceful Boston and a predictable "massacre" had resulted.[24]

"Standing armies" were not national guards, protecting the people. They were janissary troops, palace guards, predatory mercenaries loyal to the power source—the Crown, the executive, the President, anyone in authority to whom they were loyal or who would pay them. So it had been said in the 1690s; so it had been said in 1768; and so it was said two decades later. The good people of South Carolina, a speaker in that state's convention warned, will certainly resist the despotism of the Constitution, as threatening to liberty as Archbishop Laud's doctrine of "non-resistance" had been. And what will result? "Your standing army, like Turkish janizaries enforcing despotic laws, must ram it down their throats with the points of bayonets." Surely, a Pennsylvanian "Democratic Federalist" wrote in one of the most powerful replies to Wilson's October 6 speech—surely

> the experience of past ages and the . . . most celebrated patriots have taught us to dread a standing army above all earthly evils. Are we then to go over all the thread-bare, common place arguments that have been used without success by the advocates of tyranny, and which have been for a long time past so gloriously refuted! Read the excellent *Burgh* in his

political disquisitions on this hackneyed subject, and then say
whether you think that a standing army is necessary in a free
country.

Even the *"aristocratical"* David Hume, the writer stated, believed that
a standing army was *"a mortal distemper in a government."* Wilson's
"thread-bare, hackneyed argument" for a standing army, the writer
concluded, "has been answered over and over in different ages, and
does not deserve even the smallest consideration." One scarcely
needed to argue the issue, the dangers were so obvious and well
known. "Brutus" contented himself simply with quoting at great length
the famous, often reprinted speech on reducing the army that William
Pulteney had delivered to the House of Commons in 1732.

As for the supposed safeguard of the state militias, to the antifederalists the idea made a mockery of reason. Not only did the Constitution specifically allow Congress to nationalize the state troops,
hence absorb them into the standing army, but there was nothing to
prevent the President from using them as if they *were* standing armies,
since he had the power to deploy them anywhere: Virginia's troops
could be shipped off to Massachusetts to put down political opposition there, Rhode Island's to Pennsylvania—or for that matter to Cuba
or Timbuctoo—wherever the President's adventures might lead him.
Even worse: the national government, George Mason said, referring
specifically to events in Pennsylvania forty years earlier, might cun-
ningly neglect the state militias, fail to arm them, or otherwise im-
mobilize them, so that in time, when the people felt the need for
military protection, they would throw themselves on the mercy of the
national government and cry out, " 'Give us a standing army!' " A fan-
tasy? "Those things which *can* be," the Presbyterian preacher David
Caldwell said in the North Carolina convention, *"may* be." "I do not
. . . say Congress *will* do" the evil he feared, Abraham Holmes of
Plymouth County declared in the Massachusetts convention, "but,
sir, I undertake to say that Congress . . . *may* do it; and if they do
not, it will be owing *entirely*—I repeat it, it will be owing *entirely*—to
the goodness of the men, and not in the *least degree* owing to the
goodness of the Constitution." And the goodness of men being a
hopelessly frail reed, evil possibilities must be eliminated at the start.
A standing army, once established, will be uncontrollable.[25]

Limitless taxation, corrupted representation, a specious sharing of sovereignty that would end in absolutism, standing armies—these were not new issues, but ancient issues that had been fought over a generation earlier in precisely the same terms and that had resulted in revolution. Similarly familiar—notorious—was the omission, in Article III, of jury trials in civil cases, a repudiation, it seemed to the antifederalists, of the central safeguard of common law procedure, reminiscent of the Crown's advancement of prerogative courts in its effort, in the 1760s and 1770s, to assert its power over the colonies. Familiar, too, was the issue of Congressmen paying their own salaries: "Before the Revolution," Dr. John Taylor told the Massachusetts convention, "it was considered as a grievance that the governors, etc., received their pay from Great Britain. They could not, in that case, feel their dependence on the people, when they received their appointments and salaries from the crown." Rawlins Lowndes, in South Carolina, objecting to the lack of popular control over Congressional salaries, had a vivid memory of the precedent, recalling "what a flame was raised in Massachusetts, on account of Great Britain assuming the payment of salaries to judges and other state officers; and that this conduct was considered as originating in a design to destroy the independence of their government."[26]

The fear of "secret services" money dispensed in covert operations by the executive through hidden slush funds—one of the Crown's most dangerous practices—was also revived, along with the sense that the President's pardoning power was a legal re-creation of the ancient precept that the king can do no wrong. Like the king, the President, under Article II, Section 2, was empowered to pardon anyone "for offenses against the United States, except in cases of impeachment." So the President, George Mason wrote, could "screen from punishment those whom he had secretly instigated to commit the crime, and thereby prevent a discovery of his own guilt," a maneuver that would be the less dangerous for him since—Luther Martin pointed out—trials of Presidential impeachments were to be conducted by the Senate, "a privy council to the President" whose "leading and influential members may have advised or concurred in the very measures for which he may be impeached"—Senators who would, in addition, still be hopeful of lucrative presidential appointments. Such trials, moreover, were to be presided over by a chief justice nominated by the President "probably . . . not so much for his eminence in legal knowledge and for his integrity, as from favouritism and influence, since the President, knowing that in case of. impeachment the chief justice is to preside at his trial, will naturally wish to fill that office with a person of whose voice and influence he shall consider himself secure."[27]

So the antifederalists' vision of the dangers they faced was deeply colored by their recollections of the past. "The same causes produces [*sic*] the same effects," a Massachusetts debater argued, recalling the Boston Massacre in a discussion of standing armies. Like Patrick Henry, they feared the anticipated creation of federal customs officers because: "the experience of the mother country leads me to detest them." Like James Winthrop, in his eighteen-part "Agrippa" series, they recalled that at the heart of the disaster of British rule had been Parliament's effort to impose uniformity on the great variety of life in this distant periphery, an effort that would have to be repeated, catastrophically, by Congress and by the federal courts if the national government were in any degree to rule the diverse nation effectively. Artificial uniformity of any kind *would* be, just as it *had been*, catastrophic: a uniform trade policy would destroy the successes of regional enterprise; a uniform naturalization law would violate the need either of some states to import people rapidly or of others "to keep their blood pure." And in the end any such effort would require the imposition of armed might, which would lead inevitably—as it always had in the past—to turmoil and civil war.[28]

It was all a familiar story, with a predictable outcome to people who had been through it all before. Amos Singletary—referred to affectionately as our "Honourable Old Daddy" by his colleagues in the Massachusetts ratifying convention—reminded the delegates that he had been "on the stage in the beginning of our troubles, in the year 1775," and *he* recalled, even if no one else did, precisely what had happened. If, at that time, he declared, "any body had proposed such a constitution as this . . . it would have been thrown away at once—it would not have been looked at." For could not Congress under the Constitution do precisely what people like himself had gone to war to prevent—assert a limitless right to tax and to "bind us in all cases whatever"? So they cited leading documents of the earlier, pre-Revolutionary debates. They quoted Stephen Hopkins's *Rights of*

Colonies Examined, John Dickinson's *Farmer's Letters*, James Burgh's *Political Disquisitions*, Hutchinson's debates with the Massachusetts Assembly; and they invoked the ancient deities—Hampden, Sidney, Pym, Wilkes—and denounced the ancient villains—Hutchinson, Hillsborough, Bute, even those fabled apologists of "passive obedience and non-resistance" in the time of Charles I, Robert Sibthorpe and Roger Mainwaring.[29]

But the historical dimension of the antifederalists' condemnation of the Constitution had a subtler and more powerful element. One unquestionably fundamental belief in the received tradition which had been brought into focus during the pre-Revolutionary struggle with Britain was the conviction that the only truly free states were republics, where people ruled themselves through freely elected representatives; that republics, necessarily delicate structures, could survive only in small units since they required uniformity of opinion, or at least a rough consensus, force being necessary to control clangorous diversity; and that the animating principle of republics was virtue. The ultimate sources of these ideas they rarely cited. Their chief authority, insofar as they needed any authority to document what seemed to them such obvious ideas, was Montesquieu, whose name recurs far more often than that of any other authority in all of the vast literature on the Constitution. He was the fountainhead, the ultimate arbiter of belief, his ideas the standard by which all other measures were set. They reverted to his authority at every turn, and through his eyes saw the moral impossibility of creating a massive republic.

For the antifederalists, no less than the federalists, had a thoroughly realistic sense of human nature, and never deluded themselves that any people could be entirely virtuous or that any political population could be principally animated by public spirit. Patrick Henry, the most ardent of the antifederalist spokesmen, based his philosophy of government on the universal force and moral validity of what he called "self-love." It is the heart of his most passionate and eloquent oration, which lasted for two days in the Virginia convention—a speech that must have been electrifying when Henry reached his peroration: "Must I give my soul, my lungs, to Congress? Congress must have our souls; the state must have our souls. This is dishonorable and disgraceful."

The devil in it all, he declared, was the *implied* powers of the "necessary and proper" clause combined with the innate evil of human nature. "Implication is dangerous because it is unbounded: if it is admitted at all, and no limits be prescribed, it admits of the utmost extension" because the lust for power, the passion for dominance, will exploit every possibility. Constitutional checks and balances cannot possibly eliminate or even effectively constrain the evil of human nature. The only counterforce that counts, Henry said, is "self-love."

> Tell me not of checks on paper; but tell me of checks founded on self-love. . . . fair, disinterested patriotism and professions of attachment to rectitude have never been solely trusted to by an enlightened, free people. If you depend on your President's and Senators' patriotism, you are gone. . . . The real rock of political salvation is self-love, perpetuated from age to age in every human breast and manifested in every action. If they can stand the temptations of human nature, you are safe . . . there is no danger. But can this be expected of human nature? Without real checks, it will not suffice that some of them are good . . . the wicked will be continually watching: consequently you will be undone . . . I dread the depravity of human nature. . . . I will never depend on so slender a protection as the possibility of being represented by virtuous men.

Britain's freedom has survived, Henry concluded, not because of the people's virtue but because the monarch's "self-love, [his] self-interest," coincides with the advancement of the nation's prosperity. The monarch remains monarch for life, and his narrowest self-interest is therefore nourished by the nation's successes and good fortune. But "the President and Senators have nothing to lose. They have not that interest in the preservation of the government that the kings and lords have in England. They will, therefore, be regardless of the interests of the people."[30]

Henry's language was peculiarly his own, but his belief that "man is a fallen creature, a fallible being" was universal among the antifederalists. His colleague Mason, "considering the natural lust of power so inherent in man," feared above all that "the thirst of power will prevail to oppress the people." In North Carolina, one antifederalist said "the depravity of mankind" militates against any confidence that the people's representatives would have sufficient virtue and wisdom to regulate affairs properly, another that "it is the nature of mankind to be tyrannical" and hence he feared "the depravity of human nature, the predominant thirst for power which is in the breast of everyone." And in New York the pseudonymous "Cato" wrote that "ambition and voluptuousness aided by flattery will teach magistrates . . . to have separate and distinct interests from the people," a sentiment stated with even greater force by other antifederalists in that state, in Massachusetts, and in South Carolina.[31]

It was because of their fear of human depravity, of mankind's selfish neglect of the public good and passionate devotion to the narrowest self-interest, that the antifederalists were certain that an extended republic, of continental dimensions, could never survive as a free state and would end either as a military dictatorship or as a junta of ruthless aristocrats. The logic of this process was variously expounded, variously phrased, but the conclusion was everywhere the same and always derived from the same received tradition of pre-Revolutionary thought. For most, it was largely a matter of citing what "Brutus," in the first of his notable series to the people of New York, called "the opinion of the greatest and wisest men who have ever thought or wrote on the science of government," principally Montesquieu, whose classic formulation in *The Spirit of the Laws* he quoted:

> "It is natural to a republic to have only a small territory, otherwise it cannot long subsist. In a large republic there are men of large fortunes, and consequently of less moderation . . . he has interest of his own; he soon begins to think that he may be happy, great and glorious by oppressing his fellow citizens, and that he may raise himself to grandeur on the ruins of his country. In a large republic, the public good is sacrificed to a thousand views. . . . In a small one, the interest of the public is easier perceived, better understood, and more within reach of every citizen; abuses are of less extent, and of course are less protected."

A sentiment, "Brutus" said, concurred in by Beccaria, exemplified by Greek and Roman history, and simply self-evident. It was perfectly, palpably, logical. A free republic, he patiently explained, must be ruled by laws written by the representatives of the people.

> Now, in a large extended community it is impossible to have
> a representation possessing the sentiments . . . to declare the
> minds of the people without having it so numerous and un-
> wieldly [*sic*] as to be subject in great measure to the incon-
> veniency of a democratic government. The territory of the
> United States is of vast extent. . . . Is it practicable for a coun-
> try so large and so numerous as they will soon become to
> elect a representation that will speak their sentiments without
> their becoming so numerous as to be incapable of transacting
> public business? It certainly is not.

And he went on to discourse on the varieties of climate, economic
interests, religion, manners and habits of the vast and scattered American population which might, he thought, one day far in the future,
reach a total of 30 million souls.[32]

Others developed variations on this basic theme. For "Cato," who
quoted the same passage of *The Spirit of the Laws* and cited the same
examples from classical antiquity (examples helpfully furnished by
Montesquieu), agreed with "Brutus," but added that factionalism in an
extended republic would lead inevitably to a standing army. For factionalism would produce the threat of secession, and that in turn
would require the creation of "a permanent force, to be kept on foot"
in order to preserve the state, a necessity created also by the difficulty
of executing revenue laws, always the source of opposition to a government, "on the extremes" of the extended realm. Where a military
force ruled, "will not political security, and even the opinion of it, be
extinguished? Can mildness and moderation exist in a government
where the primary incident in its exercise must be force? Will not
violence destroy confidence . . . ?" The "Federal Farmer" had more
dramatic apprehensions. In a huge republic, the legislative body would
be an uncontrollable mob, and the effectiveness of the sprawling court
system would dissipate on the far-flung frontier, so that the rule of
law would survive inversely with the distance from the seat of government. The result? "Either neglected laws, or a military execution
of them. . . . Neglected laws must first lead to anarchy and confusion;
and a military execution of laws is only a shorter way to the same
point—despotic government." For James Winthrop the issue came
down to the inevitable violation of local interests by a nation-state of

continental size. And for George Mason it was simply a matter of recorded history. In the whole of history, he declared, "there never was a government over a very extensive country without destroying the liberties of the people . . . popular governments can only exist in small territories. Is there a single example on the face of the earth to support a contrary opinion?"[33]

Upon all of this, rooted in fears formulated in the pre-Revolutionary past, the antifederalists mounted their assault on the Constitution. The newspapers teemed with their condemnations of a constitution that would legalize vast governmental powers, and that failed even to include a Bill of Rights that might stand as a protector of the individual liberties that had been won in the Revolution and that the national government was now being empowered to destroy. Nothing was more unaccountable to them than the absence of a Bill of Rights in a constitution known to be a design for a government potentially far more powerful than any the American people had ever known before. The federalists' argument that *all* rights were reserved to the people because government would have only specified powers made little impression on them. Did no one know history? Patrick Henry asked. Did no one recall that in Britain the people and the Crown had struggled for a century over the uncertainties of *implied* rights until the matter had finally been settled in the acceptance of an *explicit* Bill of Rights—and that that had been precisely the first thing the American people had thought of when they had been faced with the necessity of protecting themselves against Parliament's power? Given the powers accorded the new national government in the Constitution, it was said time after time, unless there were a Bill of Rights,

> we are totally insecure in all of them; and no man can promise himself with any degree of certainty that his posterity will enjoy the inestimable blessings of liberty of conscience, of freedom of speech and of writing and publishing their thoughts on public matters, of trial by jury, of holding themselves, their houses and papers free from seizure and search upon general suspicion or general warrants; or in short that they will be secured in the enjoyment of life, liberty and property without depending on the will and pleasure of their rulers.

The whole system, the "Federal Farmer" insisted—and with him almost every other antifederalist—should be "bottomed" on a Bill of Rights that declared the people's "unalienable and fundamental rights" in such a way as to set limits to the power of government and to serve as an alarm when legislators and rulers overreached their proper bounds.[34]

III

Such was the challenge that faced the federalist leaders in the ratification struggle. Their task was complex. They had, first, to convince doubters that the existing situation under the Articles of Confederation was disastrous, verging on chaos, and that only a radical strengthening of the powers of the central government would solve the nation's problems. They had, next, to explain the details of the proposed government and show how it met the current needs without destroying the liberties America had fought for, and without injuring local interests, at least in the long run. Somehow, too, they had to prove that in the mechanics of government the new nation-state would not absorb or otherwise destroy the state governments, which were seen as the protectors of the people's liberties.

But beyond all of that they had an overriding problem. They had to reach back into the sources of the received tradition, confront the ancient, traditional fears that had lain at the heart of the ideological origins of the Revolution, and identify and reexamine the ancient formulations that stood in the way of the present necessities: take these ideas and apprehensions apart and where necessary rephrase them, reinterpret them—not reject them in favor of a new paradigm, a new structure of thought, but reapply them and bring them up to date. They did not leave the cave, they corrected it. They would have been astonished to hear that they were initiating a change from something scholars would later call "civic humanism" or "classical republicanism" to another, something that would be called "liberalism," or that they were chiefly interested in preserving patrician rule derived from the older tradition. They were neither more nor less determined to protect private property as a foundation of personal freedom and to advance economic enterprise than their predecessors and opponents, and they were no less committed to the need for disinterested "virtue" in government. Both they and their opponents were working within the broad pattern of political thought inherited from the early days of the Revolution, but the urgencies the federalists felt led them to reassess the impediments to the creation of a national state which they found embedded in that enveloping tradition.

This could not easily be done. Aside from the intellectual demands of thinking through the ancient formulations, the task required imagination, boldness, freedom from fear. One of the most revealing themes that runs through the voluminous writings of the federalists is the exhortation to rise to the extraordinary occasion before them by thinking freshly and fearlessly about the problems they faced, and above all not to brood on groundless fears, not to view every change as the stroke of doom and imagine catastrophe around every corner. Catastrophe will be found everywhere, Timothy Pickering warned, "if we give a loose to our imaginations." "Where in the name of common sense," Hamilton wrote,

> are our fears to end if we may not trust our sons, our brothers, our neighbours, our fellow-citizens? What shadow of danger can there be from men who are daily mingling with the rest of their countrymen and who participate with them in the same feelings, sentiments, habits, and interests? . . . In reading many of the publications against the Constitution a man is apt to imagine that he is perusing some ill-written tale or romance which, instead of natural and agreeable images, exhibits to the mind nothing but frightful and distorted shapes—gorgons, hydras, and chimeras dire—discoloring and disfiguring whatever it represents and transforming every thing it touches into a monster.

"Events merely possible," Hamilton said on another occasion, "have been magnified by distempered imagination into inevitable realities, and the most distant and doubtful conjectures have been formed into a serious and infallible prediction." Stop thinking in extremes, he warned; don't abandon a wise government for "a fantastical Utopia." And don't argue "against a measure from a remote possibility of its being abused. Human sagacity cannot devise any law but what, in its operations, may in some instances bear hard." But it was not easy to purge the antifederalists of what Judge Hanson called their "trumpery of fictions" and Hamilton their hopeless infatuation with "halcyon scenes of the poetic or fabulous age." A mind like R. H. Lee's, a writer in Virginia declared, "which delights . . . to indulge itself in *political reveries*, is capable of conceiving any idea, however absurd, and being startled by any danger, however visionary." Madison, as always, spoke soberly and succinctly: "We must limit our apprehensions," he said quietly in the Virginia debates, "to certain degrees of probability," and then in a passage of what was for him extreme rhetoric, he sought to switch the role of the imagination from stirring up morbid fantasies of impending doom to assisting in the construction of "a government for posterity." "Hearken not," he wrote in one of the early *Federalist* papers,

> to the voice which petulantly tells you that the form of government recommended for your adoption is a novelty in the political world . . . shut your ears against this unhallowed language. Shut your hearts against the poison which it conveys. . . . Is it not the glory of the people of America that whilst they have paid a decent regard to the opinions of former times and other nations, they have not suffered a blind veneration for antiquity, for custom, or for names to overrule the suggestions of their own good sense, the knowledge of their own situation, and the lessons of their own experience?
> . . . Had no important step been taken by the leaders of the Revolution for which a precedent could not be discovered, no government established of which an exact model did not present itself, the people of the United States might, at this moment, have been numbered among the melancholy victims of misguided councils, must at best have been labouring under the weight of some of those forms which have crushed the liberties of the rest of mankind.[35]

It was with these injunctions in mind—to dismiss morbid fears of impending doom and to think ahead imaginatively but also realistically—that the federalists turned to the major problems their inheritance had created for them. Some of the problems were blatant, glaring. They were creating a national army, distinct from the state militias. But would these national troops not be, as the antifederalists claimed, the bloodthirsty, venal janissaries, the dreaded palace guards that Americans had been endlessly warned of and which they believed they had themselves confronted in the Revolutionary War? The question had to be answered.

For Noah Webster, commissioned publicist of the federalist cause, the question was simply unreal: "the principles and habits of the Americans are directly opposed to standing armies; and there is as little necessity to guard against them by positive constitutions as to prohibit the establishment of the Mahometan religion." Is Mahometanism prohibited in the state constitutions? No. And is Christianity in danger as a consequence? Do the states outlaw standing armies? No (with a couple of exceptions). And is civilian government in the states threatened by military coups d'état?

But the venerable arguments could not simply be dismissed out of hand. The issue had to be carefully considered. All national, peacetime armies, Tench Coxe explained a month after the Constitution had been unveiled, are *not* "standing armies." The American army would have no existence aside from the people's will, since military appropriations were to last for only two years, and to be made by the House of Representatives, *"the immediate delegates of the people."* Further, the army would have no monopoly of military force. The state militias would not only "form a *powerful check* upon the regular troops, and will generally be sufficient *to overawe them"* but will make a large national army unnecessary—which would be so in any case because of America's *"detached* situation" geographically. Finally, he said, there is all the difference in the world "between the troops of a commonwealth like ours, *founded on equal and unalterable principles,* and those of a royal government, where ambition and oppression are *the profession of the king."* In a free state a military officer is simply *"the occasional servant of the people, employed for their defense";* in a monarchy he is always the instrument of the schemes of oppression or conquest which obsess the mind of his royal master.[36]

These were the main themes, but other writers sought to focus more sharply on the crux. "The fallacy lies here," Timothy Pickering wrote: in Europe large standing armies exist to maintain the power of absolute and hereditary monarchs and therefore by definition "are instruments to keep the people in slavery." An army in America would serve only to protect the people who themselves maintain it through representatives who would share in any suffering such troops might create. In Britain "the armies are *his* [the king's] *armies*, and their direction is solely by him without any control. . . . Here the army, when raised, is the army of the people." Judge Hanson, who condemned the "clamour against standing armies" as "a mere pretext for terrifying you, like children, with spectres and hobgobblins," touched on another, more pragmatic point which became a standard federalist argument. If there were no standby national army, one would have to be created overnight in the case of sudden invasion or other emergencies, and it might well prove to be too little and too late. If the only armed force were the militia, Francis Corbin elaborated in the Virginia convention, the results would be either a disastrous neglect of farming or a fatal ignorance and incompetence in arms. But the militia would be *part* of the nation's armed might, and that mixture of a citizen militia and a professional national army was vital. Either alone, Wilson Nicholas argued in the Virginia convention, would be a danger: an unemployed standing army would be a public menace, a militia would in itself be wholly incapable of stopping an invasion by a "powerful, disciplined army." Further, a militia army would favor the rich, who could buy substitutes for personal service, and burden the poor, who could not. So let the rich bear the burden of financing the professional army, and the poor the burden of services when needed. The result of such a mixed military establishment will be military competence and no danger, the ideal situation which the Constitution had designed.[37]

It is in the context of this wide-ranging reexamination of the ancient threat of "standing armies" that Hamilton's discussion of the subject in a series of well-known *Federalist* papers can best be understood. It is clear at once that much of what he wrote was commonplace. He too stressed America's physical isolation, which would not necessitate a large army, any more than Britain's island situation had required one. And he too stressed the concurrent and yet competitive role that the state militias would have. But his writing on this subject is nevertheless unique. Cutting through the visionary fears, the "gorgons, hydras, and chimeras dire," he analyzed the real, operative process by which military power, in the projected constitutional system, could become a threat.

How, he asked, could a danger actually—not theoretically—arise? Suppose a President were determined to build a janissary army to suppress liberty. How could it be done? Short of a complete coup d'état, such an army could be created only "by progressive augmentations" of Congressional appropriations, which would take time and would require that a conspiracy between executive and legislature be sustained through successive transformations in the representative body. Now, can one realistically believe that that could happen? Would an incoming Congressman instantly "commence a traitor to his constituents and to his country"? Would no one be shrewd enough "to detect so attrocious a conspiracy, or bold or honest enough to apprise his constituents of their danger"? If that were really the case, one should forget about representation and live under governments no larger than counties. And beyond all that, how could such a plot, developed over years, be concealed? What benign excuse could be convincingly given for such a visible buildup? None would make sense. In fact the people would not be deceived, and the project and its projectors would be quickly destroyed.

Hamilton, and other federalists following him, did not dismiss the danger of standing armies—the ancient fear persisted: "I am a mortal enemy to standing armies," one of the federalists' most fervent defenders of the armed forces clauses of the Constitution concluded, "in time of peace particularly." Their aim was to show, by close analysis, that while a national army was necessary, the *regular* army of the United States would not—could not—be a *"standing"* army in the traditional sense. If it ever became that, freedom would already—for other, deeper reasons—have been destroyed: at that point "there will not be a particle of virtue in the people; they will be ripe for the most corrupt government."[38]

This hardheaded realism was the essence of the federalists' response to the opposition. Point by point they took on the objections based on inherited notions and probed their applicability in the American situation.

The key doctrine of federalism could survive criticism only to the extent that it could somehow be distinguished from the ancient belief that *imperium in imperio* was an illogical and unresolvable "solecism." So they reexamined that old formula, took it apart, and showed, not its falsity, but its irrelevance in the American situation. The antifederalists, Hamilton wrote, obsessed with "artificial distinctions and syl-logistic subtleties," reiterated the ancient maxim that *imperium in imperio* is a "political monster." But in operation, he wrote, the states and the national governments would not clash. The "supreme law of the land" clause would have the effect of linking the states' officers, no less than the nation's officers, to the enforcement of federal law and hence lead to a functional merger of—not conflict between—the two levels of authority. There would be no fatal clash, as "Brutus" feared, between the taxing powers of states and nation. The nation's taxing power is specified, and under Article I, Section 10, the states retained all other taxing powers. The two governments would inter-sect only where they exercised *concurrent* powers, and *concurrence* is not the *repugnancy* that lay at the heart of the ancient precept. Simple prudence and "reciprocal forbearances" would permit a harmonious relationship, and if the national government invaded areas of taxation reserved to the states, such action would be void, and the people would make this clear.[39]

Oliver Ellsworth, the future chief justice, cut deeper into the prob-lem, and in the course of a remarkable address in the Connecticut ratifying convention explained the essential role of judicial review in resolving the ancient problem. It is said, Ellsworth declared, that Congress and the states cannot coexist in legislative powers. "I ask, *why* can they not? It is not enough to *say* that they cannot. I wish for some reason." There is no more reason for them to conflict than there is for New York City's laws to conflict with those of New York State or London's with Britain's. But, he then said, in a classic statement of judicial review,

> if the general legislature should at any time overleap their limits, the judicial department is a constitutional check. If the United States go beyond their powers, if they make a law which the Constitution does not authorize, it is void; and the judicial power, the national judges, who to secure their im-partiality are to be made independent, will declare it to be void. On the other hand, if the states go beyond their limits, if they make a law which is an usurpation upon the general government, the law is void, and upright independent judges will declare it to be so.

And all the federalists agreed that the law would be enforced not against states (that would be civil war, and would involve the innocent along with the guilty) but against individual people, who collectively were the very source of the authority under which the government would be acting. If that were not the case, Madison wrote at the end of a learned discourse on the political miseries of the United Netherlands, then you would indeed have the hopeless situation of "a sovereignty over sovereigns, a government over governments, a legislation for communities as contradistinguished from individuals" which, just "as it is a solecism in theory, so in practice it is subversive of the order and ends of civil polity, by substituting *violence* in place of *law*, or the destructive *coertion* of the *sword* in place of the mild and salutary *coertion* of the *magistracy.*" The ancient precept was not wrong; the Constitution simply avoided the dangers of dual sovereignties, real as they were.[40]

But federalism as a solution to the venerable problem of dual sovereignties was part of a larger issue: the theoretical problem of creating a republic of large, potentially continental size. To the vehement antifederalist insistence, drawn directly from the received tradition, that almost every authority and the entire experience of mankind proved that republics could survive only as small-scale polities, the federalists countered, first, that the national government had only limited and specified powers; the states, which retained all the rest, remained republics of small dimensions; and it would be the states that would continue to regulate the affairs of everyday life. But they themselves recognized the limits of this argument: national law would be supreme where it applied and therefore the national government would have effective power over the use of coercive force, over justice, and over the economy. So they turned to the ancient precept itself, probed its logic and validity, and ended by demonstrating its irrelevance for the American system.

Their mood was typified by Edmund Randolph's remark in the Virginia convention that he was not impressed "that some of the most illustrious and distinguished authors" said that republicanism is impractical in a country of large extent: "I reply, that authority has no weight with me till I am convinced that, not the dignity of names but the force of reasoning, gains my assent." The famous examples and analogies—Switzerland, particularly—did not apply.

> The extent and situation of that country [Switzerland] is to-
> tally different from ours; their country is surrounded by pow-
> erful, ambitious, and reciprocally jealous nations; their territory
> small, and soil not very fertile.

He was convinced that if American laws were made with integrity
and executed with wisdom, the extent of the country would be no
problem. Francis Corbin too, in the same debate, rejected what he
called the "old worn-out idea that a republican government is best
calculated for a small territory. . . . How small must a country be to
suit the genius of republicanism? In what particular extent of country
can a republican government exist? . . . Too small an extent will render a republic weak, vulnerable, and contemptible. Liberty, in such
a petty state, must be on a precarious footing; its existence must
depend on the philanthropy and good nature of its neighbors." He
believed that the centralized national government would tend to concentrate and conciliate conflicting opinions within a single forum, better organized and disciplined than thirteen scattered policy-making
bodies attempting to fuse their formulated views into a national policy. And yet the heterogeneity would guarantee that a majority would
never concur sufficiently to oppress a minority. Hamilton too asked
how small a country must be to satisfy Montesquieu's prescription. If
you think about it carefully, Hamilton said, the dimensions Montesquieu must have had in mind were far short of those of the present
states. Did the antifederalists now propose, accordingly, to split up
the states "into an infinity of little jealous, clashing, tumultuous com-
monwealths, the wretched nurseries of unceasing discord and the
miserable objects of universal pity or contempt"? What an "infatuated
policy" that would be—what "a desperate expedient."[41]

But these were general and vague approaches to a problem that
required much more specific formulations. The American nation, it
was quickly pointed out, would not be a singular but a compound
entity, a *confederate* republic, each unit of which (the states) would be
relatively small yet the whole large enough to protect itself and serve
the society's common needs. True, as James Wilson said, creating a
"confederate republic . . . left us almost without precedent or guide,
and consequently without the benefit of that instruction which in
many cases may be derived from the constitution and history and

experience of other nations." For the Swiss and Dutch examples, he agreed, were irrelevant; so too were the examples of classical antiquity. But the *theory*, at least, of confederate republics was not unknown. Montesquieu himself, Hamilton pointed out early in the debate, had developed the idea as a way of "extending the sphere of popular government and reconciling the advantages of monarchy with those of republicanism." And he had also suggested an example of " 'an excellent confederate republic,' " namely, the Lycian (c. second century B.C.), whose central body had in fact had "the most delicate species of interference in [the individual states'] internal administration." That strange conglomeration of cities and republics was, however, a very strained example or parallel; nevertheless, the theory of confederate republics was valid—for reasons the ancients and Montesquieu could never have conceived of. For America alone had developed fully the "vital principle" of representation—"the chain of communication between the people and those to whom they had committed the exercise of the powers of government." And that principle rendered all earlier considerations of size irrelevant. Representation made possible a perfect compromise: a confederated state large enough to protect itself but small enough to retain the freedoms of a republic.[42]

These were singular notes in a developing harmony of opinion. The great crescendo was eventually sounded at a higher level by Madison and Hamilton in several of their most famous *Federalist* papers—but they were preceded by John Stevens's premonitory "Americanus" papers. Stevens, a New Jersey lawyer who would later frame the first patent laws and attain fame as an engineer and developer of steam transport, attacked the insistence that "the axioms of Montesquieu, Locke, etc., in the science of politics are as irrefragable as any in Euclid," and ridiculed the idea of hunting for precedents in Europe. It would be "downright madness to shackle ourselves with maxims and principles which are clearly inapplicable to the nature of our political institutions. The path we are pursuing is new, and has never before been trodden by man." It was the venerated ancient theorists, the systematizers, who posed the most difficult problems. To concede to their "maxims and principles . . . would be an unpardonable indiscretion." What mattered most was America's unique historical experience. Montesquieu's ideas, after all, had been formed in the

Old World: "Had he been an American, and now living, I would stake my life on it, he would have formed different principles."

In the new nation, Stevens explained, representation—"the hinge on which all republican governments must move"—will obviate the confusions of democracy in a state of large size, and bicameralism and the "revisory power" of the executive and judiciary will further inhibit the development of the "turbulent spirit." But there were deeper reasons for seeing the large size of a republican nation as a positive advantage. "The gusts of passion," Stevens wrote, twenty days before the publication of Madison's *Federalist* X, destructive in a small territory, dissipate in a large state. Small republics

> ever have been, and from the nature of man always will be, liable to be torn to pieces by faction. When the citizens are confined within a narrow compass, as was the case of Sparta, Rome, etc., it is within the power of a factious demagogue to scatter sedition and discontent instantaneously thro' every part of the state.

But in an extensive federal system like that of the United States, factions lose their force before they reach the seat of government. "The different powers are so modified and distributed as to form mutual checks upon each other," thus preventing a plebiscitarian upheaval. The people at large will not need to maintain eternal vigilance. Their representatives and the internal checks of the system itself will do the job for them, and therefore all that is required of the people is to participate in frequent elections and attend closely to their own personal interests. The American government, for its success, will require

> nothing more of its subjects than that they should study and pursue merely their own true interest and happiness. . . . A government thus founded on the broad basis of human nature, like a tree which is suffered to retain its native shape, will flourish for ages with little care or attention.

In this vein Stevens's ideas developed, fructified, in complex ways. Feeling his way through venerable Old World precedents that he felt obliged to reconsider—to think through, test, and where necessary reformulate—he ridiculed the idea that analogies between Britain and America were useful except insofar as both nations' histories prove that "it is impossible to subjugate a numerous and free people spread over a wide extent of country without the intervention and concurrence of adventitious and extrinsic causes." He condemned again and again the "faction, instability, and frequent revolutions" inherent in small republics, and argued that large republics can contain and control insurrections better than small ones, and thereafter can create reconciliation more readily. He denied that there were more jarring interests in large states than in small and declared that an "infinite number and variety of distinct and jarring interests . . . necessarily prevail among the individuals of a society in a state of civilization." If the government does not serve to reconcile these clashing interests, "I say there is an end of every thing . . . we must then relinquish all our ideas of the efficiency of government as mere chimeras."[43]

Stevens, of course, was no Madison or Hamilton. But like both of them he pounded away at the necessity of reconsidering inherited formulations, testing them for their applicability in the American setting, and excoriated utopianism and self-validating theorizing. His one favorable citation of Montesquieu is a passage in which the Frenchman disparaged Harrington, whom Stevens himself attacked directly together with Plato and Sir Thomas More for having "amused themselves with forming visionary schemes of perfected governments . . . no better than romances." Hamilton, equally blistering on abstract, systematic speculation, pointed out that the tiny republics of classical antiquity were in fact scenes of constant and often fatal squabbling; only the larger confederacies had any stability. And as for the fear that law and order would be unenforceable on America's far borderlands, that, he said, was "a palpable illusion of the imagination." People on the borderlands will be equally well represented in the central government, will be equally well informed on the effectiveness of their representatives in serving their interests, and in addition their interests will be vigilantly protected by the state governments, if only "from the rivalship of power." But beyond all that, Hamilton wrote, there is the simple fact that distance will not create different interests in kind.

> . . . the citizens who inhabit the country at and near the seat
> of government will, in all questions that affect the general

liberty and prosperity, have the same interest with those who are at a distance; and . . . will stand ready to sound the alarm when necessary, and to point out the actors in any pernicious project. The public papers will be expeditious messengers of intelligence to the most remote inhabitants of the union.[44]

But it was left to Madison, first in his extraordinary letter to Jefferson (October 24) and then in two of his finest *Federalist* papers (X and LI)—to give this whole line of argument its ultimate range, depth, and intellectual elegance. He did not simply assume faction and interest—most commentators, antifederalists as well as federalists, did that.[45] He defined them, and showed that they were "sown in the nature of man" and manifested particularly in the inescapable inequalities in the distribution of property. Then he logically reduced the possibility of coping with faction to controlling its effects, and demonstrated that that would be possible only in extended republics. That was so, he argued, partly because America's unique electoral system would tend to produce local representatives of "most attractive merit and the most . . . established characters" capable of grasping and pursuing "great and national objects," but principally because "the greater number of citizens and extent of territory" in a large republic would reduce the possibility that any one faction would become dominant and hence be in a position to oppress the rest.

> Extend the sphere, and you take in a greater variety of parties and interests; you make it less probable that a majority of the whole will have a common motive to invade the rights of other citizens; or if such a common motive exists, it will be more difficult for all who feel it to discover their own strength, and to act in unison with each other.

And he went on to illustrate the moderating effect of distance and numbers on inflammatory religious sects and on "a rage for paper money, for an abolition of debts, for an equal division of property, or for any other improper or wicked project."

It is surprising that there should ever have been any confusion about what Madison was saying and meaning in his most famous *Federalist* paper. Nothing he said about factionalism or its material basis was new or controversial. Antifederalist as well as federalist assumed the same. Nor was he introducing any shift in basic ideology, or anticipating something modern scholars would call liberalism or interest-group politics; and he was neither opposing "civic humanism" nor exalting it.[47] He was doing what John Stevens had been doing before him, what James Wilson and Alexander Hamilton were doing too, and what many other, lesser figures—Edmund Randolph, Francis Corbin, James Bowdoin, Charles Pinckney—were also doing, namely, showing the inapplicability in America of the inherited notion that republics can survive only on a small scale. For all of the federalists who commented at length on the problem of size, the safety of republican government lay in extension, not contraction; all of them believed that in a system like America's the greater the numbers and the extent of territory, the more solidly based and the safer free government would become. None of this had to be learned from Madison. The difference between Madison and the other federalist writers who tackled the problem of size lay not in the point of the arguments but in the style and quality of argumentation. No other writer had Madison's cogency, penetration, knowledge, and range.

Nor did they need him to show them the way on the larger and engrossing question of virtue and republicanism. Federalists and antifederalists both agreed that man in his deepest nature was selfish and corrupt; that blind ambition most often overcomes even the most clear-eyed rationality; and that the lust for power was so overwhelming that no one should ever be entrusted with unqualified authority. The difference between the two parties lay in the conclusion they reached with respect to the extent and power of a central government. Because the antifederalists saw corruption and the lust for power everywhere, they argued that the more exiguous the power available, the less harm the manipulation of power could do. The federalists argued that the problem in the American situation had been exaggerated. Yes, people were innately evil and self-seeking, and yes, no one could be trusted with unconfined power. That was as true in America as anywhere else. But under the Constitution's checks and balances power would be far from unconfined, and for such a self-limiting system there would be virtue enough for success.

Madison had begun his statements on this question in *Federalist* LV and LVI, published in mid-February 1788: "As there is a degree of depravity in mankind," he then wrote, "which requires a certain degree of circumspection and distrust, so there are other qualities in human nature which justify a certain portion of esteem and confidence." Four months later he elaborated the point in what was for him a remarkable outburst. It was touched off by Mason's insistence, in the Virginia ratifying convention, that legislators will do everything mischievous they can think of and fail to do anything good. Why is it not as reasonable, Madison replied, to assume that they will as readily do good as evil?—not that one should "place unlimited confidence in them, and expect nothing but the most exalted integrity and sublime virtue." And then followed this statement of his basic philosophy:

> I go on this great republican principle, that the people will have virtue and intelligence to select men of virtue and wisdom. Is there no virtue among us? If there be not we are in a wretched situation. No theoretical checks, no form of government, can render us secure. To suppose that any form of government will secure liberty or happiness without any virtue in the people is a chimerical idea.[48]

Other federalists, equally convinced of the power of self-interest, greed, and corruption, said the same. Washington wrote Lafayette that the guarantee that the American government would never degenerate into despotism lay in the ultimate virtue of the American people. John Dickinson asked, "will a virtuous and sensible people choose villains or fools for their officers? Or, if they should choose men of wisdom and integrity, will these lose both or either, by taking their seats? If they should, will not their places be quickly supplied by another choice? Is the like derangement again, and again, and again, to be expected? Can any man believe that such astonishing phenomena are to be looked for?" Similarly, the federalist Reverend Mr. West in the Massachusetts convention demanded to know whether it was likely that people would "choose men to ruin us. . . . May we not rationally conclude that the persons we shall choose to administer [the Constitution] will be, in general, good men?"—a sentiment that astonished his adversary, General Samuel Thompson, who thought it "quite contrary to the common language of the clergy, who are continually representing mankind as reprobate and deceitful, and that we really grow worse and worse day after day." Even the archconservative Fisher Ames, ever fearful of the destructiveness of pure democracy, conceded, in justifying republicanism, that "the people always mean right; and, if time is allowed for reflection and information, they will do right." But it was Hamilton—clear in his belief that in the proportion that riches and luxury prevail, virtue will tend to become a mere "graceful appendage of wealth, and the tendency of things will be to depart from the republican standard"—who nevertheless most strongly reinforced Madison's balanced view of human nature: "The supposition of universal venality in human nature," he wrote in *Federalist* LXXVI, "is little less an error in political reasoning than the supposition of universal rectitude. The institution of delegated power implies that there is a portion of virtue and honor among mankind, which may be a reasonable foundation of confidence. And experience justifies the theory."[49]

So, the federalists argued, virtue existed sufficient for the purposes of a government of checks and balances—in fact, *must* exist, as Madison said, in "any form of government" that secured liberty and happiness. It followed, therefore, that the peculiar identification of virtue with republicanism—the hitherto unquestioned precept whose authority could be traced back to classical antiquity—was simplistic: not wrong, but misapplied. Without virtue "*no* form of government can render us secure." But the critique of the received tradition could go much deeper. A few—not many—of the federalists went beyond the standard federalist formulation, which assumed the existence of basic virtue, and probed more deeply the logic and presuppositions of the ancient formulation.

This deeper critique had begun from a peculiar angle even before the Constitution had been written. In 1784–85 a twenty-four-year-old American law student in London, William Vans Murray, wrote six essays in defense of the American state governments which appeared in pamphlet form in Philadelphia while the convention was still at work and were then reprinted in the *American Museum* at about the time the Constitution was published. Their purpose was to examine what Murray called the "false theory," the "hackneyed assertion," that "democratic forms required a tone of manners unattainable and unpreservable in a society where commerce, luxury, and the arts have disposed the public mind to the gratifications of refinement"—the error, in other words, that "what is usually understood by the term virtue, as fancifully displayed by Montesquieu, is the root of democracy" and that "the progress of luxury" destroys it. The American situation, Murray wrote, defies such "system mongers," and he devoted his entire second essay—a discourse of well over 4,000 words—to demonstrating the falseness of the belief that virtue was incompatible with wealth and luxury or peculiarly necessary for a free state in an advanced civilization.

It all went back to Montesquieu, Murray wrote, and the trouble with Montesquieu is that he had "never studied a free democracy." If he had, he would have realized that "a greater share of virtue is not [more] necessary to a democratic than to a monarchial form." It wasn't really a question of virtue: virtue was necessary for both forms. But spartan asceticism, being based on a "love of poverty . . . [which] could operate but in very small societies of men," is not the only form of virtue. In fact, in the growing affluence of democratic America not only has freedom flourished but the development of the human race had advanced, giving the lie to the idea that the spirit of a "simple age, uncultivated and rude, was essential to that very form which . . . is best adapted to the plenitude of human felicity." "Liberty and . . . the fullest dispersion of luxury through every vein of the body politic are in all degrees and respects compatible with each other." Montesquieu had simply not probed deeply enough: "great as he was and venerable as he will ever be, [he] was too fond of hypothesis. . . . He was too mechanical, too geometrical"; his writing shows the "ingenuity of a great mind which fritters away its powers in conceit."[50]

With all of this, Noah Webster, one of the federalists' most active publicists, agreed, but for him Murray's critique did not go far enough. In 1785, in his *Sketches of American Policy*, he too had questioned the precept "that *virtue* is the foundation of republics." What was meant by virtue? "The great Montesquieu," Webster assumed, had meant "*patriotism*, or disinterested public spirit and love of one's country." But had that ever, truly, existed in human society? If *that* is what virtue means, and if one is talking about actual, operational human motivation, then virtue has never been, and is not now, the peculiar attribute or "principle" of *any* form of government, republican, monarchical, or aristocratic. There is only one "real principle that is predominat in every individual and directs all his actions," Webster wrote, and that is "self-interest," and "self-interest" operates differently in different forms of government.

Two years later Webster elaborated. In his pamphlet *An Examination into the Leading Principles of the Federal Constitution . . . by a Citizen of America,* which he wrote at the request of the federalist leadership shortly after the ratification debate had begun, he said that Murray had been right in his criticism of Montesquieu, but he had failed to show the correct principles that had eluded the great man. After an introductory passage of much learning followed by a refutation of various criticisms of the Constitution, Webster developed his view of liberty, and then turned to the concept of power. "In what," he asked, "does *real* power consist?" Not simply military force, and not cultural forces like religion. "The answer is short and plain—in *property.*" The "inseparable connexion between property and dominion" can be seen throughout Roman history and throughout British history. "Wherever we cast our eyes we see this truth, that *property* is the basis of *power.*" Therefore *"a general and tolerably equal distribution of landed property is the whole basis of national freedom,"* and it is that that Montesquieu, wise as he was, had never understood.

> The system of the great Montesquieu will ever be erroneous till the words *property or lands in fee simple* are substituted for *virtue,* throughout his *Spirit of Laws. Virtue,* patriotism, or love of country never was and never will be, till men's natures are changed, a fixed, permanent principle and support of government. . . . An equality of property, with a necessary alienation constantly operating to destroy combinations of powerful families, is the very *soul of a republic.* While this continues, the people will inevitably possess both *power* and *freedom;* when this is lost, power departs, liberty expires, and a commonwealth will inevitably assume some other form.

All the rest—"liberty of the press, trial by jury, the Habeas Corpus writ, even Magna Charta itself"—though no doubt "palladia of freedom," were all "inferior considerations when compared with a general distribution of real property among every class of people. . . . Let the people have property and they *will* have power. . . . The liberties of America, therefore, and her forms of government, stand on the broadest basis." Abstract virtue—absolutely disinterested love of country—is unreal and has nothing to do with the matter.[51]

But it was the fervent federalist John Stevens, writing a month after Webster's pamphlet appeared, who poured the bitterest scorn on applying the classical dicta on republicanism to the American situation. Everything Stevens wrote in the early numbers of the "Americanus" series was explicitly or implicitly a criticism of Montesquieu, but in the fifth paper (December 12, 1787) he confronted the central issues directly. Aside from its being "evidently defective" as a work of "philosophic precision," *The Spirit of the Laws* had been written to soften the rigors of monarchy, hence it was largely irrelevant in America. Montesquieu's three-fold classification of the types of government—republican, monarchical, and despotic—jumbles up distinctive categories, and his definition of the principles, or "springs of action which set these different species of government in motion," is "certainly a very fanciful piece of business . . . an ingenious conceit." By the virtue that he believed animated republics Montesquieu had meant ascetic self-denial and "an enthusiastic attachment to the political system of the country we inhabit." But one had only to look at the results in his favorite example, the "monstrous political prodigy" of Sparta, to see "the absurdities mankind are capable of." If Americans tried to imitate the Spartans, "we should soon become mere nests of hornets. . . . Away with this Spartan virtue and black broth; we'll have none of them."

There were, Stevens wrote, only two truly animating principles, and they were everywhere the same "though compounded in various degrees" for the different types of government: *fear*, or the dread of punishment; and *attachment*—that is, "customs, manners, habits, prejudices." Further, Montesquieu's notion that ambition is pernicious in a republic is precisely wrong: no form of government needs the "laudable desire of excelling in whatever we undertake" as much as a republic. "Montesquieu may talk of virtue as the spring of action in a republican government, but I trust its force would be found too feeble to produce great exertions without the aid of ambition. . . . It is ambition that constitutes the very life and soul of republican government. As fear and attachment insure obedience to government, so does ambition set its wheels in motion."[52]

I V

So the federalists questioned the classical formulation that bound republicanism in some unique way to the principle of virtue. For
most, it was sufficient to say that some degree of virtue was necessary
for *any* free and secure government whatever its constitutional form,
and that there was virtue enough in republican states to make the
complex system of the Constitution work. But a few others went
further, probed the meaning of "virtue," denied its applicability if defined either as asceticism, disinterested patriotism, or the denial of
personal ambition, and suggested more realistic principles of political
motivation and of the means of securing the permanence of free republican governments. All of this was part of the effort to come to
terms with their inheritance. They felt the necessity to build a power
center in the national government, but their inherited understanding
of the dangers to liberty—fragile in its nature and easily destroyed—
warned them against any such effort. At the Philadelphia convention,
with exquisite care and with delicate nuances, they devised a complex
constitution that would generate the requisite power but would so
distribute its flow and uses that no one body of men and no one
institutional center would ever gain a monopoly of force or influence
that could dominate the nation.[53] But that blueprint for a self-
correcting power system, which they labored to explain in the mi-
nutest detail throughout the vast ratifying debate, was not enough.
Something more was required. Their ideological inheritance, which
so clearly warned them of the dangers of what they were doing and
which fueled the antifederalists' objections to the Constitution, had
to be confronted and assessed. The past would have to be laid to
rest; not rejected in favor of some other, different set of beliefs, but
refined, renewed, brought up to date—worked out, fulfilled.

Embarked as they were on a project they believed was without
precedent in human history[54]—to construct a potentially powerful
state, but one that would preserve the liberties of the people—they
clung to the basic ideology of the early Revolution, but where necessary turned its monitory, negative formulations to affirmative purposes. Anachronisms were weeded out; irrelevancies in the American
situation were discarded; distended abstractions were lanced and
drained of distortions; and the hard realities of the real, functioning

world were everywhere revealed. Change was inevitably involved, but the movement of change was return as well as departure: revision, refinement, and reapplication of an earlier tradition, not repudiation.

So they dissipated the fear of "standing armies," not by abandoning the fear of military rule but by showing the irrelevance of that peculiar and distinctive concept "standing armies" in the American situation. They recognized the need for a regular, professional army, but they insisted that it remain under strict civilian control: the military must always, Tench Coxe wrote in the course of his defense of a national army, "be regarded *with a watchful eye,* for it is a profession that is liable to dangerous perversion."[55] So they showed the irrelevance of the ancient "solecism" *imperium in imperio*; but despite Hamilton's assurances and despite the federalist structure of the Constitution, they continued to believe that a concurrence of powers *could* mean a repugnancy; that in certain situations you *could* have—to repeat Madison's words—"a sovereignty over sovereigns, a government over governments," and when you did you would find *"violence* in place of *law,* or the destructive *coertion* of the *sword* in place of the mild and salutary *coertion* of the *magistracy."* For, Madison prophetically insisted, "if a compleat supremacy some where is not necessary in every society, a controuling power at least is so, by which the general authority may be defended against encroachments of the subordinate authorities and by which the latter may be restrained from encroachments on each other." The supremacy of Britain's *Parliament* had not been necessary "for the harmony of that empire," but the Crown's negative "or some equivalent controul" *had* been necessary if "the unity of the system" were to have been preserved. The federalists did not dismiss the problem of dual sovereignties; they saw its deeper meanings, used it, and transformed it.[56]

Federalism was a possible, not a certain, solution; its essence was not automatic harmony but an uncertain tension which statecraft alone could maintain. For the federalists there was no other solution, since they, as much as the eloquent antifederalist "Brutus," feared any comprehensive government whose power could be exercised without limitation. In their mind's eye they too could imagine and they too shuddered at the thought of a national government that could creep into every corner of the country, "wait upon the ladies at their toilett . . . accompany them to the ball, the play, the assembly . . . enter the house of every gentleman, watch over his cellar, wait upon his cook in the kitchen, follow the servants into the parlour, preside over the table, and note down all he eats and drinks . . . attend him to his bed-chamber, and watch him while he sleeps." This they too, no less than their opponents, continued to believe was the ultimate tyranny.[57]

So, similarly, the federalists tested for its practical reality the venerable abstraction that the peculiar distinction and animating principle of republics is somehow "virtue"—showed the ambiguities and the unreality of such a schematic notion. But they never abandoned the belief that only an informed, alert, intelligent, and uncorrupted electorate would preserve the freedoms of a republican state, and that sufficient virtue existed to sustain the American republic. So too they scotched the fear of an effective national executive, showed its necessity and benignity in the American situation. But they continued to believe, as deeply as any of the militants of '76, that power corrupts; that, in the words of the conservative Edward Rutledge of South Carolina, "the very idea of power included a possibility of doing harm";[58] that any release of the constraints on the executive—any executive—was an invitation to disaster; and that an unfettered collaboration between the executive and the military or the "secret services" was a certain catastrophe.

It was thus that the federalists corrected the cave—enlarged its dimensions, reshaped it, modernized it. We live in that more spacious world. Thanks to them, and to their antifederalist opponents who helped keep them close to their ideological origins, we know what obstacles are there, and so may weave and flitter, dip and soar in perfect courses through the blackest air. In that spirit we too—in the very happiest intellection—may continue to correct the cave.

Notes to Chapter 10

For incisive criticisms of various drafts of this essay, I wish to thank Linda Kerber, Thomas C. Grey, Drew McCoy, Michael Kammen, Jack Rakove, James Henretta, and Pauline Maier. The scrutiny of this phalanx of fine historians has saved me from errors both large and small and sent me scrambling to improve infelicities of all kinds. In the end I was obliged to leave unchanged points I know they disagree with; but the essay has greatly benefited from their comments.

1 The poem appeared first in *Things of This World* (1956) and is reprinted here with the kind permission of the publisher, Harcourt Brace Jovanovich, Inc.

2 Bernard Bailyn, *The Ideological Origins of the American Revolution* (Cambridge, Mass., 1967); idem, ed., *Pamphlets of the American Revolution, 1750–1776* (Cambridge, Mass., 1965–), I; idem, "Religion and Revolution: Three Biographical Studies," above, pp. 104–49; idem, *The Ordeal of Thomas Hutchinson* (Cambridge, Mass., 1974), Chaps. 3, 6; idem, ed., "A Dialogue between an American and a European Englishman (1768)," *Perspectives in American History*, 9 (1975), 343–410.

3 Gordon S. Wood, *The Creation of the American Republic, 1776–1787* (Chapel Hill, 1969), esp. Parts 2 and 3.

4 For a survey of some of the issues involved, concentrating on the uses made of the Revolution "as a rhetorical strategy" in the ratifying debate, each side attempting thereby to influence public opinion in its favor, see Frederick R. Black, "The American Revolution as 'Yardstick' in the Debates on the Constitution, 1787–1788," *Proceedings of the American Philosophical Society*, 117, no. 3 (June 15, 1973), 162–85. In this essay I do not consider the debate on the Constitution as rhetoric, but as reality; I concentrate on the conceptual problems that framed the Founders' understanding; and I stress the continuities in the basic ideology of the Revolution: the way in which the antifederalists reinvoked the inherited ideas and attitudes and applied them to present problems, and the way the federalists, within the same system of thought, reconsidered—adjusted, modernized, and renewed—the familiar precepts. For an excellent presentation of a similar view carried into the decade after the Constitution, see Lance Banning, "Republican Ideology and the Triumph of the Constitution, 1789–1793," *William and Mary Quarterly*, 31 (April 1974), 167–88, and also Banning's fuller treatment in his *Jeffersonian Persuasion* (Ithaca, 1978)

and his careful updating of the issues in *Reviews in American History*, 17 (June 1989), 199–204.

5 Jonathan Elliot, ed., *The Debates in the Several State Conventions, on the Adoption of the Federal Constitution* . . . (2d ed.; 4 vols., Washington, D.C., 1836); Paul L. Ford, ed., *Essays on the Constitution of the United States* . . . *1787–1788* (Brooklyn, N.Y., 1892); idem, ed., *Pamphlets on the Constitution of the United States* . . . *1787–1788* (Brooklyn, N.Y., 1888); Walter H. Bennett, ed., *Letters from the Federal Farmer to the Republican* (University, Ala., 1978). Of the many reprintings of the complete *Federalist* papers, the edition by Jacob E. Cooke (Middletown, Conn., 1961) is technically the most useful and will be the edition quoted in references to the last ten papers (LXXVI–LXXXV). Papers I–LXXV appear among the other commentaries on the Constitution so far published in the *Documentary History* series cited in note 6 immediately below, and will be quoted from that edition.

6 Cecelia M. Kenyon, ed., *The Antifederalists* (Indianapolis, 1966); Herbert J. Storing, ed., *The Complete Anti-Federalist* (Chicago, 1981); Merrill Jensen, John P. Kaminski, and Gaspare J. Saladino, eds., *The Documentary History of the Ratification of the Constitution* (Madison, Wis., 1976–   ). An essay in the front matter of the first volume reviews the earlier publishing history of the sources of the ratification controversy. Four volumes to date (XIII–XVI) of the series contain Commentaries on the Constitution, public and private, as distinct from the debates and other materials directly related to the ratifying conventions. These documents are numbered in a single sequence and will be referred to below as CC followed by the number in the sequence. Thus James Wilson's speech of Oct. 6, 1787, will be identified as such, followed by: *Doc. Hist.*, XIII, CC 134.

7 Knox to John Sullivan, New York, Jan. 19, 1788, *Doc. Hist.*, XV, CC 461.

8 John P. Kaminski, "Antifederalism and the Perils of Homogenized History: A Review Essay," *Rhode Island History*, 42 (1983), 35.

9 Herbert J. Storing, "The 'Other' Federalist Papers: A Preliminary Sketch," *Political Science Reviewer*, 6 (1976), 216–47.

10 Washington to Hamilton, Aug. 28, 1788, in Harold C. Syrett and Jacob E. Cooke, eds., *Papers of Alexander Hamilton* (New York, 1961–79), V, 207; Webster, review of *The Federalist*, quoted in *Doc. Hist.*, XVI, 451 n.; "Marcus" [Iredell], IV, ibid., CC 616.

11 For the text of Wilson's speech and references to the controversy that followed, see ibid., XIII, CC 134.

12 King to Jeremiah Wadsworth, New York, Dec. 23, 1787, ibid., XV, CC 368; for Hanson's comments, see ibid., pp. 521–22. Criticism like Hanson's must have been widespread since the antifederalists thought it useful to develop it into an elaborate spoof. In a letter purportedly written in confidence by Benjamin Rush to Hamilton, Rush first congratulates Hamilton on their success in bribing the printers to suppress all antifederalist writings, and then adds: "I wish, Sir, I could prevail on Publius not to be so prolix; if his pieces were shorter, they would answer much better; besides, they want that spirit of declamation necessary to excite the public atten-

tion. Most people here say (and, I am sorry, with too much justice) that the pieces contain nothing but plagiarisms from history and British politics, and general sentiments that apply more forcibly against the constitution than for it. My dear sir, let me entreat you to have the plan changed. . . ." *Newport* (R.I.) *Mercury*, March 24, 1788, p. 4. For other antifederalist abuse of the more heavy-handed Federalist papers which "would jade the brain of any poor sinner," see Robert A. Rutland, "The First Great Newspaper Debate . . . 1787–88," *Proceedings of the American Antiquarian Society*, 97, Part 1 (April 1987), 53, and *Doc. Hist.*, XIII, pp. 493n.

The enormous importance accorded the *Federalist* papers is largely a twentieth-century phenomenon (though on the uses made of them in the antebellum period, see Rakove's essay in Kessler, ed., *Saving the Republic*, cited directly below). Recognized now as this country's most distinguished work of political theory, it provides abundant material for a large academic industry. The endless outpouring of scholarly writing on the series inundates everything written on the history of the Constitution and on American political thought. A complete bibliography would include hundreds, perhaps thousands, of items. These studies, growing ever more sophisticated, approach now an exquisite refinement of analysis that would have amazed the harried authors, who wrote polemically, to help win a political battle. Among the more notable recent studies are Morton White's technical philosophical analysis, *Philosophy, The Federalist, and the Constitution* (New York and Oxford, 1987); Daniel W. Howe's psychological analysis, "The Political Psychology of *The Federalist*," *William and Mary Quarterly*, 44 (July 1987); the fourteen essays in Charles R. Kessler, ed., *Saving the Revolution: The Federalist Papers and the American Founding* (New York and London, 1987); and David Epstein's *The Political Theory of the Federalist* (Chicago, 1984).

13 Ellsworth, speech in the Connecticut convention (Jan. 7, 1788), *Doc. Hist.*, III, 553 (the speech appears also in ibid., XV, CC 420, and in Elliot, *Debates*, II, 190–97); Wilson's speeches in the Pennsylvania convention (Dec. 1, 7, 1787), ibid., II, 450–51, 517. Stevens's "Americanus" papers and the federalists' struggle with the received tradition are discussed in this essay, Part III. By the end of January 1788 the question of judicial review had become a prominent and controversial issue, as it had not been in the Philadelphia convention. The Supreme Court's power to define "the sense of every article of the Constitution" and its freedom from "any fixed or established rules" or from correction by any superior power were savagely and brilliantly attacked—in words that would be repeated in every generation thereafter—by "Brutus" in seven of his sixteen essays published in New York, Jan. 31–March 20, 1788. Ibid., XV, CC 489; XVI, CC 510, 530, 551, 576, 598, 632. (On the disputed authorship of the "Brutus" essays, see ibid., XIII, CC 178.) *The Federalist*'s replies, by Hamilton, who as a New York lawyer had earlier presumed the power of judicial review in arguing a case in that state's courts, came late, in LXXVIII, LXXXI, and LXXXII (May 28, 1788), though Hamilton had anticipated some of his later arguments in XXII (Dec. 14, 1787). "Americanus" too preceded *The Federalist*'s arguments in his clear and forceful statement of judicial review published on Jan. 21

(paper VII, cited below, n. 43). For Hanson's feeble responses to "Brutus," in his *Remarks on the Proposed Plan* . . . (Annapolis, 1788), see *Doc. Hist.*, XV, CC 490 (p. 536).

14 Cecelia M. Kenyon, "Men of Little Faith: The Anti-Federalists on the Nature of Representative Government," *William and Mary Quarterly*, 3rd ser., 12 (1955), 3–43.

15 Tredwell's forceful speech, prepared for the July 2, 1788, session of the New York ratifying convention but apparently not delivered, appears in Elliot, *Debates*, II, 396–406, quotations at p. 401. For a similar interpretation of the antifederalists' thought, in the context of the transit of generations, see Pauline Maier, *The Old Revolutionaries* (New York, 1980), pp. 282 ff.

16 "A Columbian Patriot" [Mercy Otis Warren], *Observations on the Constitution*, in *Doc. Hist.*, XVI, CC 581 (pp. 282, 283, 284, 276, 277). The genealogy of parties, linking present opponents to the enemies of '76, could be argued on both sides. Thus a federalist squib in Pennsylvania identified seven characteristics shared by the antifederalists and the *Tories* of '76, among which were: denunciations of conventions and town meetings as mere mob actions; insistence that they, the antifederalists, alone understood the true principles of government; and harping on imaginary grievances. "It is to be hoped the Antifederalists will end their career as some of the Tories, whom they resemble in so many particulars, have done, viz.—in poverty—in exile." *Doc. Hist.*, II, 157.

17 Luther Martin's *The Genuine Information* is an expansion of his speech in the Maryland Assembly, Nov. 29, 1787, justifying his behavior in the Philadelphia convention (*Doc. Hist.*, XIV, CC 304B). It has a complicated publishing history. Issued first in twelve parts (Dec. 28, 1787–Feb. 8, 1788), it was reissued as a pamphlet in April 1788 but with two additional letters and two further essays. Cf. *Doc. Hist.*, XV, CC 389. The quotations from Bryan's "Centinel" are from no. XII (*Doc. Hist.*, XV, CC 470), where he explicitly defends his characterization of the federalists as *"conspirators."* The term, he writes, "was not, as has been alledged, rashly or inconsiderately adopted; it is the language of dispassionate and deliberate reason, influenced by the purest patriotism. The consideration of the nature and construction of the new constitution naturally suggests the epithet; its justness is strikingly illustrated by the conduct of the patrons of this plan of government." And he goes on to say—in a perfect paradigm of conspiratorial psychology—that if there had been any doubt that there was a conspiracy on foot the federalists' "uneasiness" at the charge would clearly prove it: "innocence would have nothing to dread from such a stigma." Bryan continued his "unmasking" of the federalists' conspiracy in later numbers of the "Centinel." The climax came with the attack on Franklin in no. XVII, where he declares himself finally satisfied that he has fully revealed the federalists' "insidious design of enslaving and robbing their fellow-citizens, of establishing those odious distinctions between the well born and the great body of the people, of degrading the latter to the level of slaves and elevating the former to the rank of nobility." *Doc. Hist.*, XVI, CC 642. For Rufus King and the Cincinnati, see ibid., p. 528. Cf. Bailyn, "A Note on Conspiracy," *Ideological Origins*, pp. 144–59.

18 Conflated from "Philadelphiensis," V, IX, XI (ibid., XV, CC 356; XVI, CC 507, 609).

19 Ibid., XVI, 475.

20 "Brutus," VII, ibid., XV, CC 411. Henry's speeches in the Virginia convention, Elliot, *Debates*, III, 56, 386. The former—June 5—speech, printed, though with omissions, on pp. 35–64 of Elliot's *Debates*, was one of Henry's shorter orations, but it must have taken well over an hour to deliver. For the speech he delivered a short time later, which stretched over the better part of two days of the convention's time, see pp. 241–42. On the national debt: "Brutus," VIII, *Doc. Hist.*, XV, CC 437.

21 Mason's remarks on federalism, which he amplified on various occasions, appear in Elliot, *Debates*, III, 29. "An Old Whig" [George Bryan?], VI, *Doc. Hist.*, XIV, CC 292. For the earlier Tory denunciation of pre-Revolutionary dual-sovereignty notions, indistinguishable from the antifederalists' attacks on the Constitution's federalism, see Bailyn, *Ideological Origins*, pp. 219–23.

22 "Brutus," V, VI, continued in VII, *Doc. Hist.*, XIV, CC 343; XV, CC 384 (the florid passage), and CC 411. Judge Hanson later commented on "Brutus's" peroration, calling it "the mere phrenzy of declamation, the ridiculous conjuration of spectres and hobgobblins!" Ibid., XV, CC 490A (p. 545). Almost every leading antifederalist at one time or another elaborated on the impossibility of maintaining concurrent, federal powers for any length of time, and predicted that "the state governments must be annihilated, or continue to exist for no purpose." E.g., "Federal Farmer," II, *Doc. Hist.*, XIV, CC 242, quotation at p. 29. So too did fence straddlers like Samuel Adams, unsure of what position to take and considering both sides carefully (Adams to R. H. Lee, Dec. 3, 1787, ibid., CC 315). For other antifederalist endorsements of the old, and long since repudiated, belief that external and internal spheres of power could be effectively distinguished, see "An Old Whig," VI, ibid., CC 292 (p. 218); and "Brutus," V, ibid., CC 343 (p. 427). For Hamilton's criticism of the idea, see *Federalist* XXX; for Wilson's, arguing against William Findley's invocation of the colonists' arguments against Parliament's efforts to impose "internal taxes or excises," see his summation in the Pennsylvania convention, Dec. 11, 1787, *Doc. Hist.*, II, 557–58. Cf. Bailyn, *Ideological Origins*, pp. 212 ff.

23 Charles Turner, speech in the Massachusetts convention, Elliot, *Debates*, II, 30–32; Henry, speech in the Virginia convention, ibid., III, 324.

24 "Federal Farmer," III, *Doc. Hist.*, XIV, CC 242 (pp. 38–39); Bailyn, *Ideological Origins*, pp. 61–63, 112–19.

25 "A Columbian Patriot" [Warren], *Observations*, *Doc. Hist.*, XVI, CC 581 (p. 280); Mason, speech in the Virginia convention, Elliot, *Debates*, III, 378–81 (for the full documentation of Mason's view of standing armies and the threat to militia troops, see Robert A. Rutland, ed., *Papers of George Mason*, *1725–1792* [Chapel Hill, 1970], III, 1073–81); Patrick Dollard, speech in the South Carolina convention, Elliot, *Debates*, IV, 338; "A Democratic Federalist," *Doc. Hist.*, XIII, CC 167 (p. 390) (on Burgh, see Bailyn, *Ideological Origins*, p. 41 and references there); "Brutus," VIII, *Doc. Hist.*, XV, CC 437 (pp. 337–38); "Federal Farmer," III, *ibid.*, XIV, CC 242

(p. 39); Caldwell, speech in the North Carolina convention, Elliot, *Debates*, IV, 62 (emphasis added); Holmes, speech in the Massachusetts convention, ibid., II, 111 (emphasis in original).

26 Taylor, speech in the Massachusetts convention, ibid., II, 53; Lowndes, speech in the South Carolina convention, ibid., IV, 289.

27 William Symmes, Jr., to Peter Osgood, Jr., Andover, Mass., Nov. 15, 1787, *Doc. Hist.*, XIV, CC 262, at p. 111; "Brutus," III, ibid., CC 264 (pp. 123–24); Mason, "Objections to the Constitution," ibid., CC 276A (p. 151); Martin, *Genuine Information*, IX, ibid., XV, CC 484 (pp. 496–97). Suppose, wrote "Cincinnatus" in his fifth essay (ibid., XIV, CC 307), the Privy Council in England, the official advisory body to the king, "were vested with the sole power of trying impeachments. Would any man say that this would not render that body absolute, and impeachment, to all popular purposes, nugatory?" The most elaborate reply to Mason's and Martin's specific charges against the pardoning power was Iredell's "Marcus" III essay (ibid., XVI, CC 596), in which he concedes that it is *possible* a President would pardon a co-conspirator to "prevent a discovery of his own guilt," but not probable, if only because the pardoned accomplice would then be free to testify against the President with no fear of retribution. Further, the President would be more, not less, exposed if he pardoned his accomplice than if he let the law take its course. In any case, against any possible danger the pardoning power might have, Iredell argued, must be put the necessity of protecting the nation's secret agents when revealed as collaborators by the enemy in time of war and subject to popular fury for their apparent treason. No one else—neither the courts nor the juries—could rescue such a "useful but dishonourable character"; for him, the "prerogative of mercy in the chief magistrate of a great country ought to be at hand." See also "Impartial Citizen," V, *Doc. Hist.*, VIII, 428–30; *Federalist* LXIX and LXXIV [Hamilton], ibid., XVI, CC 617, 644.

28 Samuel Nasson, speech in the Massachusetts convention, Elliot, *Debates*, II, 137; Henry, speech in the Virginia convention, ibid., III, 147; "Agrippa" [Winthrop], IV, V, and esp. VI and VII, in Ford, *Essays*, pp. 63 ff., quotation from IX, p. 79.

29 Singletary, speech in the Massachusetts convention, Elliot, *Debates*, II, 101; *United States Chronicle* (Providence, R.I.), Aug. 5, 1788 (quoting Hopkins); "An Old Whig," III (referring to "the publications of the years 1774, 1775, 1776, and 1777"), *Doc. Hist.*, XIII, CC 181; "Centinel," II, III, ibid., CC 190; XIV, CC 243; Robert Whitehill, speech in the Pennsylvania convention, ibid., II, 527; on Burgh, n. 25 above; Henry, speeches in the Virginia convention, Elliot, *Debates*, III, 396, 411; "A Columbian Patriot" [Warren], *Doc. Hist.*, XVI, CC 581 (esp. pp. 281–82). Cf. Bailyn, *Ideological Origins*, pp. 28–29, 53.

30 Henry, speech in the Virginia convention, Elliot, *Debates*, III, 148, 149, 164, 165, 327. For another antifederalist's similar view of "the principle of self-love," see "Brutus," IV, *Doc. Hist.*, XIV, CC 306; for a federalist's version, see "A Countryman" [Roger Sherman], II, *Doc. Hist.*, XIV, CC 284.

31 Mason, speech in the Virginia convention, Elliot, *Debates*, III, 32; speeches of Joseph McDowell and William Lenoir in the North Carolina convention, ibid., IV,

150, 203–4; "Cato," V, *Doc. Hist.*, XIV, CC 286; Charles Turner, speech in the Massachusetts convention, Elliot, *Debates*, II, 30–32; Patrick Dollard, speech in the South Carolina convention, ibid., IV, 337. Cf. Paine, *Common Sense*, quoted in Bailyn, *Ideological Origins*, p. 143, and "A Georgian," *Doc. Hist.*, III, 236.

32 "Brutus," I, ibid., XIII, CC 178, quotations at pp. 417, 418. For an identical argument, see "Agrippa" [Winthrop], IV, in Ford, *Essays*, pp. 63–65.

33 "Cato," III, *Doc. Hist.*, XIII, CC 195; "Federal Farmer," II, ibid., XIV, CC 244 (quotation at p. 29); "Agrippa' [Winthrop], esp. VII, in Ford, *Essays*, p. 73; Mason, speech in the Virginia convention, Elliot, *Debates*, III, 30. For the use of Montesquieu as the great authority on such matters, see Paul M. Spurlin, *Montesquieu in America, 1760–1801* (University, La., 1940), Chap. 6.

34 Henry, speech in the Virginia convention, ibid., p. 150; "An Old Whig," V, *Doc. Hist.*, XIII, CC 224; "Federal Farmer," II, ibid., XIV, CC 242 (quotation at 27).

35 Pickering to Charles Tillinghast, Philadelphia, Dec. 24, 1787, ibid., CC 288C (p. 197); *Federalist* XXIX [Hamilton], ibid., XV, CC 429; Hamilton, speech in the New York convention, Elliot, *Debates*, II, 262–63, 320; "Impartial Citizen," V, *Doc. Hist.*, VIII, 428; "Aristides" [Hanson], *Remarks*, ibid., XV, CC 490A (at p. 536); *Federalist* XXX [Hamilton], ibid., CC 391 (p, 164); "Cassius," in *Virginia Independent Chronicle*, April 2, 1788; Madison, speech in the Virginia convention, Elliot, *Debates*, III, 433; *Federalist* XIV [Madison], *Doc. Hist.*, XIV, CC 310.

36 [Noah Webster], *An Examination into the Leading Principles of the Federal Constitution . . . by a Citizen of America* (Philadelphia, [1787]), pp. 152–53; "An American Citizen" [Coxe], IV, ibid., XIII, CC 183A.

37 Pickering to Tillinghast, ibid., XIV, CC 288C (p. 203); Samuel Holden Parsons to William Cushing, Middletown, Conn., Jan. 11, 1788, ibid., III, 641; "Aristides" [Hanson], *Remarks*, ibid., XV, CC 490A (at p. 532); "Marcus" [Iredell], IV, ibid., XVI, CC 616 (at p. 385); Corbin and Nicholas, speeches in the Virginia convention, Elliot, *Debates*, III, 112–13, 389–90.

38 *Federalist* VIII and XXVI [Hamilton], *Doc. Hist.*, XIV, CC 274; XV, CC 366; "An Impartial Citizen," VI, ibid., VIII, 498.

39 *Federalist* XXII, XV, XXVII, XXXII–XXXIII [Hamilton], ibid., XIV, CC 347, 312; XV, CC 378, 405.

40 Ellsworth, speech in the Connecticut convention, ibid., XV, CC 420 (at pp. 278–79) (cf. above, n. 13); *Federalist* XX [Madison], ibid., XIV, CC 340. Madison's view of federalism as a fulfillment and resolution of the ancient fear of dual sovereignty was a commonplace in federalist thought. Thus the Connecticut lawyer Samuel Holden Parsons, writing a month after the publication of *Federalist* XX, expressed the same idea in similar words, explaining that dual sovereignty is a political absurdity only when both powers are "coextensive in their objects." Towns, surely, or counties have legislative powers *for some purposes*: does that mean a state cannot exist and legislate too? Parsons to Cushing, Jan. 11, 1788 (above, n. 37), p. 644.

41 Randolph and Corbin speeches in the Virginia convention, Elliot, *Debates*, III, 85, 69, 107, 108; *Federalist* IX, *Doc. Hist.*, XIV, CC 277 (p. 160).

42 Wilson, speech in the Pennsylvania convention, ibid., II, 352–53, 355; *Federalist* IX

[Hamilton], ibid., XIV, CC 277; see also Bowdoin, speech in the Massachusetts convention, Elliot, *Debates*, II, 128. Further on Montesquieu's concept of a confederated republic as a possible solution to the problem of size, see Spurlin, *Montesquieu*, pp. 196–200.

43 Stevens's seven "Americanus" essays, not yet included in the *Doc. Hist.* series, were published in the *New York Daily Advertiser*, Nov. 2, 23, 30; Dec. 5–6, 12, 1787; and Jan. 12, 21, 1788. The quotations and specific citations in the text are from nos. I–IV, VI.

44 *Federalist* LXXXIV [Hamilton], Cooke, ed., pp. 582, 583. (Cf. n. 5 above.)

45 For the passionate antifederalist James Winthrop's defense of state sovereignty in terms of protecting local interest groups, see "Agrippa," VII, in Ford, *Essays*, p. 73: "It is only by protecting local concerns that the interest of the whole is preserved. No man when he enters society does it from a view to promote the good of others, but he does it for his own good. All men having the same view are bound equally to promote the welfare of the whole." For a federalist's view of "interest," published three days before the appearance of *Federalist* X, see "Philanthrop," *Doc. Hist.*, III, 468–70 ("surely real true self interest, considered on a large extensive scale, is public good").

46 Madison to Jefferson, Oct. 24, 1787, in Robert A. Rutland et al., eds., *Papers of James Madison* (Chicago and Charlottesville, 1973–), X, 205–20; *Federalist* X, LI, *Doc. Hist.* XIV, CC 285; XVI, CC 503. The famous passage quoted at length is from CC 285, at p. 181.

47 It is worth nothing that *Federalist* X, far from constituting a sudden new theory of politics, was the expansion of ideas Madison had long been considering. It was in his pre-convention memorandum "Vices of the Political System of the United States" (April 1787) that he had first recorded his concern for "the insecurity of private rights" in majoritarian republics and argued that the larger the sphere of the republic, the greater the probability that factions would check and neutralize each other and the less likely that any one of them would be a threat to the preservation of private rights. When he came to deal with the operational mechanics of the Constitution, he used the idea of extended spheres in a more specific way, to justify his proposal, which the convention rejected, of a Congressional veto over state legislation deemed to be in conflict with the Constitution, federal laws and regulations, and individual rights. Why would Congress not itself be factious, partial, unfair, even exploitative in using such a veto? Why would it be impartial? When, in his letter to Jefferson of Oct. 24, he came to answer that question and hence to justify his advocacy of a Congressional veto, he explained that the multitude of interests and factions in America's extended republic would guarantee Congress's impartiality. No one group would be able fully to control Congress, hence no one group would be in a position to use Congress's veto for its own, selfish purposes. Madison thought so highly of this justification of his defeated idea of a Congressional veto that he excerpted that entire section of the letter in his own hand, apparently for later use. He did not wait long to re-use it. Within a month he took over this passage, written to Jefferson to justify the Congressional veto, and developed it along the lines of his earlier,

more general "Vices," simply to argue, in *Federalist* X (Nov. 22), that an extended republic reduced rather than increased the dangers of factionalism; and he used it again, similarly, in *Federalist* LI (Feb. 6, 1788). Madison would have been surprised to learn that these familiar ideas, of factionalism and its relation to extended spheres, would at one point, generations later, be hailed as the advent of a new political science, at another as the justification for patrician rule. Cf. *Papers of James Madison*, X, 205–6; the excerpted passage is at pp. 209–14.

48 *Federalist* LV, ibid., XVI, CC 525 (at pp. 114–15); Madison, speech in the Virginia convention, Elliot, *Debates*, III, 536–37.

49 Washington to the Marquis de Lafayette, Mount Vernon, Feb. 7, 1788, *Doc. Hist.*, XVI, CC 509; "Fabius" [Dickinson], IX, in Ford, *Pamphlets*, p. 215; West, Thompson, and Ames speeches in the Massachusetts convention, Elliot, *Debates*, II, 32–33, 33–34, 10; Winfred E. A. Bernhard, *Fisher Ames* (Chapel Hill, 1965), pp. 6, 73; Gerald Stourzh, *Alexander Hamilton and the Idea of Republican Government* (Stanford, Calif., 1970), pp. 70–74, quotation at p. 71; *Federalist* LXXVI, Cooke, ed., pp. 513–14. Cf. Hamilton's earlier statement *(Federalist* XXII, *Doc. Hist.*, XIV, CC 347) that only "minds animated and guided by superior virtue" can overcome the natural corruptibility of ordinary people suddenly elevated to positions of power in a republic, and on such minds, protected and favored by a proper constitution, the survival of freedom will depend.

50 Murray, "Political Sketches," *American Museum*, II, no. 3 (Sept. 1787), 220, 227, 228, 230, 231, 232. Cf. Alexander deConde, "William Vans Murray's *Political Sketches:* A Defense of the American Experiment," *Mississippi Valley Historical Review*, 41 (1954–55), 623–40. Murray was a political disciple of John Adams, who was ambassador in London when Murray was writing his essays, and addressed the essays to Adams. Adams himself was then writing his *Defence of the Constitutions . . . of the United States of America* (3 vols., 1787–88), which similarly disparages Montesquieu's ideas. In a long passage in Volume III (1788), Adams followed Murray's ideas closely and, independently of Webster and Stevens, developed views similar to theirs as well. Honor and fear, he wrote, were as much a part of republics as of monarchies and despotisms, and virtue and honor were similarly parts of despotisms. And he too challenged Montesquieu's definition of virtue as the absence of ambition and avarice or as selfless patriotism. Every republic has been animated by ambition and avarice, he wrote, and it is unrealistic to think of frugality or the pure love of country as the principles of republics. No one was ever frugal or entirely selfless in patriotism "but from necessity." Liberty can be secure only under a government "which unites all the virtue, honor, and fear of the citizens, in a reverence and obedience to the laws . . . all orders, and ranks, and parties [must be] compelled to prefer the public good before their own." Montesquieu's ideas, he concluded, are "imaginations of his own, derived from the contemplation of the reveries of Xenophon and Plato." Adams, *Works . . .*, ed. Charles Francis Adams (Boston, 1850–56), VI, 206–16, quotations at 208, 211.

51 Webster, *Sketches* (facsimile ed., New York, 1937), p. 24 n.; *Examination*, in Ford, *Pamphlets*, pp. 57, 59, 60—echoed in Webster's "To the Dissenting Members of the

Late Convention of Pennsylvania" (Dec. 31, 1787), *Doc. Hist.*, XV, CC 399 (p. 195). For the federalists' request to Webster, see Thomas FitzSimmons to Noah Webster, Philadelphia, Sept. 15, 1787, in Noah Webster Coll., New York Public Library; reproduced in microfiche addenda to *Doc. Hist.*, II, at mf. pp. 707–8.

52 "Americanus" [Stevens], VI, *New York Daily Advertiser*, Dec. 12, 1787; remarks on Sparta are in paper I, Nov, 2, 1787. Cf. Hamilton's comment in *The Continentalist* (1782) that it is folly to urge pure disinterestedness in republican politics: "We might as soon reconcile ourselves to the Spartan community of goods and wives, to their iron coin, their long beards, or their black broth . . . it is as ridiculous to seek for models in the simple ages of Greece and Rome, as it would be to go in quest of them among the Hottentots and Laplanders." Quoted in Stourzh, *Hamilton*, p. 70.

53 All of the federalists' discussions of the Constitution are, in one way or another, commentaries on power, its uses and abuses; but for a particularly clear and cogent discussion of power, in the abstract and in practice, see "A Landholder" [Ellsworth], III, *Doc. Hist.*, XIV, CC 272.

54 Typically, Wilson's speech in the Pennsylvania convention, *Doc. Hist.*, III, 352–53, and that convention's general sentiment, p. 367; *Federalist* XIV [Madison], ibid., XIV, CC 310.

55 "An American Citizen" [Coxe], IV, ibid., XIII, CC 183A, at p. 435.

56 *Federalist* XX [Madison], ibid., CC 340; Madison to Jefferson, Oct. 24, 1787 (cited above, n. 46), pp. 209–10.

57 See above, quotation on pp. 235–36.

58 Speech of Edward Rutledge in the South Carolina convention, Elliot, *Debates*, IV, 276.

Original Publications

All but the last of the essays in this volume were published previously. Under their original titles, and in the form in which they were first written, they appeared in the following journals and books. The last essay was originally presented in much briefer form as the McCallum Lecture, 1987, Pembroke College, Oxford, and as a paper at the American Historical Association convention in December of that year.

1. "Butterfield's Adams: Notes for a Sketch," *William and Mary Quarterly*, 19 (1962).
2. "Boyd's Jefferson: Notes for a Sketch," *New England Quarterly*, 33 (1960).
3. "Success of the Acquisitive Man: Portrait of the Provincial Bourgeois": the second Trevelyan Lecture of 1971, Cambridge University, published as Chapter 1 in *The Ordeal of Thomas Hutchinson* (Harvard University Press, 1974). (Reference to Hutchinson's role as Harvard Overseer, courtesy Thomas Siegel.)
4. "Common Sense," in *Fundamental Testaments of the American Revolution* (Library of Congress, 1973).
5. "The Index and Commentaries of Harbottle Dorr," *Proceedings of the Massachusetts Historical Society*, 85 (1973).
6. "Religion and Revolution: Three Biographical Studies," *Perspectives in American History*, 4 (1970).
7. "1776: A Year of Challenge—A World Transformed," *Journal of Law & Economics*, 19 (1976).
8. "Political Experience and Enlightenment Ideas in Eighteenth-Century America," *American Historical Review*, 67 (1962).
9. "The Central Themes of the American Revolution: An Interpretation," in Stephen G. Kurtz and James H. Hutson, eds., *Essays on the American Revolution* (University of North Carolina Press, 1973).

Index

Index

Index

Bowdoin, James, 259
Boyd, Julian P., 22, 24
Braxton, Carter, 160
Breed's Hill, *see* Bunker Hill
Britain, *see* Great Britain
British constitution, *see* constitution, British
Brown, John, *Estimate of the Manners and Principles of the Times*, 83
"Brutus" (*pseud.*), 234–5, 235–6, 238, 243–4, 252, 270, 272
Bryan, Samuel, 233, 271
Bunker Hill (Breed's Hill) (Mass.), battle of (1775), 68, 122
Burgh, James, 190
   Political Disquisitions, 241
Burke, Edmund, 141, 145, 156, 177, 194, 217, 219
Burnet, Gilbert, *History of My Own Time*, 54
Bute, Earl of, *see* Stuart, John
Butterfield, Lyman, 4, 13
Byrd, William, II, 196

Caesar, Caius Julius, 58
Caldwell, David, 238
Caner, Henry, 56, 132
Carroll, Charles, 104
Cartwright, Maj. John, *Take Your Choice!*, 156–7, 183
Catanoch, John, 170
"Cato" (*pseud.* of New York writer), 243, 244
"Cato" (*pseud.* of Trenchard and Gordon): *Letters*, 190
"Centinel" (*pseud.* of S. Bryan), 233, 271
Chalmers, George, 45
Charles I, 142, 147
Chartist movement (Britain), 219
Chatham, Earl of, *see* Pitt, William
Chathamites (Britain), 182

checks and balances, 227
   Adams (J.) on, 21
   "Americanus" (Stevens) on, 256
   in British constitution, 70, 77–8, 140
   federalists' reliance on, 259, 260, 261
   Henry (P.) on, 242
   Paine on, 76–7
Cheeseborough, David, 63
Cherokee Indians, 172
China, trade with, 215
Church of England, *see* Anglican church
Cicero, Marcus Tullius, 58
"Cincinnatus" (*pseud.*), 273
"Civis" (*pseud.*), 140, 141
Clarke, Richard, 127, 128, 129–30
Clarke, Samuel, 109–10, 126
Coke, Sir Edward, 139
Common Sense (Paine), 67–84, 153–4, 162, 183
Condorcet, Marie-Jean-Antoine-Nicolas de Caritat, Marquis de, 156
Congress (U.S.)
   elections to, 233, 236
   salaries of members, 239
Connecticut
   convention to ratify federal constitution, 252
   migration westward from, 171, 172
   religious pluralism, 192–3
"Consistent Whig" (*pseud.* of Dorr), 86
constitution, British
   Bentham on, 158
   Eliot (A.) on, 112
   informality and inefficiency of, 180–1
   Johnson on, 142, 148
   Mayhew on, 133
   as model for American constitutions, 160, 201
   Paine's *Common Sense* on, 72, 77–8, 82, 153–4, 183

A NOTE ABOUT THE AUTHOR

Bernard Bailyn did his undergraduate work at Williams College and his graduate work at Harvard, where he has taught since 1949 and where, since 1981, he has been the Adams University Professor. His previous publications include *The New England Merchants in the Seventeenth Century; The Origins of American Politics; Education in the Forming of American Society; Pamphlets of the American Revolution; The Ideological Origins of the American Revolution*, which received the Pulitzer and Bancroft prizes in 1968; *The Ordeal of Thomas Hutchinson*, which won the 1975 National Book Award for History; *The Peopling of British North America;* and *Voyagers to the West*, which won the Pulitzer Prize in 1986.

A NOTE ON THE TYPE

This book was set in a modern adaptation of a type designed by William Caslon (1692–1766). The first of a famous English family of type designers and founders, he was originally an apprentice to an engraver of gunlocks and gun barrels in London. In 1716 he opened his own shop, for silver chasing and making bookbinders' stamps. The printers John Watts and William Bowyer, admirers of his skill in cutting ornaments and letters, advanced him money to equip himself for type founding, which he began in 1720.

In style Caslon was a reversion to earlier type styles. Its characteristics are remarkable regularity and symmetry, and beauty in the shape and proportion of the letters; its general effect is clear and open but not weak or delicate. For uniformity, clearness, and readability it has perhaps never been surpassed. After Caslon's death his eldest son, also named William (1720–1778), carried on the business successfully. Then followed a period of neglect of nearly fifty years. In 1843 Caslon type was revived by the firm of Caslon for William Pickering and has since been one of the most widely used of all type designs in English and American printing.

Composed by Creative Graphics, Inc.,
Allentown, Pennsylvania

Printed and bound by R.R. Donnelley & Sons,
Harrisonburg, Virginia

Designed by Anthea Lingeman